Renaissance Thought:
Dante and Machiavelli

MACHIAVELLI

DANTE

Renaissance Thought

DANTE & MACHIAVELLI

MONUMENTS OF WESTERN THOUGHT

Edited by **Norman F. Cantor** and **Peter L. Klein,** Brandeis University

GINN-BLAISDELL   A Xerox Company

Waltham, Massachusetts | Toronto | London

FOREWORD

The basis of a university education is an understanding of the great writings that have shaped Western civilization. The aim of this twelve-volume series is to make these doctrines of Western thought available to the student in the most convenient and readily comprehensible form. Each volume presents carefully selected texts by the two major thinkers of a particular historical period. In choosing the texts, the entire works of each thinker have been drawn upon, and passages from both familiar and unfamiliar writings are presented to bring the reader to an understanding of the central thought of the author. Following the selections are commentaries by leading modern scholars on the works studied. Many of these statements are drawn from books which are available only in the very best libraries. Again, these modern commentaries are carefully edited to present the main points as succinctly as possible. The first two chapters of each volume delineate the relevant historical context and biographical information and suggest the main outlines of the two thinkers' arguments, thus providing a framework for the student's own analysis of the texts. The source texts are followed by study guide questions which challenge the student's understanding of the arguments he has been reading and force him to go back and analyze the texts again. These study guides will also serve as a basis for class discussion. The modern commentaries are similarly followed by study guides, requiring the student to consider the merits of the authors' critiques.

We believe that the richness of the material selected and the pedagogical principles that have determined the organization of each volume will enable the student to carry away from his study a sophisticated understanding of the imperishable ideas the two great thinkers have propounded. The student who studies all twelve volumes will have an excellent basis for comprehending the fundamental thought of Western civilization.

N. F. C.
P. L. K.

CONTENTS

Renaissance Thought:
Dante and Machiavelli

1
THE HISTORICAL CONTEXT

From the middle of the thirteenth century to the early years of the sixteenth century, the distinctive form of political organization in Northern Italy was the city-state, or commune, of which Florence, Milan, Venice, and Sienna were the most important. In the 1250's the attempt by the German emperor to control the Italian communes effectively came to an end after a century of intermittent warfare—in which the papacy had given the communes valuable assistance in repelling northern domination; and until the French invasion of 1494, the Italian cities were left to work out their own destiny. During these two and a half centuries the Italian cities were the scene of a great efflorescence in education, art, literature, and philosophy, which was inspired by the forms of classical art and thought. The intellectual leaders of this cultural expansion referred, therefore, to a "rebirth" of art and letters, and this era has ever since been known as the age of the Renaissance. In many ways the Renaissance built upon medieval learning and forms of thought, but modern scholars agree that a great turning point in theory, attitudes, and literary and artistic style occurred in Northern Italy between 1250 and 1500 and that in several highly significant ways modern thought has its source in the Italian Renaissance.

The doctrines of the Renaissance thinkers immediately reflect the political, economic, and social conditions that prevailed in the Italian cities from 1250 to the early sixteenth century. The government of an Italian city was sovereign over the lives and interests of its subjects. The medieval feudal state was limited by the rights and privileges of various groups and classes and by a vague recognition that the state was subject to a moral law dictated by the church. The Renaissance state gave supreme and absolute power to the holder, or holders, of political authority, and no class or family could resist the civil law. The Italians came to believe that social order and the welfare of the community demanded that no special vested interest resist the sovereign political authority. This belief represents a great advance to political modernity—to the idea and practice of sovereignty that underlies

1

all modern state functioning. By the fifteenth century the feeling was also becoming widespread that the state could not recognize the sanctions of the church or even a moral consciousness as limitations to its authority. For better or worse, this amoral political doctrine has been characteristic of many, although not all, modern governments.

The state was central to the lives of Italians in the Renaissance period because it protected and fostered their extremely profitable capitalist economic interests. Since the tenth century the Italians had been the dominant group in the commercial life of Western Europe. The Italian cities had begun to grow wealthy in the tenth and eleventh centuries by acting as middlemen in the trade between the East (the Islamic world, Byzantium, and the Far East) and the rest of Western Europe. By the fourteenth century the northern merchants were challenging the Italian leadership in Mediterranean and Eastern trade, but until the sixteenth century Italian mercantile superiority was clearly maintained. In addition to their commercial enterprises, the Italian cities had invested heavily in industries, of which the most important was Florentine textile production, and great profits were also gained in this field. Finally, Italian economic activity had led to the development of banking institutions and to the techniques of financial capitalism. Again, until the end of the fifteenth century the Italians, particularly the Florentines, were the most sophisticated and most successful bankers and moneylenders in Europe, with the pope and several kings as their clients.

The capital gained from these vast enterprises enriched certain great families in every Italian city, and inevitably it was these families who dominated the government of the communes and took the lead in patronage of the arts and letters—indeed, they produced important writers and thinkers from among their own scions. For an understanding of the Italian Renaissance, it is important to realize that these high bourgeoisie were a group who had advanced far beyond crude calculation and money-grubbing; they had become, in fact, a new aristocracy. The Italian capitalist families took over the refined style of life that had been developed by the French aristocracy of the thirteenth century and improved upon it. This style had decreed that social and political leadership depended not only upon wealth and birth but also upon nobility of mind—education in the best literature, a rhetorical way of speaking, and refined manners. The Italian merchant and banking families gave their sons (and sometimes their daughters as well) an intensive education in the Latin classics in order that the aristocratic style and temperament might be inculcated in the rising generation. The humanistic education begun by these families was to dominate the European school system until the twentieth century, and still has strong support today.

The products of this wealthy social background and this humanistic educational system saw themselves as the continuators, almost the reincarnation, of the great men of classical antiquity. The classical ideal of excellence became the Renaissance ideal of *virtù*; the best man was he who fulfilled all the potentialities of his being, who cultivated all the arts, and exercised political and military leadership as well. This ideal was also to have a long tradition in the Western world: it is the basis of the idea of the gentleman—the true aristocrat who strives for refinement and excellence in all aspects of both intellectual and physical life.

The great achievement of the Renaissance was recognition of individual as opposed to group values, of personality as opposed to collectivity, and it was this new self-consciousness and recognition of individual needs and possibilities that so sharply distinguished Renaissance from medieval culture.

However, it was precisely because of this individualism that the Renaissance communes finally failed to maintain their stability and independence. The struggle for leadership and preferment among the great individuals that the high bourgeois families produced tore the Renaissance states apart. The political history of these societies is marked by constant factionalism, feuding, and ugly power struggles. By the fifteenth century many of the communes had abandoned government by a council of leading families and had surrendered power to a *podesta*, a military dictator, who at least could provide domestic tranquillity. When the newly reorganized French monarchy invaded Italy in 1494, the Italian cities could not agree on a common program of alliance and defence, such as that which had repulsed the German emperor between 1150 and 1250. The French invasion was followed by the incursion of forces led by the Habsburg emperor of Spain and Germany, and Northern Italy by 1525 was the scene of a wide conflict between northern powers for the right to control the wealth and intellectual resources of the communes.

The great age of Italian culture was over by 1525, but in the previous 250 years, the communes had inspired and fostered many of the most imperishable monuments of European art and literature. And the city of Florence had produced the two greatest Renaissance thinkers, Dante Alighieri and Niccolo Machiavelli, although the communal government was ungenerous to both of its famous sons. Dante is the exponent of the early Renaissance thought that marks the transition from the church and group-centered medieval world to the state and individual-centered Renaissance culture. Machiavelli is the great theorist of the High (or full) Renaissance in which the potentialities of statism and humanism are carried to their ultimate conclusion and presented in forms that helped to shape modern European civilization.

Having treated the politics and society of the Renaissance from a very general point of view, we must now descend into the murky waters of Florentine affairs, for it was as political exiles from Florence that both Dante Alighieri and Niccolo Machiavelli viewed the world. Like all other communes, Florence was originally dominated by a patrician class known as magnates or *grandi*; these magnates justified their privileges by serving as mounted knights in the communal army. In the thirteenth century this class was sharply divided between those who supported the Italian policy of the German emperor Frederick II and those who sided with the papacy; the former were called Ghibellines and the latter, Guelphs. The opposition between the two was so strong that, even after the death of Frederick II, the Guelph-Ghibelline feud continued to constitute the core of Italian, and particularly Florentine, history for the next 50 years. On Frederick's death in 1250, the Guelph party seized control of the government. Within ten years the Ghibellines, rallying behind the cause of King Manfred, Frederick's illegitimate son, put an end to Guelph hegemony. When Pope Clement IV entered the struggle and excommunicated Manfred, he offered the crown of Sicily and Naples to Charles of Anjou, brother of the French king, and fortune once again favored the Guelphs. In 1267 the pope and Charles of Anjou succeeded in their common endeavor, and once again the Guelphs were back in power. To assure the continuance of their supremacy, the Guelphs proceeded to annihilate their Ghibelline opponents by driving them into exile, confiscating their houses and goods, and so impoverishing them that they never were able to recover.

In spite of the reactionary government, Florence entered a period of unprecedented prosperity. As Guelphs, the merchant-bankers of Florence secured a practical monopoly of the lucrative business of collecting papal revenue and acting as bankers for the papacy. The collection of papal revenue brought the Florentine merchant companies into contact with England and English wool, with the result that a great weaving industry grew up in Florence alongside the already established industry which finished cloth imported from the Netherlands and Northern France. The political significance of this economic prosperity was two-fold: first, it created a continuing supply of new and wealthy merchants eager to participate in the spoils of government; second, it concentrated considerable power in the hands of the merchant and craft guilds.

In 1282 the seven leading merchant guilds, whose members constituted the business elite of the town, joined forces with the five leading craft guilds and seized control of the government of Florence. To solidify their reign, they created a new executive office consisting of six priors, who were to be chosen from their own ranks. These priors served in office for two months and, during their incumbency, lived together in a private house as a single family. During the next ten years the government of the priors maintained a precarious existence, constantly threatened by the old, landed aristocracy which they had pushed aside. Finally, in 1293, the government of the priors, under the leadership of Gieno della Bella, promulgated the most famous and enduring act of Florentine constitutional history, the Ordinances of Justice. There were two separate parts to this act. The first part elaborated and strengthened the new guild government. The second part disenfranchised the older nobility by identifying active citizenship with membership in the guilds and by rendering ineligible for the office of priorate all families, any member of which had acquired the honor of knighthood within the past 20 years. A violent feud sprang up within the Guelph party between the Whites, who were moderate constitutionalists and favored acceptance of the Ordinance of Justice, and the reactionary Blacks. In 1302 the Blacks carried through an armed revolution with the aid of French troops sent by Pope Boniface VIII. A reign of terror followed in which hundreds of White Guelphs—Dante among them—were condemned to death or exile.

Then when the German emperor Henry VII came down into Italy for a few months, exiled Whites, such as Dante, hoped that he would revive imperial ambitions to control Northern Italy, or at least intervene in Florence so as to restore the Whites to their native city. But the German empire was only a shadow of its former power. Henry went quietly back to Germany, and Dante and his political colleagues were not allowed to return to Florence.

Unlike the other communes of Italy, Florence preserved its republican constitution until the end of the Renaissance. But in the fourteenth and fifteenth centuries behind the republican facade there always stood a small group of wealthy merchants who actually controlled the state. By the 1430's, power fell within the province of single individuals, the heads of the Medici family. Thus, like the other communes, Florence, during the fourteenth and fifteenth centuries, developed into a territorial state governed by a prince. Cosimo Medici, as head of the merchant oligarchy, came to power in 1434 and for the 30 years until his death controlled the government of Florence. Cosimo retained his control by two means; he supervised the random selection of all important officials, and, to meet special problems, he called extraordinary reforming assemblies to which only his followers were admitted as delegates. Another key to Cosimo's power was his own temperament. He was a very successful banker due to his cautious and conservative nature; he was wise enough to let others enjoy the spotlight of power; and he preferred peace to war. Upon Cosimo's death, his eldest son, Piero, was set at the head of the oligarchy and, consequently, at the head of the government. Piero had his father's banker's mentality and wisely followed his prudent policy. But chronic gout, the family malady, cut short Piero's life; after only five years in power, his son, Lorenzo, replaced him as head of the oligarchy. Lorenzo, educated as a gentleman, unfortunately lacked the caution and sobriety of his merchant forbears. In his hands, not only did the family's personal wealth decline, but he managed to squander the family fortune by embarking upon a number of reckless diplomatic schemes. Yet, by his own skill, the family reputation, and the good fortunes of history, Lorenzo managed to retain his power until his death in 1492; within two years his son and heir, Piero, was driven out of Florence.

The hiatus in the long Medici control over Florentine government inaugurated a period of political upheaval and conflict that was exacerbated greatly by French and Spanish invasions. It was during this era of change and conflict that Machiavelli was a Florentine civil servant; he drew upon his experience of political life in the commune in developing his theories about the state.

2

AN INTRODUCTION TO THE LIFE AND WORK OF DANTE AND MACHIAVELLI

An Introduction to Dante

The Florentine political purge of 1302 marked a crucial point in the life of Dante Alighieri (1265–1321), for, like Machiavelli's, his life was divided into two parts: before his exile and after his exile. Dante was born in Florence in May, 1265. His family, it was thought, was descended from the Roman founders of the city. A long family tree was probably their most notable achievement, for in Dante's time they belonged to the lesser nobility, were of rather modest means, and like most of the city's lesser nobility and artisans, were Guelph. Despite the family's modest social standing, Dante was able to pursue his studies and live the life of a gentleman. In 1289 he served the commune in the cavalry at the battle of Campaldino, which was the last important victory for the citizen army of Florence before the mercenary system took hold.

While still a young man, Dante began his career as a poet and composed love poetry, as was the fashion of the day. Out of this period came his *Vita Nuova*, which, although ostensibly an autobiographical account of his love for a Florentine gentlewoman named Beatrice, is, in fact, a secular expression of the cult of the Virgin Mary. It was also in this period that Dante devoted considerable time to the study of the Latin poets, particularly Virgil, whom he acknowledged as the source of the "beautiful style" that made him famous, and to the study of philosophy, which he abandoned after three years, "having overtaxed his eyes with too much reading."

Dante did not devote his attention exclusively to poetry and philosophy; as a young gentleman, he was also interested in the politics of Florence. Although the Ordinances of Justice in 1293 effectively barred Dante's class from holding office, a mitigating constitutional provision in 1295 granted nobles of a certain rank the privilege of being elected to the councils of the people and to the priorate, if they registered in the rolls of the guilds. Thus, Dante joined the guild of physicians and apothecaries, and shortly thereafter served in the special council of the

7

people. In 1300, Dante was elected to the priorate; although the two-month office provided little time for creating enduring enemies, it was an unfortunate moment to be in office, for the storm clouds of war were breaking over Florence. In 1302 Dante left Florence in exile, accused of graft, embezzlement, opposition to the pope, and disturbance of the peace of Florence.

Dante's two greatest works, *De Monarchia* and the *Divine Comedy*, were both written during his exile. The shock of expulsion from his native city and his bitterness and disappointment forced Dante to reconsider his views on the individual and society, and these two works exhibit a maturity and profundity that is lacking in his early lyric poetry. In his early poetry, written in Florence, Dante perpetuates the romantic motifs of twelfth- and thirteenth-century French literature. In his two later works (the *Divine Comedy* is an epic poem in the Italian vernacular; *De Monarchia* is a Latin prose treatise) Dante establishes a consistent and comprehensive view of social and personal values.

The *Divine Comedy* is in outline—but only in outline—a summation of the medieval world view and is heavily indebted to the philosophy of Thomas Aquinas. The Roman poet Virgil, symbolizing reason and classical humanism, leads Dante through hell to the entrance to purgatory; Dante, like Thomas, is saying that reason can show us how to achieve a life that meets minimal moral standards. Beatrice, representing the beatific vision of the church, leads the poet through purgatory and the lower levels of heaven; this is as much as the church can provide. It is St. Bernard, representing the mystical experience, who guides Dante through the higher circles of heaven. If the structure of the *Divine Comedy* is a summation of the medieval ethos, there are several doctrines in it that signal a break with the traditional teachings of the church. Siger of Brabant, the radical disciple of the Arab philosopher Averroes and the antagonist of Thomas Aquinas at the University of Paris, is placed in heaven. In *De Monarchia* Dante indicates his sympathy with the heretical Averroist doctrine of collective, as opposed to individual, immortality. Pope Boniface VIII, Dante's contemporary and the spokesman for papal supremacy over the state, is placed in hell. The Donation of Constantine, the forged document of the eighth century that gave the pope claims to secular rule in Italy, is bitterly regretted by Dante. Above all, what is radical in the *Divine Comedy* is the theme of personal search for salvation, of personal quest for fulfillment. The church helps in this quest, but reason and individual feelings are also indispensable. It is the personal search for value and meaning, and not obedience to external ecclesiastic authority, that gives life its purpose and dignity; this is Dante's basic theme. And this idea was to become the prime motif of Renaissance thought.

The organization and style of the *Divine Comedy* are as complex as the theme. Dante, like so many of his age, believed that numbers had a special, divine meaning; three and ten were the most important, the former symbolizing the Trinity, and the latter, perfection. Thus, the *Comedy* is divided into three canticles, each dealing with an other-worldly realm—Inferno, Purgatory, and Paradise; each canticle has 30 cantos, with one canto as an introduction to the entire poem—totaling exactly ten times ten, or 100. Even the rhyme scheme operates on the principle of three; furthermore, the Inferno, a vast abyss in the center of the earth, is divided into nine circles, plus the vestibule; there are as many divisions in Purgatory, a high mountain which rises from the ocean in the southern hemisphere; and Paradise has nine heavens plus the empyrean.

The *De Monarchia*, being a didactic work, is more blatantly radical than the *Divine Comedy*. Dante removes from the church its control over the state, and gives to secular political authority the ultimate sanction in society. This view, too, inaugurates a prime theme in Renaissance thought. Dante came to this view partly because of his unhappy personal experience. While in exile Dante altered his political views; convinced that the evils of Italian politics were attributable to the church's meddling in temporal affairs and to the lack of a supreme secular ruler, Dante became a champion of the German imperial cause. He saw the possibility of his vision becoming a reality when it appeared that Henry VII of Germany was planning an invasion of Italy. In a letter Dante wrote: "Rejoice, sorrowful Italy, for thy bridegroom hastens to the marriage, and you that weep oppressed, lift up your hearts, because your salvation is nigh, and all of you, Italians, rise to meet your king, . . ." Thus, *De Monarchia* was intended as a theoretical defense of Henry VII's conquest of Italy.

The imperial conquest never occurred; Dante's expectations were again grimly frustrated. Insofar as the *De Monarchia* was intended to justify Henry VII's conquest of Florence, the treatise rapidly became obsolete and pointless. But Dante had ranged much further in his argument than the needs of the current political situation. He examined the general principles of political life, and he justified the sovereign authority of the emperor partly on grounds of social need: only the authority of state could provide peace and order. This view became central to the political vision of the Renaissance and the dominant assumption in all modern political thinking.

An Introduction to Machiavelli

Lorenzo Medici's son, Piero, was driven from Florence by the terrible saint, Savonarola, who preached against moral laxity and the decay of religion, moving the people to overthrow their masters. Within six years the pope had Savonarola burned at the stake, and Florence set about reorganizing its republic. Named as second chancellor was Niccolo Machiavelli (1469–1527), a young man with no reputation and very little experience, but with a brilliant intellect. Machiavelli was to spend 14 years as second chancellor and special envoy, at the end of which time he was exiled from the government. Like Dante, Machiavelli composed his greatest works after his exile. Today Machiavelli is remembered for his observations on political life; but to his contemporaries he was also known for his enjoyment of life, particularly of political discourse and of women. He was of medium height, thin, and bold in his bearing; his hair was black and his skin pale; his most outstanding feature was an ironical smile which always seemed to hover on his lips. From his father he acquired a love of books, and he was a close student of the Latin classics; the two pillars of Machiavelli's thought were his knowledge of Roman history and his experience as second chancellor.

The second chancery was not a very important place, although it did have a redeeming virtue: it was one of the few places where a Florentine could follow the day-to-day political fortunes of Italy. It was in his special commissions that Machiavelli acquired his knowledge of politics. The first few years of the sixteenth century were decisive years for Italy; both France and Spain were preparing to invade Italy, and Cesare Borgia, the bastard son of Pope Alexander VI, was waging war in the papal states. Florence was in the center of the storm. There were alliances to be made and to be broken, and a course of action to be planned. Machiavelli had earned a reputation for his clear and concise reports and uncanny appraisals of complex situations. Therefore, he was sent from court to court in order to observe and assess the situation and advise Florence. All this came to an end in 1511, when the Spanish army, acting in consort with the pope, defeated Florence. The condition of surrender was that the Medici should be restored to Florence. Once the government was reorganized there was no longer a need for the republican secretary, Machiavelli, and he was dismissed from office. But, this was only the beginning of his troubles. Not only did the pro-Medici government dismiss him, but they sought blame, punishment, and revenge.

Banished from government, and self-exiled in a country home, Machiavelli, who had been accustomed to moving in courts of princes and pondering the affairs of state, settled down to his new life:

> I rise in the morning with the sun, and I go off to a wood of mine which I am having cut down, where I stop for two hours to see what was done the day before and to talk to the woodcutters who always have some trouble on hand either among themselves or with their neighbours. . . . Leaving the wood I go to a spring and thence to some bird-traps of mine. I have a book with me, Dante or Petrarch or one of the minor poets,

Tibullus, Ovid or the like. I read about their amorous passions and their loves, I remember my own, and dwell enjoyably on these thoughts for a while. Then I go on to the road and into the tavern. I talk to the passers-by, I ask what news of their villages, I hear all sorts of things, and observe the various tastes and ideas of men. In the meanwhile it is time for dinner, and with my folk I eat what food this poor farm and miserable patrimony of mine provides. When I have eaten I go back to the tavern. Here I find the host, and usually a butcher, a miller, and a couple of kiln-men. With them I degrade myself all day at *cricca* and tric-trac, and this gives rise to a thousand arguments and endless vexations with insulting words, and most times there is a fight over a penny, and we can be heard shouting from as far away as San Casciano. And so, surrounded by these lice, I blow the cobwebs out of my brain and relieve the unkindness of my fate, content that she trample on me in this way to see if she is not ashamed to treat me thus.

When evening comes I return home and go into my study, and at the door I take off my daytime dress covered in mud and dirt, and put on royal and curial robes; and then decently attired I enter the courts of the ancients, where affectionately greeted by them, I partake of that food which is mine alone and for which I was born; where I am not ashamed to talk with them and inquire the reasons of their actions; and they out of human kindness answer me, and for four hours at a stretch I feel no worry of any kind; I forget all my troubles, I am not afraid of poverty or of death. I give myself up entirely to them. And because Dante says that understanding does not constitute knowledge unless it is retained in the memory, I have written down what I have learned from their conversation and composed a short work *de Principatibus*. . . .

It was in the early years of his exile, under these conditions and in this mood, that Machiavelli wrote the *Prince*. Machiavelli had high hopes for his *Prince*: if only presented to the right patron, he thought it might gain a position in government for him. The key to Florentine government was through the Medici, and Machiavelli tried dedicating his work to one member of the family after another, writing about each as if he alone were the true prince. Machiavelli's plan failed; but throughout the rest of his life he continued to seek reentry into Florentine government; but when at last the Medici offered him a commission, it was not to enter government but to write a history of Florence.

Machiavelli never regained his political office. But *The Prince* and another and much more elaborate treatise written during his exile, *The Discourses* (designed as a commentary on the work of the Roman historian Livy), taken together with his *History of Florence* and some more strictly belletristic works, have gained for him the position as the leading social and historical thinker of the Italian Renaissance and the founder of modern political theory.

Machiavelli was first and foremost what he professed to be: a classical humanist. He was an idealistic republican who wanted statesmen to work for the welfare of society. But his experience in Florentine politics, the lessons he learned as ambassador to the court of the crafty French king, his observation of the career of Cesare Borgia—the most dramatic political leader of the day—and his close study of Roman history convinced Machiavelli that the high moral ideals that men profess are often ignored and, in fact, betrayed in day-to-day political action. He therefore set out to establish the realities of power politics and to prescribe how ambitious men actually obtain and retain power in the state. To the end of his life, however, Machiavelli never abandoned his hopes for a better political order, and he envisioned the coming of a great leader who would save Italy from foreign invaders and unite the Italian cities in a national state that would serve the commonweal.

As an historian, Machiavelli followed the lines of interpretation set down by the Greco-Roman historians. He believed in a cyclic view of political development—in the degeneration, reconstruction, and then further degeneration of governments. He made the focus of his history the deeds of great men, and for him the dimension and subject of history was the rise and fall of political authority. These were to remain the motifs of historical literature until the nineteenth century, and they are still the most common themes in historical writing. Machiavelli was, therefore, the founder of modern historiography as well as of modern political science.

3
SELECTIONS FROM DANTE'S WORK

Divine Comedy

Inferno

*In addition to being an account of Dante's journey through hell, purgatory,
and paradise, the* Divine Comedy *is an allegory of sin and salvation, a
political treatise concerning Florentine politics and European church-state
relations, a handbook for the aristocratic ethos of courtly love, and, not least,
a poem of exquisite literary and artistic beauty. The following selections,
which present the essential intellectual and stylistic features of the* Inferno,
Purgatory, *and* Paradise, *should be read on these multiple levels.*

CANTO 1

> Midway in our life's journey, I went astray
> from the straight road and woke to find myself
> alone in a dark wood. How shall I say
>
> what wood that was! I never saw so drear,
> so rank, so arduous a wilderness!
> Its very memory gives a shape to fear.
>
> Death could scarce be more bitter than that place!
> But since it came to good, I will recount
> all that I found revealed there by God's grace.
>
> How I came to it I cannot rightly say,
> so drugged and loose with sleep had I become
> when I first wandered there from the True Way.

SOURCE: *The Inferno* by Dante Alighieri, translated by John Ciardi. Copyright,
1954, by John Ciardi. Reprinted by permission of The New American Library,
Inc., New York.

But at the far end of that valley of evil
   whose maze had sapped my very heart with fear!
   I found myself before a little hill

and lifted up my eyes. Its shoulders glowed
   already with the sweet rays of that planet
   whose virtue leads men straight on every road,

and the shining strengthened me against the fright
   whose agony had wracked the lake of my heart
   through all the terrors of that piteous night.

Just as a swimmer, who with his last breath
   flounders ashore from perilous seas, might turn
   to memorize the wide water of his death—

so did I turn, my soul still fugitive
   from death's surviving image, to stare down
   that pass that none had ever left alive.

And there I lay to rest from my heart's race
   till calm and breath returned to me. Then rose
   and pushed up that dead slope at such a pace

each footfall rose above the last. And lo!
   almost at the beginning of the rise
   I faced a spotted Leopard, all tremor and flow

and gaudy pelt. And it would not pass, but stood
   so blocking my every turn that time and again
   I was on the verge of turning back to the wood.

This fell at the first widening of the dawn
   as the sun was climbing Aries with those stars
   that rode with him to light the new creation.

Thus the holy hour and the sweet season
   of commemoration did much to arm my fear
   of that bright murderous beast with their good omen.

Yet not so much but what I shook with dread
   at sight of a great Lion that broke upon me
   raging with hunger, its enormous head

held high as if to strike a mortal terror
    into the very air. And down his track,
      a She-Wolf drove upon me, a starved horror

ravening and wasted beyond all belief.
    She seemed a rack for avarice, gaunt and craving.
      Oh many the souls she has brought to endless grief!

She brought such heaviness upon my spirit
    at sight of her savagery and desperation,
      I died from every hope of that high summit.

And like a miser—eager in acquisition
    but desperate in self-reproach when Fortune's wheel
      turns to the hour of his loss—all tears and attrition

I wavered back; and still the beast pursued,
    forcing herself against me bit by bit
      till I slid back into the sunless wood.

And as I fell to my soul's ruin, a presence
    gathered before me on the discolored air,
      the figure of one who seemed hoarse from long silence.

At sight of him in that friendless waste I cried:
    "Have pity on me, whatever thing you are,
      whether shade or living man." And it replied:

"Not man, though man I once was, and my blood
    was Lombard, both my parents Mantuan.
      I was born, though late, *sub Julio*, and bred

in Rome under Augustus in the noon
    of the false and lying gods. I was a poet
      and sang of old Anchises' noble son

who came to Rome after the burning of Troy.
    But you—why do *you* return to these distresses
      instead of climbing that shining Mount of Joy

which is the seat and first cause of man's bliss?"
    "And are you then that Virgil and that fountain
      of purest speech?" My voice grew tremulous:

"Glory and light of poets! now may that zeal
and love's apprenticeship that I poured out
on your heroic verses serve me well!

For you are my true master and first author,
the sole maker from whom I drew the breath
of that sweet style whose measures have brought me honor.

See there, immortal sage, the beast I flee.
For my soul's salvation, I beg you, guard me from her,
for she has struck a mortal tremor through me."

And he replied, seeing my soul in tears:
"He must go by another way who would escape
this wilderness, for that mad beast that fleers

before you there, suffers no man to pass.
She tracks down all, kills all, and knows no glut,
but, feeding, she grows hungrier than she was.

She mates with any beast, and will mate with more
before the Greyhound comes to hunt her down.
He will not feed on lands nor loot, but honor

and love and wisdom will make straight his way.
He will rise between Feltro and Feltro, and in him
shall be the resurrection and new day

of that sad Italy for which Nisus died,
and Turnus, and Euryalus, and the maid Camilla.
He shall hunt her through every nation of sick pride

till she is driven back forever to Hell
whence Envy first released her on the world.
Therefore, for your own good, I think it well

you follow me and I will be your guide
and lead you forth through an eternal place.
There you shall see the ancient spirits tried

in endless pain, and hear their lamentation
as each bemoans the second death of souls.
Next you shall see upon a burning mountain

souls in fire and yet content in fire,
   knowing that whensoever it may be
   they yet will mount into the blessed choir.

To which, if it is still your wish to climb,
   a worthier spirit shall be sent to guide you.
   With her shall I leave you, for the King of Time,

who reigns on high, forbids me to come there
   since, living, I rebelled against his law.
   He rules the waters and the land and air

and there holds court, his city and his throne.
   Oh blessed are they he chooses!" And I to him:
   "Poet, by that God to you unknown,

lead me this way. Beyond this present ill
   and worse to dread, lead me to Peter's gate
   and be my guide through the sad halls of Hell."

And he then: "Follow." And he moved ahead
in silence, and I followed where he led.

CANTO 2

The light was departing. The brown air drew down
   all the earth's creatures, calling them to rest
   from their day-roving, as I, one man alone,

prepared myself to face the double war
   of the journey and the pity, which memory
   shall here set down, nor hesitate, nor err.

O Muses! O High Genius! Be my aid!
   O Memory, recorder of the vision,
   here shall your true nobility be displayed!

Thus I began: "Poet, you who must guide me,
   before you trust me to that arduous passage,
   look to me and look through me—can I be worthy?

You sang how the father of Sylvius, while still
   in corruptible flesh won to that other world,
   crossing with mortal sense the immortal sill.

But if the Adversary of all Evil
    weighing his consequence and who and what
    should issue from him, treated him so well—

that cannot seem unfitting to thinking men,
    since he was chosen father of Mother Rome
    and of her Empire by God's will and token.

Both, to speak strictly, were founded and foreknown
    as the established Seat of Holiness
    for the successors of Great Peter's throne.

In that quest, which your verses celebrate,
    he learned those mysteries from which arose
    his victory and Rome's apostolate.

There later came the chosen vessel, Paul,
    bearing the confirmation of that Faith
    which is the one true door to life eternal.

But I—how should I dare? By whose permission?
    I am not Aeneas. *I* am not Paul.
    Who could believe me worthy of the vision?

How, then, may I presume to this high quest
    and not fear my own brashness? You are wise
    and will grasp what my poor words can but suggest."

As one who unwills what he wills, will stay
    strong purposes with feeble second thoughts
    until he spells all his first zeal away—

so I hung back and balked on that dim coast
    till thinking had worn out my enterprise,
    so stout at starting and so early lost.

"I understand from your words and the look in your eyes,"
    that shadow of magnificence answered me,
    "your soul is sunken in that cowardice

that bears down many men, turning their course
    and resolution by imagined perils,
    as his own shadow turns the frightened horse.

To free you of this dread I will tell you all
　　of why I came to you and what I heard
　　when first I pitied you. I was a soul

among the souls of Limbo, when a Lady
　　so blessed and so beautiful, I prayed her
　　to order and command my will, called to me.

Her eyes were kindled from the lamps of Heaven.
　　Her voice reached through me, tender, sweet, and low.
　　An angel's voice, a music of its own:

'O gracious Mantuan whose melodies
　　live in earth's memory and shall live on
　　till the last motion ceases in the skies,

my dearest friend, and fortune's foe, has strayed
　　onto a friendless shore and stands beset
　　by such distresses that he turns afraid

from the True Way, and news of him in Heaven
　　rumors my dread he is already lost.
　　I come, afraid that I am too-late risen.

Fly to him and with your high counsel, pity,
　　and with whatever need be for his good
　　and soul's salvation, help him, and solace me.

It is I, Beatrice, who send you to him.
　　I come from the blessed height for which I yearn.
　　Love called me here. When amid Seraphim

I stand again before my Lord, your praises
　　shall sound in Heaven.' She paused, and I began:
　　'O Lady of that only grace that raises

feeble mankind within its mortal cycle
　　above all other works God's will has placed
　　within the heaven of the smallest circle;

so welcome is your command that to my sense,
　　were it already fulfilled, it would yet seem tardy.
　　I understand, and am all obedience.

But tell me how you dare to venture thus
   so far from the wide heaven of your joy
   to which your thoughts yearn back from this abyss.'

'Since what you ask,' she answered me, 'probes near
   the root of all, I will say briefly only
   how I have come through Hell's pit without fear.

Know then, O waiting and compassionate soul,
   that is to fear which has the power to harm,
   and nothing else is fearful even in Hell.

I am so made by God's all-seeing mercy
   your anguish does not touch me, and the flame
   of this great burning has no power upon me.

There is a Lady in Heaven so concerned
   for him I send you to, that for her sake
   the strict decree is broken. She has turned

and called Lucia to her wish and mercy
   saying: 'Thy faithful one is sorely pressed;
   in his distresses I commend him to thee.'

Lucia, that soul of light and foe of all
   cruelty, rose and came to me at once
   where I was sitting with the ancient Rachel,

saying to me: 'Beatrice, true praise of God,
   why dost thou not help him who loved thee so
   that for thy sake he left the vulgar crowd?

Dost thou not hear his cries? Canst thou not see
   the death he wrestles with beside that river
   no ocean can surpass for rage and fury?

No soul of earth was ever as rapt to seek
   its good or flee its injury as I was—
   when I had heard my sweet Lucia speak—

to descend from Heaven and my blessed seat
   to you, laying my trust in that high speech
   that honors you and all who honor it.'

She spoke and turned away to hide a tear
　　that, shining, urged me faster. So I came
　　and freed you from the beast that drove you there,

blocking the near way to the Heavenly Height.
　　And now what ails you? Why do you lag? Why
　　this heartsick hesitation and pale fright

when three such blessed Ladies lean from Heaven
　　in their concern for you and my own pledge
　　of the great good that waits you has been given?''

As flowerlets drooped and puckered in the night
　　turn up to the returning sun and spread
　　their petals wide on his new warmth and light—

just so my wilted spirits rose again
　　and such a heat of zeal surged through my veins
　　that I was born anew. Thus I began:

"Blesséd be that Lady of infinite pity,
　　and blesséd be thy taxed and courteous spirit
　　that came so promptly on the word she gave thee.

Thy words have moved my heart to its first purpose.
　　My Guide! My Lord! My Master! Now lead on:
　　one will shall serve the two of us in this.''

He turned when I had spoken, and at his back
I entered on that hard and perilous track.

CANTO 3

I AM THE WAY INTO THE CITY OF WOE.
I AM THE WAY TO A FORSAKEN PEOPLE.
I AM THE WAY INTO ETERNAL SORROW.

SACRED JUSTICE MOVED MY ARCHITECT.
I WAS RAISED HERE BY DIVINE OMNIPOTENCE,
PRIMORDIAL LOVE AND ULTIMATE INTELLECT.

ONLY THOSE ELEMENTS TIME CANNOT WEAR
WERE MADE BEFORE ME, AND BEYOND TIME I STAND.
ABANDON ALL HOPE YE WHO ENTER HERE.

These mysteries I read cut into stone
above a gate. And turning I said: "Master,
what is the meaning of this harsh inscription?"

And he then as initiate to novice:
"Here must you put by all division of spirit
and gather your soul against all cowardice.

This is the place I told you to expect.
Here you shall pass among the fallen people,
souls who have lost the good of intellect."

So saying, he put forth his hand to me,
and with a gentle and encouraging smile
he led me through the gate of mystery.

Here sighs and cries and wails coiled and recoiled
on the starless air, spilling my soul to tears.
A confusion of tongues and monstrous accents toiled

in pain and anger. Voices hoarse and shrill
and sounds of blows, all intermingled, raised
tumult and pandemonium that still

whirls on the air forever dirty with it
as if a whirlwind sucked at sand. . . .

CANTO 19

O Simon Magus! O you wretched crew
who follow him, pandering for silver and gold
the things of God which should be wedded to

love and righteousness! O thieves for hire,
now must the trump of judgment sound your doom
here in the third fosse of the rim of fire!

We had already made our way across
to the next grave, and to that part of the bridge
which hangs above the mid-point of the fosse.

O Sovereign Wisdom, how Thine art doth shine
in Heaven, on Earth, and in the Evil World!
How justly doth Thy power judge and assign!

I saw along the walls and on the ground
   long rows of holes cut in the livid stone;
   all were cut to a size, and all were round.

They seemed to be exactly the same size
   as those in the font of my beautiful San Giovanni,
   built to protect the priests who come to baptize;

(one of which, not so long since, I broke open
   to rescue a boy who was wedged and drowning in it.
   Be this enough to undeceive all men.)

From every mouth a sinner's legs stuck out
   as far as the calf. The soles were all ablaze
   and the joints of the legs quivered and writhed about.

Withes and tethers would have snapped in their throes.
   As oiled things blaze upon the surface only,
   so did they burn from the heels to the points of their toes.

"Master," I said, "who is that one in the fire
   who writhes and quivers more than all the others?
   From him the ruddy flames seem to leap higher."

And he to me: "If you wish me to carry you down
   along that lower bank, you may learn from him
   who he is, and the evil he has done."

And I: "What you will, I will. You are my lord
   and know I depart in nothing from you wish;
   and you know my mind beyond my spoken word."

We moved to the fourth ridge, and turning left
   my Guide descended by a jagged path
   into the strait and perforated cleft.

Thus the good Master bore me down the dim
   and rocky slope, and did not put me down
   till we reached the one whose legs did penance for him.

"Whoever you are, sad spirit," I began,
   "who lie here with your head below your heels
   and planted like a stake—speak if you can."

I stood like a friar who gives the sacrament
  to a hired assassin, who, fixed in the hole,
  recalls him, and delays his death a moment.

"Are you there already, Boniface? Are you there
  already?" he cried. "By several years the writ
  has lied. And all that gold, and all that care—

are you already sated with the treasure
  for which you dared to turn on the Sweet Lady
  and trick and pluck and bleed her at your pleasure?"

I stood like one caught in some raillery,
  not understanding what is said to him,
  lost for an answer to such mockery.

Then Virgil said: "Say to him: 'I am not he,
  I am not who you think.'" And I replied
  as my good Master had instructed me.

The sinner's feet jerked madly; then again
  his voice rose, this time choked with sighs and tears,
  and said at last: "What do you want of me then?

If to know who I am drives you so fearfully
  that you descend the bank to ask it, know
  that the Great Mantle was once hung upon me.

And in truth I was a son of the She-Bear,
  so sly and eager to push my whelps ahead,
  that I pursed wealth above, and myself here.

Beneath my head are dragged all who have gone
  before me in buying and selling holy office;
  there they cower in fissures of the stone.

I too shall be plunged down when that great cheat
  for whom I took you comes here in his turn.
  Longer already have I baked my feet

and been planted upside-down, than he shall be
  before the west sends down a lawless Shepherd
  of uglier deeds to cover him and me.

He will be a new Jason of the Maccabees;
    and just as that king bent to his high priests' will,
    so shall the French king do as this one please."

Maybe—I cannot say—I grew too brash
    at this point, for when he had finished speaking
    I said: "Indeed! Now tell me how much cash

our Lord required of Peter in guarantee
    before he put the keys into his keeping?
    Surely he asked nothing but 'Follow me!'

Nor did Peter, nor the others, ask silver or gold
    of Matthew when they chose him for the place
    the despicable and damned apostle sold.

Therefore stay as you are; this hole well fits you—
    and keep a good guard on the ill-won wealth
    that once made you so bold toward Charles of Anjou.

And were it not that I am still constrained
    by the reverence I owe to the Great Keys
    you held in life, I should not have refrained

from using other words and sharper still;
    for this avarice of yours grieves all the world,
    tramples the virtuous, and exalts the evil.

Of such as you was the Evangelist's vision
    when he saw She who Sits upon the Waters
    locked with the Kings of earth in fornication.

She was born with seven heads, and ten enormous
    and shining horns strengthened and made her glad
    as long as love and virtue pleased her spouse.

Gold and silver are the gods you adore!
    In what are you different from the idolator,
    save that he worships one, and you a score?

Ah Constantine, what evil marked the hour—
    not of your conversion, but of the fee
    the first rich Father took from you in dower!"

And as I sang him this tune, he began to twitch
   and kick both feet out wildly, as if in rage
   or gnawed by conscience—little matter which.

And I think, indeed, it pleased my Guide: his look
   was all approval as he stood beside me
   intent upon each word of truth I spoke.

He approached, and with both arms he lifted me,
   and when he had gathered me against his breast,
   remounted the rocky path out of the valley,

nor did he tire of holding me clasped to him,
   until we reached the topmost point of the arch
   which crosses from the fourth to the fifth rim

of the pits of woe. Arrived upon the bridge,
   he tenderly set down the heavy burden
   he had been pleased to carry up that ledge

which would have been hard climbing for a goat.
Here I looked down on still another moat.

CANTO 28

Who could describe, even in words set free
   of metric and rhyme and a thousand times retold,
   the blood and wounds that now were shown to me!

At grief so deep the tongue must wag in vain;
   the language of our sense and memory
   lacks the vocabulary of such pain.

If one could gather all those who have stood
   through all of time on Puglia's fateful soil
   and wept for the red running of their blood

in the war of the Trojans; and in that long war
   which left so vast a spoil of golden rings,
   as we find written in Livy, who does not err;

along with those whose bodies felt the wet
   and gaping wounds of Robert Guiscard's lances;
   with all the rest whose bones are gathered yet

at Ceperano where every last Pugliese
   turned traitor; and with those from Tagliacozzo
   where Alardo won without weapons—if all these

were gathered, and one showed his limbs run through,
   another his lopped off, that could not equal
   the mutilations of the ninth pit's crew.

A wine tun when a stave or cant-bar starts
   does not split open as wide as one I saw
   split from his chin to the mouth with which man farts.

Between his legs all of his red guts hung
   with the heart, the lungs, the liver, the gall bladder,
   and the shriveled sac that passes shit to the bung.

I stood and stared at him from the stone shelf;
   he noticed me and opening his own breast
   with both hands cried: "See how I rip myself!

See how Mahomet's mangled and split open!
   Ahead of me walks Ali in his tears,
   his head cleft from the top-knot to the chin.

And all the other souls that bleed and mourn
   along this ditch were sowers of scandal and schism:
   as they tore others apart, so are they torn.

Behind us, warden of our mangled horde,
   the devil who butchers us and sends us marching
   waits to renew our wounds with his long sword

when we have made the circuit of the pit;
   for by the time we stand again before him
   all the wounds he gave us last have knit.

But who are you that gawk down from that sill—
   probably to put off your own descent
   to the pit you are sentenced to for your own evil?"

"Death has not come for him, guilt does not drive
   his soul to torment," my sweet Guide replied.
   "That he may experience all while yet alive

I, who am dead, must lead him through the drear
and darkened halls of Hell, from round to round:
and this is true as my own standing here."

More than a hundred wraiths who were marching under
the sill on which we stood, paused at his words
and stared at me, forgetting pain in wonder.

"And if you do indeed return to see
the sun again, and soon, tell Fra Dolcino
unless he longs to come and march with me

he would do well to check his groceries
before the winter drives him from the hills
and gives the victory to the Novarese."

Mahomet, one foot raised, had paused to say
these words to me. When he had finished speaking
he stretched it out and down, and moved away.

Another—he had his throat slit, and his nose
slashed off as far as the eyebrows, and a wound
where one of his ears had been—standing with those

who stared at me in wonder from the pit,
opened the grinning wound of his red gullet
as if it were a mouth, and said through it:

"O soul unforfeited to misery
and whom—unless I take you for another—
I have seen above in our sweet Italy;

if ever again you see the gentle plain
that slopes down from Vercelli to Marcabò,
remember Pier da Medicina in pain,

and announce this warning to the noblest two
of Fano, Messers Guido and Angiolello:
that unless our foresight sees what is not true

they shall be thrown from their ships into the sea
and drown in the raging tides near La Cattolica
to satisfy a tyrant's treachery.

Neptune never saw so gross a crime
   in all the seas from Cyprus to Majorca,
   not even in pirate raids, nor the Argive time.

The one-eyed traitor, lord of the demesne
   whose hill and streams one who walks here beside me
   will wish eternally he had never seen,

will call them to a parley, but behind
   sweet invitations he will work it so
   they need not pray against Focara's wind."

And I to him: "If you would have me bear
   your name to time, show me the one who found
   the sight of that land so harsh, and let me hear

his story and his name." He touched the cheek
   of one nearby, forcing the jaws apart,
   and said: "This is the one; he cannot speak.

This outcast settled Caesar's doubts that day
   beside the Rubicon by telling him:
   'A man prepared is a man hurt by delay.' "

Ah, how wretched Curio seemed to me
   with a bloody stump in his throat in place of the tongue
   which once had dared to speak so recklessly!

And one among them with both arms hacked through
   cried out, raising his stumps on the foul air
   while the blood bedaubed his face: "Remember, too,

Mosca dei Lamberti, alas, who said
   'A thing done has an end!' and with those words
   planted the fields of war with Tuscan dead."

"And brought about the death of all your clan!"
   I said, and he, stung by new pain on pain,
   ran off; and in his grief he seemed a madman.

I stayed to watch those broken instruments,
   and I saw a thing so strange I should not dare
   to mention it without more evidence

but that my own clear conscience strengthens me,
that good companion that upholds a man
within the armor of his purity.

I saw it there; I seem to see it still—
a body without a head, that moved along
like all the others in that spew and spill.

It held the severed head by its own hair,
swinging it like a lantern in its hand;
and the head looked at us and wept in its despair.

It made itself a lamp of its own head,
and they were two in one and one in two;
how this can be, He knows who so commanded.

And when it stood directly under us
it raised the head at arm's length toward our bridge
the better to be heard, and swaying thus

it cried: "O living soul in this abyss,
see what a sentence has been passed upon me,
and search all Hell for one to equal this!

When you return to the world, remember me:
I am Bertrand de Born, and it was I
who set the young king on to mutiny,

son against father, father against son
as Achitophel set Absalom and David;
and since I parted those who should be one

in duty and in love, I bear my brain
divided from its source within this trunk;
and walk here where my evil turns to pain,

an eye for an eye to all eternity:
thus is the law of Hell observed in me."

CANTO 32

If I had rhymes as harsh and horrible
as the hard fact of that final dismal hole
which bears the weight of all the steeps of Hell,

I might more fully press the sap and substance
   from my conception; but since I must do
   without them, I begin with some reluctance.

For it is no easy undertaking, I say,
   to describe the bottom of the Universe;
   nor is it for tongues that only babble child's play.

But may those Ladies of the Heavenly Spring
   who helped Amphion wall Thebes, assist my verse,
   that the word may be the mirror of the thing.

O most miscreant rabble, you who keep
   the stations of that place whose name is pain,
   better had you been born as goats or sheep!

We stood now in the dark pit of the well,
   far down the slope below the Giant's feet,
   and while I still stared up at the great wall,

I heard a voice cry: "Watch which way you turn:
   take care you do not trample on the heads
   of the forworn and miserable brethren."

Whereat I turned and saw beneath my feet
   and stretching out ahead, a lake so frozen
   it seemed to be made of glass. So thick a sheet

never yet hid the Danube's winter course,
   nor, far away beneath the frigid sky,
   locked the Don up in its frozen source:

for were Tanbernick and the enormous peak
   of Pietrapana to crash down on it,
   not even the edges would so much as creak.

The way frogs sit to croak, their muzzles leaning
   out of the water, at the time and season
   when the peasant woman dreams of her day's gleaning—

Just so the livid dead are sealed in place
   up to the part at which they blushed for shame,
   and they beat their teeth like storks. Each holds his face

bowed toward the ice, each of them testifies
  to the cold with his chattering mouth, to his heart's grief
  with tears that flood forever from his eyes.

When I had stared about me, I looked down
  and at my feet I saw two clamped together
  so tightly that the hair of their heads had grown

together. "Who are you," I said, "who lie
  so tightly breast to breast?" They strained their necks,
  and when they had raised their heads as if to reply,

the tears their eyes had managed to contain
  up to that time gushed out, and the cold froze them
  between the lids, sealing them shut again

tighter than any clamp grips wood to wood,
  and mad with pain, they fell to butting heads
  like billy-goats in a sudden savage mood.

And a wraith who lay to one side and below,
  and who had lost both ears to frostbite, said,
  his head still bowed: "Why do you watch us so?

If you wish to know who they are who share one doom,
  they owned the Bisenzio's valley with their father,
  whose name was Albert. They sprang from one womb,

and you may search through all Caïna's crew
  without discovering in all this waste
  a squab more fit for the aspic than these two;

not him whose breast and shadow a single blow
  of the great lance of King Arthur pierced with light;
  nor yet Focaccia; nor this one fastened so

into the ice that his head is all I see,
  and whom, if you are Tuscan, you know well—
  his name on the earth was Sassol Mascheroni.

And I—to tell you all and so be through—
  was Camicion de' Pazzi. I wait for Carlin
  beside whose guilt my sins will shine like virtue."

And leaving him, I saw a thousand faces
   discolored so by cold, I shudder yet
   and always will when I think of those frozen places.

As we approached the center of all weight,
   where I went shivering in eternal shade,
   whether it was my will, or chance, or fate,

I cannot say, but as I trailed my Guide
   among those heads, my foot struck violently
   against the face of one. Weeping, it cried:

"Why do you kick me? If you were not sent
   to wreak a further vengeance for Montaperti,
   why do you add this to my other torment?"

"Master," I said, "grant me a moment's pause
   to rid myself of a doubt concerning this one;
   then you may hurry me at your own pace."

The Master stopped at once, and through the volley
   of foul abuse the wretch poured out, I said:
   "Who are you who curse others so?" And he:

"And who are *you* who go through the dead larder
   of Antenora kicking the cheeks of others
   so hard, that were you alive, you could not kick harder?"

"I *am* alive," I said, "and if you seek fame,
   it may be precious to you above all else
   that my notes on this descent include your name."

"Exactly the opposite is my wish and hope,"
   he answered. "Let me be; for it's little you know
   of how to flatter on this icy slope."

I grabbed the hair of his dog's-ruff and I said:
   "Either you tell me truly who you are,
   or you won't have a hair left on your head."

And he: "Not though you snatch me bald. I swear
   I will not tell my name nor show my face.
   Not though you rip until my brain lies bare."

I had a good grip on his hair; already
  I had yanked out more than one fistful of it,
  while the wretch yelped, but kept his face turned from me;

when another said: "Bocca, what is it ails you?
  What the Hell's wrong? Isn't it bad enough
  to hear you bang your jaws? Must you bark too?"

"Now filthy traitor, say no more!" I cried,
  "for to your shame, be sure I shall bear back
  a true report of you." The wretch replied:

"Say anything you please but go away.
  And if you *do* get back, don't overlook
  that pretty one who had so much to say

just now. Here he laments the Frenchman's pride.
  I saw Buoso da Duera, 'you can report.
  Where the bad salad is kept crisp on ice.'

And if you're asked who else was wintering here,
  Beccheria, whose throat was slit by Florence,
  is there beside you. Gianni de' Soldanier

is further down, I think, with Ganelon,
  and Tebaldello, who opened the gates of Faenza
  and let Bologna steal in with the dawn."

Leaving him then, I saw two souls together
  in a single hole, and so pinched in by the ice
  that one head made a helmet for the other.

As a famished man chews crusts—so the one sinner
  sank his teeth into the other's nape
  at the base of the skull, gnawing his loathsome dinner.

Tydeus in his final raging hour
  gnawed Menalippus' head with no more fury
  than this one gnawed at skull and dripping gore.

"You there," I said, "who show so odiously
  your hatred for that other, tell me why
  on this condition: that if in what you tell me

you seem to have a reasonable complaint
　　against him you devour with such foul relish,
　　I, knowing who you are, and his soul's taint,

may speak your cause to living memory,
　　God willing the power of speech be left to me."

CANTO 33

The sinner raised his mouth from his grim repast
　　and wiped it on the hair of the bloody head
　　whose nape he had all but eaten away. At last

he began to speak: "You ask me to renew
　　a grief so desperate that the very thought
　　of speaking of it tears my heart in two.

But if my words may be a seed that bears
　　the fruit of infamy for him I gnaw
　　I shall weep, but tell my story through my tears.

Who you may be, and by what powers you reach
　　into this underworld, I cannot guess,
　　but you seem to me a Florentine by your speech.

I was Count Ugolino, I must explain;
　　this reverend grace is the Archbishop Ruggieri:
　　now I will tell you why I gnaw his brain.

That I, who trusted him, had to undergo
　　imprisonment and death through his treachery,
　　you will know already. What you cannot know—

that is, the lingering inhumanity
　　of the death I suffered—you shall hear in full:
　　then judge for yourself if he has injured me.

A narrow window in that coop of stone
　　now called the Tower of Hunger for my sake
　　(within which others yet must pace alone)

had shown me several waning moons already
　　between its bars, when I slept the evil sleep
　　in which the veil of the future parted for me.

This beast appeared as master of a hunt
   chasing the wolf and his whelps across the mountain
   that hides Lucca from Pisa. Out in front

of the starved and shrewd and avid pack he had placed
   Gualandi and Sismondi and Lanfranchi
   to point his prey. The father and sons had raced

a brief course only when they failed of breath
   and seemed to weaken; then I thought I saw
   their flanks ripped open by the hounds' fierce teeth.

Before the dawn, the dream still in my head,
   I woke and heard my sons, who were there with me,
   cry from their troubled sleep, asking for bread.

You are cruelty itself if you can keep
   your tears back at the thought of what foreboding
   stirred in my heart; and if you do not weep,

at what are you used to weeping?—The hour when food
   used to be brought, drew near. They were now awake,
   and each was anxious from his dream's dark mood.

And from the base of that horrible tower I heard
   the sound of hammers nailing up the gates:
   I stared at my sons' faces without a word.

I did not weep: I had turned stone inside.
   They wept. 'What ails you, Father, you looks so strange,'
   my little Anselm, youngest of them, cried.

But I did not speak a word nor shed a tear:
   not all that day nor all that endless night,
   until I saw another sun appear.

When a tiny ray leaked into that dark prison
   and I saw staring back from their four faces
   the terror and the wasting of my own,

I bit my hands in helpless grief. And they,
   thinking I chewed myself for hunger, rose
   suddenly together. I heard them say:

'Father, it would give us much less pain
    if you ate us: it was you who put upon us
    this sorry flesh; now strip it off again.'

I calmed myself to spare them. Ah! hard earth,
    why did you not yawn open? All that day
    and the next we sat in silence. On the fourth,

Gaddo, the eldest, fell before me and cried,
    stretched at my feet upon that prison floor:
    'Father, why don't you help me?' There he died.

And just as you see me, I saw them fall
    one by one on the fifth day and the sixth.
    Then, already blind, I began to crawl

from body to body shaking them frantically.
    Two days I called their names, and they were dead.
    Then fasting overcame my grief and me."

His eyes narrowed to slits when he was done,
    and he seized the skull again between his teeth
    grinding it as a mastiff grinds a bone.

Ah, Pisa! foulest blemish on the land
    where "si" sounds sweet and clear, since those nearby you
    are slow to blast the ground on which you stand,

may Caprara and Gorgona drift from place
    and dam the flooding Arno at its mouth
    until it drowns the last of your foul race!

For if to Ugolino falls the censure
    for having betrayed your castles, you for your part
    should not have put his sons to such a torture:

you modern Thebes! those tender lives you spilt—
    Brigata, Uguccione, and the others
    I mentioned earlier—were too young for guilt!

CANTO 34

"On march the banners of the King of Hell,"
    my Master said. "Toward us. Look straight ahead:
    can you make him out at the core of the frozen shell?"

Like a whirling windmill seen afar at twilight,
   or when a mist has risen from the ground—
   just such an engine rose upon my sight

stirring up such a wild and bitter wind
   I cowered for shelter at my Master's back,
   there being no other windbreak I could find.

I stood now where the souls of the last class
   (with fear my verses tell it) were covered wholly;
   they shone below the ice like straws in glass.

Some lie stretched out; others are fixed in place
   upright, some on their heads, some on their soles;
   another, like a bow, bends foot to face.

When we had gone so far across the ice
   that it pleased my Guide to show me the foul creature
   which once had worn the grace of Paradise,

he made me stop, and, stepping aside, he said:
   "Now see the face of Dis! This is the place
   where you must arm your soul against all dread."

Do not ask, Reader, how my blood ran cold
   and my voice choked up with fear. I cannot write it:
   this is a terror that cannot be told.

I did not die, and yet I lost life's breath:
   imagine for yourself what I became,
   deprived at once of both my life and death.

The Emperor of the Universe of Pain
   jutted his upper chest above the ice;
   and I am closer in size to the great mountain

the Titans make around the central pit,
   than they to his arms. Now, starting from this part,
   imagine the whole that corresponds to it!

If he was once as beautiful as now
   he is hideous, and still turned on his Maker,
   well may he be the source of every woe!

With what a sense of awe I saw his head
   towering above me! for it had three faces:
   one was in front, and it was fiery red;

the other two, as weirdly wonderful,
   merged with it from the middle of each shoulder
   to the point where all converged at the top of the skull;

the right was something between white and bile;
   the left was about the color that one finds
   on those who live along the banks of the Nile.

Under each head two wings rose terribly,
   their span proportioned to so gross a bird:
   I never saw such sails upon the sea.

They were not feathers—their texture and their form
   were like a bat's wings—and he beat them so
   that three winds blew from him in one great storm:

it is these winds that freeze all Cocytus.
   He wept from his six eyes, and down three chins
   the tears ran mixed with bloody froth and pus.

In every mouth he worked a broken sinner
   between his rake-like teeth. Thus he kept three
   in eternal pain at his eternal dinner.

For the one in front the biting seemed to play
   no part at all compared to the ripping: at times
   the whole skin of his back was flayed away.

"That soul that suffers most," explained my Guide,
   "is Judas Iscariot, he who kicks his legs
   on the fiery chin and has his head inside.

Of the other two, who have their heads thrust forward,
   the one who dangles down from the black face
   is Brutus: note how he writhes without a word.

And there, with the huge and sinewy arms, is the soul
   of Cassius.—But the night is coming on
   and we must go, for we have seen the whole."

Then, as he bade, I clasped his neck, and he,
    watching for a moment when the wings
    were opened wide, reached over dexterously

and seized the shaggy coat of the king demon;
    then grappling matted hair and frozen crusts
    from one tuft to another, clambered down.

Purgatory

CANTO 15

As much as, tracing from the third hour's close
    Till earliest dawn, appeareth of that sphere
    Which like a playful child no quiet knows—

So long a course the sun's declining light
    Had still to traverse—it was evening here,
    But upon earth the very noon of night.

His beams assailed us full upon the brow;
    For we had so advanced the mountain o'er,
    That towards the sunset we were moving now;

When I my forehead felt oppressed with glare
    Of dazzling light, far brighter than before;
    And stupor seized me from effect so rare.

My hands I raised to guard my aching sight,
    And o'er my forehead held them up, to hide
    The overpowering effluence of light.

As when from water or a glass, the ray
    Bounds from below unto the opposing side,
    Ascending upward in the self-same way

That it descended—equi-distant too
    From the right line a stone would take, impelled
    Through the same space, as science shows is true;

So, as it seemed, by a refracted light
    Shining in front of me was I assailed;
    Wherefore I quickly turned away my sight.

SOURCE: *The Divine Comedy of Dante Alighieri*, translated by I. C. Wright (London: G. Bell & Sons, 1883), pp. 210–227, 280–294.

"Loved sire," I asked, "what is it I discern
   Approaching tow'rds us, and from which mine eyes,
   Unable to endure the splendour, turn?"

"Marvel not, if thou still art dazzled by
   The ministering attendants of the skies—
   One comes," he said, "to summon man on high.

These glorious sights not long shall give thee pain,
   But will inspire thee with as much delight
   As nature makes thee able to sustain."

When near we came unto the angel blest,
   "Enter," with joyful voice he said; "this height
   Presents a stair far easier than the rest."

Ascending thence—behind us sang a voice:
   "Blest are the merciful," in sweetest lay,
   "And thou victorious one, do thou rejoice."

Slow up the ascent were labouring on we two—
   My guide and I; I, thinking on my way
   That from his speech some profit might accrue;

Then, turning, made I this inquiry: "What
   Could mean the spirit of Romagna, when
   He spoke of good, with others shared or not?"

Then he: "Full well he knows the cost severe
   Of his besetting sin; no marvel then
   If man he warned, to abate his suffering here.

Because your wishes to such objects tend
   As are diminished if another share,
   In envy's full blown sighs they ever end.

But if the love of the celestial sphere
   To higher objects had allured your care,
   Your breast would not be troubled by that fear.

For there the more the expression 'our' we use,
   So much more good to each one's lot will fall,
   And greater warmth will charity diffuse."

"Now," I replied, "am I far more perplexed
    Than if thou had'st not answered me at all;
    And with more troublous doubts my mind is vexed:

How can it be, that a possession, shared
    By many persons, can enrich them more
    Than if the same is but on few conferred?"

Then he: "Because thine intellectual sight
    Is wholly bent earth's objects to explore,
    Darkness thou gatherest from the all-perfect Light.

That Good ineffable which dwells above,
    As ray to lucid body swift descends,
    So, in unbounded fulness speeds to love.

The warmth it finds, the same it still bestows;
    And wide soe'er as charity extends,
    Beyond it still the eternal Virtue glows.

The more aspirants are there of the sky,
    More good there is to love, and more is loved,
    As mirrors by reflection multiply:

And if a further answer thou request,
    See Beatrice, by whom shall be removed
    This and each other longing of thy breast.

Exert thee now without delay to efface,
    E'en as the two, each still remaining wound,
    Which due contrition soonest may erase."

I was about to say, "I am content;"
    But paused, when coming to another round,
    On novel sights my curious eyes were bent.

There an extatic vision suddenly
    Seemed to enwrap me; and a multitude
    Assembled in a temple met mine eye.

And with a mother's look, methought e'en thus
    A lady cried, who on the threshold stood:
    "Why, O my son, hast thou so dealt with us?

Behold thy sire and I full many a day
   Have sought thee sorrowing." Ceased her gentle strain;
   And this first vision floated soon away.

Then came in view a matron, from whose eyes
   Were streaming down her cheeks such tears amain,
   As from indignant wrath are wont to rise.

"If of that city thou art lord," she said,
   "Whose name caused discord 'mid the heavenly race,
   And where each science doth its lustre shed,

Punish those arms that so audaciously
   Presumed our virgin daughter to embrace."
   Pisistratus all mildly made reply,

With look benevolent and temperate:
   "How shall we treat the man who wills our woe,
   If he who loves us meets so harsh a fate?"

With fury then inflamed, I saw a crowd
   Stoning a youth; and as they struck each blow,
   "Away with him, away," they cried aloud.

I saw him, as to earth he bent at last,
   Weighed down in death by the o'erpowering blows;
   But stedfast still to heaven his eyes he cast,

In that dread conflict, to the Lord above
   Praying for pardon on his ruthless foes,
   With gentle look that doth to pity move.

When to itself my mind returned again,
   And on substantial things its aim could keep,
   I found my wanderings were not wholly vain.

My guide, remarking my uncertain gait,
   Like his who tries to rouse himself from sleep,
   Cried: "What comes o'er thee? canst thou not walk straight?

Above a mile hast thou thy journey made
   With eyes half shut, and reeling to and fro,
   Like to a man by wine or slumber swayed."

"Loved sire," I said, "if thou wilt hear my tale,
  The dream I witnessed will I strive to show,
  What time my tottering limbs appeared to fail."

"Hadst thou a hundred masks upon thy face,"
  He answered me, "yet e'en thy very dreams,
  And inmost thoughts have I the power to trace.

What thou hast seen Heaven's favour did bestow,
  Thy heart to open to the peaceful streams
  Which from the Eternal Fountain ever flow.

I asked not, 'what comes o'er thee,' with the intent
  Of one whose faculty of sight is gone,
  Soon as the soul is from the body rent;

But I inquired, to urge thee to proceed:
  Thus it behoves to spur slow loiterers on,
  That when the watch returneth, they may speed."

Then towards the west we still pursued our way,
  Extending as we went our ravished sight
  Against the splendour of the evening ray;

When lo! approaching us, came gradually
  A vapour dense and dark as blackest night;
  Nor was there shelter whither we could fly:

Our eyes were dimmed, and all obscured the light.

CANTO 16

Nor gloom of Hell, nor shade of blackest night,
  When not a star illumes the barren heaven,
  And clouds of massy darkness block the light,

My face e'er covered with a veil so dense
  As did that murky smoke, around us driven,
  And to the touch, of sharpness so intense.

In vain I strove to keep my eyes unclosed,
  Until my faithful escort, drawing near,
  His shoulder to assist my steps disposed.

As one bereft of sight behind his guide
   Walks, lest he stray and meet some shock severe,
   Or aught whence greater evils may betide;

So went I through that foul and pungent air,
   List'ning my leader's words, who did not cease
   His warning: "How you quit my side, beware."

Voices I heard; and each appeared to pray
   Unto the Lamb for pardon and for peace—
   The Lamb of God that taketh sins away;

And "Agnus Dei" was their prelude still.
   All in one measure, in one voice unite;
   And perfect concord seemed to rule their will.

"Are spirits these we hear?" I then inquire.
   He gave me answer: "Thou hast guessed aright;
   They loose the fetters of their former ire."

"Now who art thou who through our smoky air
   Passest along, and speakest of our band,
   As one who still by calends counts the year?"

Thus spake a single voice; whereat my guide:
   "Return an answer to them, and demand
   If this way leadeth up the mountain's side."

And I: "Thou, who dost cleanse thee, to return
   Pure to thy great Creator, follow me;
   And things of wondrous import shalt thou learn."

"Follow I will, far as I may," he said,
   "And if the smoke permit me not to see,
   Hearing shall keep me near to thee instead."

I then began: "Enveloped in that frame
   Which death dissolves, do I ascend on high:
   And through the infernal gloom I hither came.

Since then hath God on me such grace bestowed,
   As to behold His Courts with mortal eye,
   In this most strange and unaccustomed mode,

Conceal not who you were before you died;
 And if this path may reach the opening, tell:
 By your direction we our steps shall guide."

"I was a Lombard; Marco was my name;
 I knew the world, and loved that virtue well
 To which no mortal now directs his aim.

To mount above thou takest the proper way;
 And when thou there arrivest, let me crave
 That thou forget not for my soul to pray."

Then I: "As far as promises can bind,
 I will obey thee: but one doubt I have,
 That, unexplained, is bursting in my mind.

Single before, that doubt is now made twain
 By thy opinion, rendering me more sure,
 When coupled with what elsewhere I obtain.

Lost is the world, e'en as thou sayest, indeed
 To every virtue; and is so impure,
 That evil there on every side doth beerd.

But what the cause I do entreat thee show,
 That I may understand and tell to other;
 For one, in heaven, one places it below."

A sigh profound he drew, by grief intense
 Forced into "Oh"—he then began: "O brother!
 The world is blind, and sure thou comest thence.

Ye mortals to the heavenly orbs each cause
 Ascribe; as though a first necessity
 Moved all things in obedience to its laws:

Which (were it true) in you it would destroy
 Free-will; and then unjustly should we see
 Woe dealt to evil deeds, to virtue joy.

Your movements have their impulse first from heaven;
 I say not all; but had I so asserted,
 To choose 'twixt good and evil, light is given,

And freedom of the will; which in the first
 Encounter with the stars, stands, if exerted;
 Then conquers all if it be duly nurst.

Though free, yet are ye subject to the sway
 Of higher power, that in you plants the mind,
 Which cares not starry influence to obey.

If in the paths of error then ye rove,
 The cause is in yourselves, as ye will find;
 And this more clearly I to thee will prove.

Forth from His hand, who, ere it see the day,
 Views it delighted—like some infant child,
 Weeping and smiling in its sportive way,

The artless soul springs forth—not knowing aught
 Except to turn to joy, whence it is thrilled
 Spontaneous, by its gladsome Maker taught.

Some trifling good, first tasted with delight,
 Leads it astray, and tempts it to pursue,
 Unless restrained or guided on aright.

Laws needful hence, a bridle to impose—
 A ruler hence—who of the city true
 The towers at least may from afar disclose.

Laws are there; but who keeps the laws in view?
 For know—the Shepherd who the flock doth lead
 Parts not the hoof, although the cud he chew.

And hence it is, the tribe who see their guide
 Aim at the good they value most, do feed
 On that alone, nor care for aught beside.

Ill guidance, as ye plainly may descry,
 Hath led the world in wicked paths astray;
 And not your nature's bad propensity.

To Rome, which taught the ancient world good deeds,
 Two suns were wont to point the twofold way,
 That of the world, and that to God which leads.

The one hath quenched the other—with the crook
 The sword is joined; and scarce it need be told
 How ill the twain such combination brook,

Since one no longer doth the other curb.
 Look to the grain, if credit thou withhold;
 For by its fruit is known each several herb.

The country washed by Adicë and Po
 For courtesy and valour once was famed,
 Ere Frederick had sustained his overthrow.

Securely there may pass each villain now,
 Who dared not then have shown his face, ashamed
 To talk with good men and confront their brow.

Still live there three, in whom the olden time
 Reproves the vices of these latter days;
 And much they wish to reach a happier clime—

Currado da Palazzo, good Gheràrd,
 And da Castel, who, in the Frenchman's phrase,
 Is called more properly the plain Lombard.

Know then, Rome's Church, oppressed by too much weight,
 Confounding the two governments, hath brought
 Herself into the mire with all her freight."

"Marco," I said, "thy argument is good;
 Now know I why from the heritage 'twas thought
 Better the sons of Levi to exclude.

But who is that Gheràrd, who, as you said,
 Reproves a vicious age, and seems to be
 Left as a sample of the mighty dead?"

"To dupe or try me is thy speech preferred,
 Since, Tuscan though it is," he answered me,
 "Of good Gheràrd thou seem'st not to have heard.

Him by no other surname do I know,
 Unless his daughter Gaia one prepare.
 God speed you, for no more with you I go.

Piercing the mist—behold the morning ray
    Already whitens: I must leave thee, ere
    The Angel who is yonder, comes this way."

He spake; nor further question would he hear.

CANTO 17

Remember, reader, if thou e'er hast been
    Wrapt in dark mist upon an Alpine height,
    Through which, but as a mole doth through his skin,

Thine eye could pierce—how, when the thick moist shroud
    Begins to melt away, the solar light
    Feebly and faintly penetrates the cloud;

And swift will thy imagination be
    To form a just conception, how the sun,
    Which now was setting, first appeared to me,

As, keeping even with my faithful guide,
    Forth from such murky cloud my way I won
    To the low shores whereon the rays had died.

O Fancy, in whose chain we oft are bound—
    So lost to outward things we take no thought,
    Although a thousand trumpets clang around;

What moves thee, if no impulse sense bestow?
    Light moves thee, in the clime of heaven self-wrought,
    Or by his will who sendeth it below.

Imagination painted to my sight
    Her crime who was transformed into the bird
    Excelling all that in the song delight:

And so abstracted was my mind within,
    That from without was nothing seen or heard,
    Which had the power acceptance there to win.

Into my lofty fancy then was showered
    One crucified, enraged and fierce to view,
    Such as in death his savage soul he poured.

Round him the great Ahasuerus stood,
    Esther his wife, and Mordecai the Jew,
    In word and deed pre-eminently good.

And as this vision of my fancy burst,
    Like to a bubble, which hath sudden been
    Left by the water which composed it first,

Before my sight a youthful maid arose,
    Profusely weeping, as she cried: "O queen,
    Whence came the wrathful wish thy life to close?

To save Lavinia's life, hath death been thine;
    Yet hast thou lost her; and for thee I weep,
    Mourning thy fate more bitterly than mine."

As when a sudden and o'erpowering light
    Strikes our closed eyes, and breaks upon our sleep,
    Quivering a moment ere it takes its flight;

So the imagined vision sank below,
    Soon as a splendour burst upon mine eye
    Surpassing all that on the earth we know.

I turned to view the place I now had gained,
    When cried a voice: "Ye here may mount on high,"
    Which from all other thoughts my mind restrained,

And with such eagerness inspired my breast
    To look upon the person who thus spoke,
    Nought less than actual sight had given me rest.

E'en as the sun our mortal ken weighs down,
    Its very radiance to itself a cloak,
    So here my visual power was overthrown.

"A heavenly spirit this, who up the height,
    Unasked by us, would fain our journey speed,
    Veiling his presence with excess of light.

He uses us as man himself would use;
    For he who waits entreaty, seeing need,
    Inclines his mind already to refuse.

Then let us not such invitation spurn,
  But to the mount, ere it grow dark, repair;
  We may not afterwards, till day return."

Thus spake my faithful guide—by him attended
  I bent my course up to a lofty stair:
  And ere the lowest step we had ascended,

I felt a wind upon my face, as though
  Fanned by a pinion;—and these words were said;
  "Blessed are they who peace on earth bestow."

The sun's last rays that usher in the night,
  Were now upraised so high above my head,
  That stars on every side appeared in sight.

"Why, O my virtue," to myself I said,
  When I perceived my limbs could not command
  Their former strength, "why art thou vanquished?"

Arriving at a landing, whence no more
  The staircase led above, we took our stand,
  Like to a ship when she hath come ashore.

Some little time attentively I tried
  In this new circle to distinguish sound;
  Then to the master turned again and cried:

"O my dear Father, tell what sinful blot
  Receives ablution in the present round;
  Though rest our feet—thy speech, withhold it not."

And he to me: "The love of good, curtailed
  Of its proportions, here obtains them full;
  Here plies the oar that erst through loitering failed.

But to perceive more clearly what I say,
  Direct thy thoughts to me; and thou shalt cull
  Some fruit of goodly sort from our delay.

Creator nor created being e'er
  Was wholly void of love, my son," he said,
  "Or natural love or mental, as is clear.

The natural love was aye from error free;
   The other into error may be led,
   Or through excess, or through deficiency.

To primal good while it directs its aim,
   Or secondary, keeping measure due,
   It cannot tend to aught deserving blame:

But when perverted or when too intent,
   Or slack, some goodly object to pursue,
   'Gainst the Creator is the creature bent.

Hence it is clear that Love implants the seed
   Of all the virtues that your bosoms sway,
   And also of each unbecoming deed.

Now, from the safety of the object loved
   Since Love can never turn its face away,
   So from self hatred are all things removed.

And since no one in self-existent state
   Lives, independent of his primal source,
   It follows clearly none that source can hate.

This love of ill then, (if the truth I say)
   Against its neighbour must direct its course,
   And in three modes is gendered in your clay;

One by his neighbour's fall aspires to be
   Exalted, and upon this sole account
   He longs to see him sunk to low degree.

Another is depressed through fear to lose
   Power, grace, and honour, should a rival mount;
   Whence grieving, he his neighbour's fall pursues.

Another, roused by injury, longs to wreak
   His fiery wrath, and vengeance to obtain;
   And he must needs his neighbour's misery seek:

Beneath us is this triple love subdued.
   Now of that other love some knowledge gain,
   Which keeps no measure, though it aims at good.

Some blessing indistinct is wished by each,
   In which the soul a sweet repose may find;
   Whence all essay their several good to reach:

If love too languid urges to pursue,
   Or to obtain it,—to this round assigned,
   After repentance, meet ye sufferings due.

Another good there is—not cause of bliss—
   Not full fruition—not that essence true,
   Of every good the source: the love of this,

By mortal man too lavishly indulged,
   The inmates of the higher circles rue:
   How triply shared is not by me divulged—

The search of this thou mayst thyself pursue."

CANTO 18

His reasoning ended, my exalted guide
   Attentively surveyed my countenance,
   To see if I were fully satisfied.

And I, by further cravings now possest,
   Spake not aloud, but said within: "Perchance
   He by my constant questions is opprest."

But that true father, who at once perceived
   The timid wish I had not dared to tell,
   Soon by his speech my fear to speak relieved.

Then I: "My sight, O master, gains such force
   In thy clear rays, that I discern full well
   All that is meant and taught in thy discourse.

Wherefore, sweet Father dear, I pray thee show
   That love, whence every action fraught with shame,
   And all good deeds, as thou hast told me, flow!"

"Direct the sharpened lustres of thy mind
   To me," he said, "while I their fault proclaim,
   Who think, though blind themselves, to lead the blind.

The soul, which is created prone to love,
  Awakened into action by delight,
  To all that pleases doth obedient move.

Your apprehension from some object true
  An image draws, unfolding it to sight,
  So that the soul is tempted to pursue.

And if the mind thus wrought on, is inclined,
  That inclination is a natural love,
  Newly produced by pleasure in your mind.

Thus, e'en as fire spontaneous mounts on high,
  Created apt to raise itself above,
  And reach again its storehouse in the sky;

The soul, so smitten, enters on desire—
  A spiritual motion, resting never
  Till the beloved object it acquire.

Now will appear to thee how far they err
  From truth, who love of every kind whatever,
  As in itself deserving praise, aver.

Love may itself perhaps be understood
  As always good; but still we sometimes find
  The impression bad, although the wax be good."

I answered: "Love to me is rendered plain
  By thy discourse, and my attentive mind;
  But this hath filled me with my doubts again.

For, if from outward objects love gains force,
  And such sole force to sway the mind avails,
  No merit has it, right or wrong its course."

"As far as Reason," he replied, "can reach,
  I may direct thee; but when Reason fails
  'Tis Faith that works, and Beatrice must teach.

Each spiritual essence, that is joined
  With matter that in separate state exists,
  Contains within the virtue of its kind;

Which, if it worketh not, remains unseen,
   Save in the effect: as in a plant subsists
   Life, not perceived but by the foliage green,

So, from what source the apprehension springs
   Of first ideas, vainly men inquire,
   Or whence comes passion for the first loved things.

They live in man, as instinct in the bee
   For making honey; and this first desire
   Nor praise nor censure can infer to thee.

That every other wish round this may bend,
   In you is placed a power, whose warning voice
   Should still the threshold of the will defend.

This is the source, whence praise or blame accrues,
   As good or bad affections are your choice—
   Winnowed by each, who this or that pursues.

Those who the matter fully sifted, knew
   This innate liberty, and felt its force;
   Whence moral codes for after times they drew.

Hence lay we down, that from necessity
   Each love that in you springs derives its source;
   But in yourselves the powers to check it lie.

Free-will is termed 'the noble faculty'
   By Beatrice; remember then to bear
   This, if she speak of it, in memory."

The moon, that tardily at midnight came,
   Was making now the stars appear more rare,
   In figure like a bucket all in flame—

Stemming the heaven abandoned by the sun,
   Between the Corsic and Sardinian coast,
   When Rome beholds him as his course is run:

And that kind shade who hath more fame bestowed
   On Pietola than Mantua e'er could boast,
   Had eased my mind of its oppressive load;

When I (whose doubts had all been set at rest
  By reason clear and argument refined)
  Stood like to one by drowsiness opprest.

But vanished soon this drowsiness; for now
  Came suddenly, approaching from behind,
  A troop of spirits o'er the mountain's brow:

And like the fury and the crowd displayed
  Ismenus' and Asopus' banks beside,
  Whene'er the Thebans called for Bacchus' aid;

So each, throughout this round, as I beheld,
  Urging his hurried footstep, onward hied,—
  By goodly zeal and righteous love impelled.

They reach'd us soon—so rapidly they swept;
  (For none amid that crowd immense was slack)
  And two in front cried, shouting as they wept;

"The Virgin sought the hills without delay;
  And Caesar, hastening into Spain, to attack
  Ilerda, smote Marseilles upon his way."

"Haste, haste," the others cried who near them stood,
  "Through want of love be time not thrown away;
  Grace springs anew from ardour to do good."

"O ye in whom a fervour, now acute,
  Doth haply compensate for old delay,
  Which to lukewarmness owed its primal root;

This man who lives (no idle tale I feign)
  Would with the rising sun ascend the steep;
  Then say where nearest he the stair may gain."

These words were spoken by my faithful guide;
  When, "Close behind us now the pathway keep,
  And thou shalt find the entrance," one replied,

"So anxious to pursue our course are we,
  We cannot pause;—forgiveness then we pray,
  If this our duty rudeness seem to be.

San Zeno's Abbot in Verona I,
  What time good Barbarossa's arm held sway,
  Whom Milan speaks of yet lamentingly.

He with one foot already in the grave
  Shall for that monastery shortly mourn,
  And for the abuse of power forgiveness crave;

Since he, for Shepherd of the flock proclaimed
  His son, in mind defective, and ill born,
  Nor less in person than in temper maimed."

CANTO 31

"Thou whom beyond the sacred stream I see,"
  Thus quickly she began her speech anew,
  Turning forthwith its point direct on me,

Although full sharp the side alone had seemed,
  "Answer me; is this accusation true?
  By free confession be the fault redeemed."

Confusion so o'erwhelmed me at the sound,
  The words expired within my lips, ere they
  Had through the organs their expression found.

Awhile she paused; then uttered: "Answer me,
  For not yet hath the water washed away
  The mournful traces from thy memory."

Fear and confusion, mixt together, drew
  Forth from my lips an answering "yes," so faint,
  That to perceive it, sight was needed too.

As breaks a bow before the arrow flies,
  When both the wood and cord are overbent,
  And to the mark the shaft more feebly hies;

So I beneath this heavy burden quailed,
  Pouring forth sighs and tears, a bitter flood;
  And, ere the words had reached my lips, they failed.

Whence she resumed: "To thwart those high desires
  Instilled by me, which bade thee love that Good,
  Noblest to which the soul of man aspires—

What interposing trenches didst thou find,
   What chains, that thus, foregoing liberty,
   All hope of further progress was resigned?

And what attraction, what advantages
   In other foreheads were perceived by thee,
   That taught thee those to woo instead of these?"

After the drawing of a bitter sigh,
   My lips with difficulty answer made,
   And scarce had power to fashion a reply.

Weeping, I said: "My steps were turned aside
   By the false pleasure present things displayed,
   Soon as your face was to my view denied."

"Hadst thou been silent, or refused to own
   Thy fault," she said, "our knowledge would have reached
   That fault, by One omniscient clearly known.

When tears however, gushing forth, allege
   The conscious sinner, by himself impeached,
   In this our court the wheel rebates the edge:

But that more shame may expiate thy crime,
   And with more strength thy spirit may be fraught,
   Listening the Syren's voice another time,

Dismiss the cause of tears, and hear from me,
   What different effect should have been wrought
   By the announcement of my death to thee.

No lure to equal those fair limbs of mine,
   Now unto dust returned, did ever art,
   Or nature, to attract thine eyes, design:

And if with charm of such supreme delight
   Thy doom it was, at my decease, to part,
   What mortal thing should have allured thy sight?

At the first shaft which struck thee from the bow
   Of treacherous things, thou shouldest have soared above,
   Pursuing me, not frail, as when below.

Became thee not to stoop thy wing to earth
    To wait fresh snares—some youthful maiden's love,
    Or other vanity of equal worth.

Though the young bird may twice or thrice forget,
    Yet in the view of those full-plumed, his aim
    The fowler takes in vain, or spreads his net."

As little children, with their eyes bent low,
    Stand listening—mute, through consciousness of shame,
    Convicted and repentant; even so

I stood; and she resumed: "Since but to hear
    Afflicts thee, raise thy beard, and let thine eyes
    Witness a cause of sorrow more severe."

With less resistance by the root is torn
    Some sturdy oak, when northern blasts arise,
    Or those from Afric's land, impetuous borne,

Than lifted I my chin, as she directed;
    For when instead of "face" she said my "beard,"
    I knew the venom that her speech infected:

And, stretching out my face, beheld those fair
    Primaeval creatures, which before appeared,
    Cease from the sprinkling of the flowers they bare.

And I, though scarcely was restored my sight,
    Saw Beatrice admire that Form Divine,
    Which in itself two natures doth unite.

On the green bank—her veil around her cast—
    She seemed still more her former self to outshine,
    Than, while on earth, all others she surpast.

Repentant stings so struggled in my soul,
    I contemplated now with hate and shame
    All that had swayed me with supreme control.

Such keen remorse was kindled in my breast,
    I swoon'd away; and what I then became
    She knows, whose mighty presence I confessed.

Soon as my heart fresh vigour had supplied,
  The Lady, whom before I found alone,
  I saw above me; "Hold—keep hold," she cried;

Then drew me to the stream; and as she bore
  My sinking form, her way she quickly won,
  Light as a shuttle, that dark water o'er.

Nearing the sacred bank—came on mine ear
  "Asperges me" in strain so passing sweet,
  Recall I cannot, much less write it here.

The beauteous lady straight, her arms extending,
  Embraced my head, and plunged me where 'twas meet
  That I should taste the wave; then, lowly bending,

She raised me up, and offered me, so laved,
  Within the circle of the Maids benign,
  Who, as they danced, their arms around me waved.

Nymphs are we here below, and stars in heaven:
  To Beatrice, ere from her seat divine,
  She hither came, were we for handmaids given.

We to her eyes will lead thee; but to bear
  The joyous light within, shall yonder three,
  Profound of ken, thy visual sense prepare."

Singing melodiously, commenced they thus;
  Then to the Griffon's breast conducted me,
  Where Beatrice was standing, turned to us.

"Now satisfy," they said, "thy anxious view;
  Thee have we placed before the emeralds bright,
  Whence Love erewhile his shafts against thee drew."

A thousand longings more intense than fire
  Mine eyes attracted to those eyes of light,
  Fixt on the Griffon with profound desire:

And in them, like unto the sun pourtrayed
  Within a glass, the two-fold thing was beaming—
  His either nature there by turns displayed.

Think, reader, what surprise was mine, to see
    An object, in itself so tranquil seeming,
    Bear in its image such diversity.

Whilst, filled with deepest wonder and delight,
    My soul was tasting of that heavenly food,
    Which, satisfying, wakes new appetite,

The other three irradiate forms advance:
    How great their rank their high demeanour showed
    And songs accompanied their angel dance.

"Turn, Beatrice, O turn" (this was their song)
    "Thy holy eyes unto thy faithful one,
    Who hath, to view thee, made such journey long.

Do thou at our entreaty here reveal
    Thy smile to him, and make thy beauty known—
    That second beauty thou dost now conceal."

O splendour of eternal living light!
    Who, though grown pale beneath Parnassus' shade,
    Or wont to quaff the rills from that fair height,

Would not betray the mental strain, should he
    Attempt to picture thee, thou peerless Maid,
    When, compassed with celestial harmony,

Thou in unshrouded beauty wert displayed?

CANTO 32

Bent were mine eyes with ardour so intense
    To sate their ten years' thirst, that all the while
    Lost in oblivion was each other sense:

On either side of them a wall was set,
    To exclude ought else; so did that sacred smile
    Again enthral them with its ancient net;

When towards the left my looks were forcibly
    Diverted by those Nymphs, on hearing one
    Exclaim, addressing me; "Too earnestly:"

And a sensation of o'erpowering light,
    As when the eyes are dazzled by the sun,
    Deprived me for some moments of my sight.

But when my vision was in part renewed,
    So that mine eyes were able to discern
    Objects less splendid than those lately viewed,

I saw that on the right that glorious host
    Had wheeled around; and, making now a turn,
    Before the flames and sun took up their post.

E'en as a troop, beneath their bucklers ranged
    For greater safety, turn on either hand,
    Ere their direction can be wholly changed;

So now, of that celestial armament
    Passed onward in like guise the leading band,
    Ere the triumphal car its beam had bent.

Then to the wheels those Nymphs themselves betaking,
    The Griffon moved his blessed burden thence,
    Although so gently, not a plume was shaking.

The beauteous maid who drew me o'er the tide
    Followed the wheel of less circumference,
    By Statius and myself accompanied.

As thus we passed throughout the lofty wood,
    Void through the fault of Eve, in unison
    With angel notes our journey we pursued.

About the distance that an arrow, thrice
    Loosed from the string, might compass, had we gone,
    When from the car descended Beatrice.

Then "Adam" muttered all in accents low;
    And in a circle round a tree they went,
    Stript of each leaf, without a flower to show.

Its head, which, as it rises, doth dilate
    The more, so lofty grows, that wonderment
    In Indians 'mid their groves it would create.

"Blessed, O Griffon! art thou not to rend
    This tree, which needs must be surpassing sweet,
    Since it allured our Parents to offend."

Thus cried they, as they circled round the tree;
    And He in whom the twofold natures meet;
    "Yea, so fulfilled all righteousness must be."

Then to the chariot's beam straight turning round,
    He drew it to the tree bereft of spray,
    And left it, by a twig together bound.

As, when from heaven descends the glorious light,
    Mingled with that which when the Pisces' ray
    Departs, beams forth with more effective might,

Our plants swell out, and re-enlivened are
    With its own hues, or ere the sun unite
    His fiery steeds beneath some other star;

With tints less vivid than the rose, but more
    Deep than the violet, was that plant now dight,
    Which of its foliage was so stript before.

The words they sang I could not comprehend;
    For not to earth belonged their melodies;
    Nor did I hear their notes unto the end.

Could I but sing how heavy slumber weighed,
    At tale of Syrinx' woe, the unpitying eyes,
    That dearly for their high distinction paid,

Like one who from a model draws, might I
    Depict the manner of my slumber deep;
    But to describe it, whoso will, may try.

Passing to when I woke, hence tell I, how
    A flash of splendour burst the veil of sleep,
    A voice too, crying: "Rise; what doest thou?"

As (led to view the flowerets of that tree
    For whose delicious fruit the Angels pine,
    In heaven a source of ceaseless jubilee,)

Turned back the Apostles Peter, James and John,
From sleep awakened at the Word divine,
By which had deeper sleep been overthrown;

And witnessed straight their little band grow less—
Moses departed, and Elias too—
And their great Master altered in his dress;

So I awakening, roused me from my dream,
And saw that pitying Maid stand o'er me, who
Had led my steps along the sacred stream.

And, "Where is Beatrice?" in doubt I cried.
"Beneath the new-born leaves behold her there,
Upon the root reclining," she replied;

"Behold the maidens who her form surround:
Following the Griffon, mount the rest in air
With sweeter minstrelsy and more profound."

Whether to greater length her words were brought
I know not, since before mine eyes was She
Who barred the entrance to each other thought.

Alone she sate upon the quickened ground,
As though the car were in her custody,
Which there the twofold animal had bound.

Into a circle formed themselves anon
The Nymphs, those lights supporting in their hands
Which Auster quencheth not, or Aquilon.

"Brief space this forest shall thy dwelling be;
And in that Rome where Christ himself commands
Shalt thou be fellow-citizen with me.

Whence, that the evil world some good may learn,
Look on the car, and all that meets thine eye
Forget not to record, on thy return."

These words spake Beatrice; and I, resigned
To execute her will implicitly,
E'en as she bade, applied my eyes and mind.

Ne'er from thick cloud, by force ethereal riven,
   With such velocity was lightning sent,
   When falling from the farthest bound of heaven;

As down the bird of Jove impetuous flew
   Straight through the tree, by which the bark was rent
   Much more the tender boughs and foliage new.

He struck the car with all his force, whereat
   It quailed like vessel tempest tost, and driven
   Now by the waves on this side, now on that.

Then up into the vehicle I viewed
   A she-fox leap, to greediness so given,
   She seemed rapacious of all goodly food.

But chiding her for this unseemly deed
   My Lady put her to such rapid flight,
   Her skinny bones could scarce endure the speed.

Then from the quarter whence he came before,
   The Eagle swooped into the chariot bright,
   And left it with his feathers covered o'er.

And such a voice as issues from a heart
   Grief stricken, came from heaven; and thus it said:
   "Oh, how ill freighted, little bark thou art!"

Then seemed it that the earth did gape betwixt
   The wheels; and thence in sight a Dragon sped,
   Which, turning up its tail, the car transfixed.

And like a wasp that draweth back its sting,
   So, drawing back his venomed tail, he rent
   Part of the car, and fled with joyous wing.

And as the earth with herbage is renewed,
   So the remainder an integument
   Formed of the feathers, with intention good

Haply presented; and as rapidly
   Were both the pole and wheels therewith o'erspread,
   As the lips open to express a sigh.

The sacred Structure, thus diversified,
  Through every part of it put forth a head;
  Three at the pole, and one on either side.

Horns the first three, like unto oxen, bore;
  One single horn the four among them reared;
  Nor was such monster ever seen before.

Firm as a rock upon some mountain high,
  A wanton harlot, seated there, appeared,
  Who threw on every side a wandering eye:

And lest she should be carried from that height,
  A giant sitting close to her I viewed;
  And oft they kissed each other in my sight.

But when with mine her roving eyes did meet,
  Her dread companion lashed her in fierce mood,
  E'en from the head unto the very feet.

Then did he loose the beast, with anger keen
  Incensed, and through the wood such distance drew,
  The boughs alone afforded ample screen

To hide the damsel and the monster new.

CANTO 33

"O God, the heathen have defiled thy fane,"
  Alternate now the three and now the four,
  Suffused with tears, began the holy train.

And Beatrice was listening, so subdued
  By pity, that scarce Mary's features wore
  More signs of grief, when at the cross she stood.

But when the other virgins had given place
  For her to speak, she raised herself upright,
  And answered to their words with glowing face:

"A little while—ye shall not me behold;
  And yet again, O sisters, my delight,
  A little while, and me ye shall behold."

Then all the seven in front of her she set,
  And, beckoning unto me, a wish conveyed
  That I should follow, with the sage, who yet

Remained, and that fair damsel: thus she went:
  Nor had she, I believe, the tenth step made,
  Advancing, when her eyes on mine were bent;

And with a tranquil look she said: "Come near,
  That, should I be inclined to speak to thee,
  Thou mayest be able my discourse to hear."

When, as in duty bound, I had complied,
  "Why, brother, not attempt to question me,"
  She added, "as thou journeyest by my side?"

As those, who, moved with too much reverence, strive
  To speak in presence of their betters, so
  That to the lips comes not the voice alive;

Thus it befel me, that scarce audibly,
  "O Lady," I began, "my wants ye know,
  And can a fitting remedy supply."

And thus she answered: "Banish shame and fear;
  That not like his who talketh in a dream
  Henceforth the tenor of thy words appear.

Know that the vessel which the serpent hurt,
  Was, and is not: nor let the offender deem
  That by a sop Heaven's wrath he may avert.

Without an heir the eagle not for aye
  Shall be, who left his feathers in the car,
  Whence it became a monster—then a prey:

I see full surely—therefore I declare—
  The approach of constellations, from all bar
  And hindrance free, bringing a season near,

Wherein, One, stamped five hundred ten and five,
  Angel of God—shall slay the thievish dame,
  Her giant partner too of life deprive.

And haply my narration, dark, like those
  Of Sphinx or Themis, credit may not claim,
  Since o'er the mind, like them, a cloud it throws:

But soon, this hard enigma to explain,
  The events shall be the Oedipus; nor blade
  Nor flock therefrom shall injury sustain.

Mark thou; and ever as I spend my breath,
  Be these my words to those alive conveyed
  Whose life is but a constant race to death.

And when thou writest, tell what thou hast seen
  Relating to this memorable tree,
  Which twice already there despoiled hath been.

Whoever rends it, or commits abuse,
  Offendeth God by act of blasphemy,
  Who made it sacred, solely for his use.

Through tasting it, five thousand years and more
  Yearned the first soul in longing and in woe
  For Him who in his flesh the penance bore.

Thy reason sleeps, unless it hath appeared
  For some especial cause inverted so,
  And heavenward with such soaring head upreared:

And had not idle thoughts wrought in thy mind
  As Elsa's stream; and their false pleasures been
  A Pyramus to stain it, thou wouldst find

God's justice plainly evidenced to thee:
  And in these circumstances would be seen
  The moral of the interdicted tree.

But since thine intellect is turned to stone,
  And is so dyed by sin, that at the glare
  Of these my words 'tis dazed and overthrown,

Bear them along with thee, if not expressed,
  Sketched out at least; like pilgrim wont to bear
  His staff, returning home, with palm-leaf dressed."

Then I: "As wax the impression doth retain,
  Which from the seal imprinted it derives,
  So now by thee is stamped my very brain.

But wherefore doth thy wished-for converse soar
   Above my mind, which, as the more it strives
   To reach the summit, loses it the more?"

"The school which thou hast followed," she replied,
   "I wish thee to discern, and see how far
   Its lore falls short in following me thy guide;

And see how distant from the path divine
   The ways of man—as distant e'en as are
   From earth those heavens which most exalted shine."

"I cannot recollect," I answered her,
   "Any estrangement in my love for thee;
   Nor doth my conscience tell me that I err."

"If then" (this answer with a smile she gave)
   "Thou canst not call it to thy memory,
   Think how thou lately tastedst Lethe's wave:

And as from smoke, fire surely is inferred,
   So, of a will enticed away elsewhere
   Doth this oblivion prove the guilt incurred.

Truly my words as naked now shall be,
   As haply may thine eyes be fit to bear,
   Not wont such mighty mystery to see."

With more resplendence and with slower pace
   The sun on the meridian mounted high,
   Whose aspect varies with the change of place—

When, as a scout sent out before a band
   Draws up, on seeing aught of novelty;
   E'en thus the seven fair damsels took their stand

At the far limit of a death-like shade—
   Like that beneath black boughs and foliage green
   O'er the cool streams in Alpine glens displayed.

Springing before them from the self-same source
   Methought were Tigris and Euphrates seen,
   Like friends, each loth to take a separate course.

"O light, O glory of the human race,
　　What water this, which flows with double tide
　　Forth from one fount, borne hence thro' distant space?"

To my request was made this answer: "Pray
　　Matelda to inform thee." Then replied
　　(Like one who somewhat in excuse would say)

The beauteous maid: "By me were told to him
　　Both these and other things; and sure am I
　　That Lethe's water hath not made them dim."

Then Beatrice: "Perhaps some weightier care,
　　Which oftentimes destroys the memory,
　　Hath made the intellectual eye less clear.

To Eunoë's fount do thou direct his course,
　　And, as thou art wont, revive his overthrown
　　And drooping virtue in its crystal source."

Like to some gentle soul, that frameth no
　　Excuse, but makes another's will her own,
　　At the first signal given her; even so

Advanced the beauteous lady, soon as she
　　My hand had taken; and with courteous air
　　To Statius said: "Thou bear him company."

Had I, O reader, space to write—in part
　　At least, then would I sing that beverage rare,
　　Whose sweetness ne'er had satisfied my heart:

But since the leaves, to this my second strain
　　Allowed, are full—no longer be pursued
　　The theme, and Art restrict me with her rein.

From that most sacred water back I came
　　Regenerate, like plants that are renewed
　　With foliage fresh,—made pure throughout my frame,

And with a will to mount the stars endued.

Paradise

C A N T O   3 0

Perchance six thousand miles remote from us
   Is glowing the sixth hour, and now this world
   Inclines its shadow almost to a level,

When the mid-heaven begins to make itself
   So deep to us, that here and there a star
   Ceases to shine so far down as this depth,

And as advances bright exceedingly
   The handmaid of the sun, the heaven is closed
   Light after light to the most beautiful;

Not otherwise the Triumph, which forever
   Plays round about the point that vanquished me,
   Seeming enclosed by what itself encloses,

Little by little from my vision faded;
   Thereat to turn mine eyes on Beatrice
   Only seeing nothing and my love constrained me.

If what has hitherto been said of her
   Were all concluded in a single praise,
   Scant would it be to serve the present turn.

Not only does the beauty I beheld
   Transcend ourselves, but truly I believe
   Its maker only may enjoy it all.

Vanquished do I confess me by this passage
   More than by problem of his theme was ever
   O'r come the comic or the tragic poet;

For as the sun the sight that trembles most,
   Even so the memory of that sweet smile
   My mind depriveth of its very self.

From the first day that I beheld her face
   In this life, to the moment of this look,
   The sequence of my song has ne'er been severed;

SOURCE: *The Divine Comedy of Dante Alighieri*, translated by Henry Wadsworth Longfellow (Boston: Houghton Mifflin Co., 1891), pp. 145–163.

But now perforce this sequence must desist
    From following her beauty with my verse,
    As every artist at his uttermost.

Such as I leave her to a greater fame
    Than any of my trumpet, which is bringing
    Its arduous matter to a final close,

With voice and gesture of a perfect leader
    She recommenced: "We from the greatest body
    Have issued to the heaven that is pure light;

Light intellectual replete with love,
    Love of true good replete with ecstasy,
    Ecstasy that transcendeth every sweetness.

Here shalt thou see the one host and the other
    Of Paradise, and one in the same aspects
    Which at the final judgment thou shalt see."

Even as a sudden lightning that disperses
    The visual spirits, so that it deprives
    The eye of impress from the strongest objects

Thus round about me flashed a living light,
    And left me swathed around with such a view
    Of its effulgence, that I nothing saw.

"Ever the Love which quieteth this heaven
    Welcomes into itself with such salute,
    To make the candle ready for its flame."

No sooner had within me these brief words
    An entrance found, than I perceived myself
    To be uplifted over my own power,

And I with vision new rekindled me,
    Such that no light whatever is so pure
    But that mine eyes were fortified against

And light I saw in fashion of a river
    Fulvid with its effulgence, 'twixt two banks
    Depicted with an admirable Spring.

Out of this river issued living sparks,
    And on all sides sank down into the flowers,
    Like unto rubies that are set in gold;

And then, as if inebriate with the odors,
    They plunged again into the wondrous torrent,
    And as one entered issued forth another.

"The high desire, that now inflames and moves thee
    To have intelligence of what thou seest,
    Pleaseth me all the more, the more it swells.

But of this water it behoves thee drink
    Before so great a thirst in thee be slaked."
    Thus said to me the sunshine of mine eyes;

And added: "The river and the topazes
    Going in and out, and the laughing of the herbage,
    Are of their truth foreshadowing prefaces;

Not that these things are difficult in themselves,
    But the deficiency is on thy side,
    For yet thou hast not vision so exalted."

There is no babe that leaps so suddenly
    With face towards the milk, if he awake
    Much later than his usual custom is,

As I did, that I might make better mirrors
    Still of mine eyes, down stooping to the wave
    Which flows that we therein be better made.

And even as the penthouse of mine eyelids
    Drank of it, it forthwith appeared to me
    Out of its length to be transformed to round.

Then as a folk who have been under masks
    Seem other than before, if they divest
    The semblance not their own they disappeared in,

Thus into greater pomp were changed for me
    The flowerets and the sparks, so that I saw
    Both of the Courts of Heaven made manifest.

O splendor of God! by means of which I saw
　　The lofty triumph of the realm veracious,
　　Give me the power to say how it I saw!

There is a light above, which visible
　　Makes the Creator unto every creature,
　　Who only in beholding Him has peace,

And it expands itself in circular form
　　To such extent, that its circumference
　　Would be too large a girdle for the sun.

The semblance of it is all made of rays
　　Reflected from the top of Primal Motion,
　　Which takes therefrom vitality and power.

And as a hill in water at its base
　　Mirrors itself, as if to see its beauty
　　When affluent most in verdure and in flowers,

So, ranged aloft all round about the light,
　　Mirrored I saw in more ranks than a thousand
　　All who above there have from us returned.

And if the lowest row collect within it
　　So great a light, how vast the amplitude
　　If of this Rose in its extremest leaves!

My vision in the vastness and the height
　　Lost not itself, but comprehended all
　　The quantity and quality of that gladness.

There near and far nor add nor take away;
　　For there where God immediately doth govern,
　　The natural law in naught is relevant.

Into the yellow of the Rose Eternal
　　That spreads, and multiplies, and breathes an odor
　　Of praise unto the ever-vernal Sun,

As one who silent is and fain would speak,
　　Me Beatrice drew on, and said: "Behold
　　Of the white stoles how vast the convent is!

Behold how vast the circuit of our city!
  Behold our seats so filled to overflowing,
    That here henceforward are few people wanting!

On that great throne whereon thine eyes are fixed
  For the crown's sake already placed upon it,
  Before thou suppest at this wedding feast

Shall sit the soul (that is to be Augustus
  On earth) of noble Henry, who shall come
  To redress Italy ere she be ready.

Blind covetousness, that casts its spell upon you,
  Has made you like unto the little child,
  Who dies of hunger and drives off the nurse.

And in the sacred forum then shall be
  A Prefect such, that openly or covert
  On the same road he will not walk with him.

But long of God he will not be endured
  In holy office; he shall be thrust down
  Where Simon Magus is for his deserts,

And make him of Alagna lower go!"

CANTO 31

In fashion then as of a snow-white rose
  Displayed itself to me the saintly host,
  Whom Christ in his own blood had made his bride,

But the other host, that flying sees and sings
  The glory of Him who doth enamor it,
  And the goodness that created it so noble,

Even as a swarm of bees, that sinks in flowers
  One moment, and the next returns again
  To where its labor is to sweetness turned,

Sank into the great flower, that is adorned
  With leaves so many, and thence reascended
  To where its love abideth evermore.

Their faces had they all of living flame,
And wings of gold, and all the rest so white
No snow unto that limit doth attain.

From bench to bench, into the flower descending,
They carried something of the peace and ardor
Which by the fanning of their flanks they won.

Nor did the interposing 'twixt the flower
And what was o'er it of such plenitude
Of flying shapes impede the sight and splendor;

Because the light divine so penetrates
The universe, according to its merit,
That naught can be an obstacle against it.

This realm secure and full of gladsomeness,
Crowded with ancient people and with modern,
Unto one mark had all its look and love.

O Trinal Light, that in a single star
Sparkling upon their sight so satisfies them,
Look down upon our tempest here below!

If the barbarians, coming from some region
That every day by Helice is covered,
Revolving with her son whom she delights in,

Beholding Rome and all her noble works,
Were wonder-struck, what time the Lateran
Above all mortal things was eminent,

I who to the divine had from the human,
From time unto eternity, had come,
From Florence to a people just and sane,

With what amazement must I have been filled!
Truly between this and the joy, it was
My pleasure not to hear, and to be mute.

And as a pilgrim who delighteth him
In gazing round the temple of his vow,
And hopes some day to retell how it was,

So through the living light my way pursuing
  Directed I mine eyes o'er all the ranks,
  Now up, now down, and now all round about.

Faces I saw of charity persuasive
  Embellished by His light and their own smile,
  And attitudes adorned with every grace.

The general form of Paradise already
  My glance had comprehended as a whole,
  In no part hitherto remaining fixed,

And round I turned me with rekindled wish
  My Lady to interrogate of things
  Concerning which my mind was in suspense.

One thing I meant, another answered me;
  I thought I should see Beatrice, and saw
  An Old Man habited like the glorious people.

O'erflowing was he in his eyes and cheeks
  With joy benign, in attitude of pity
  As to a tender father is becoming.

And "She, where is she?" instantly I said;
  Whence he: "To put an end to thy desire,
  Me Beatrice hath sent from mine own place.

And if thou lookest up to the third round
  Of the first rank, again shalt thou behold her
  Upon the throne her merits have assigned her."

Without reply I lifted up mine eyes,
  And saw her, as she made herself a crown
  Reflecting from herself the eternal rays.

Not from that region which the highest thunders
  Is any mortal eye so far removed,
  In whatsoever sea it deepest sinks,

As there from Beatrice my sight; but this
  Was nothing unto me; because her image
  Descended not to me by medium blurred.

"O Lady, thou in whom my hope is strong,
  And who for my salvation didst endure
  In Hell to leave the imprint of thy feet,

Of whatsoever things I have beheld,
  As coming from thy power and from thy goodness
  I recognize the virtue and the grace.

Thou from a slave hast brought me unto freedom,
  By all those ways, by all the expedients,
  Whereby thou hadst the power of doing it.

Preserve towards me thy magnificence,
  So that this soul of mine, which thou hast healed,
  Pleasing to thee be loosened from the body."

Thus I implored; and she, so far away,
  Smiled, as it seemed, and looked once more at me;
  Then unto the eternal fountain turned.

And said the Old Man holy: "That thou mayst
  Accomplish perfectly thy journeying,
  Whereunto prayer and holy love have sent me,

Fly with thine eyes all round about this garden;
  For seeing it will discipline thy sight
  Farther to mount along the ray divine.

And she, the Queen of Heaven, for whom I burn
  Wholly with love, will grant us every grace,
  Because that I her faithful Bernard am."

As he who peradventure from Croatia
  Cometh to gaze at our Veronica,
  Who through its ancient fame is never sated,

But says in thought, the while it is displayed,
  "My Lord, Christ Jesus, God of very God,
  Now was your semblance made like unto this?"

Even such was I while gazing at the living
  Charity of the man, who in this world
  By contemplation tasted of that peace.

"Thou son of grace, this jocund life," began he,
  "Will not be known to thee by keeping ever
  Thine eyes below here on the lowest place;

But mark the circles to the most remote,
  Until thou shalt behold enthroned the Queen
  To whom this realm is subject and devoted."

I lifted up mine eyes, and as at morn
  The oriental part of the horizon
  Surpasses that wherein the sun goes down,

Thus, as if going with mine eyes from vale
  To mount, I saw a part in the remoteness
  Surpass in splendor all the other front.

And even as there, where we await the pole
  That Phaeton drove badly, blazes more
  The light, and is on either side diminished,

So likewise that pacific oriflamme
  Gleamed brightest in the centre, and each side
  In equal measure did the flame abate.

And at that centre, with their wings expanded,
  More than a thousand jubilant Angels saw I,
  Each differing in effulgence and in kind.

I saw there at their sports and at their songs
  A beauty smiling, which the gladness was
  Within the eyes of all the other saints;

And if I had in speaking as much wealth
  As in imagining, I should not dare
  To attempt the smallest part of its delight.

Bernard, as soon as he beheld mine eyes
  Fixed and intent upon its fervid fervor,
  His own with such affection turned to her

That it made mine more ardent to behold.

CANTO 32

Absorbed in his delight, that contemplator
Assumed the willing office of a teacher,
And gave beginning to these holy words:

"The wound that Mary closed up and anointed,
She at her feet who is so beautiful,
She is the one who opened it and pierced it.

Within that order which the third seats make
Is seated Rachel, lower than the other,
With Beatrice, in manner as thou seest.

Sarah, Rebecca, Judith, and her who was
Ancestress of the Singer, who for dole
Of the misdeed said, '*Miserere mei*,'

Canst thou behold from seat to seat descending
Down in gradation, as with each one's name
I through the Rose go down from leaf to leaf.

And downward from the seventh row, even as
Above the same, succeed the Hebrew women,
Dividing all the tresses of the flower;

Because, according to the view which Faith
In Christ hath taken, these are the partition
By which the sacred stairways are divided.

Upon this side, where perfect is the flower
With each one of its petals, seated are
Those who believed in Christ who was to come.

Upon the other side, where intersected
With vacant spaces are the semicircles,
Are those who looked to Christ already come.

And as, upon this side, the glorious seat
Of the Lady of Heaven, and the other seats
Below it, such a great division make,

So opposite doth that of the great John,
Who, ever holy, desert and martyrdom
Endured, and afterwards two years in Hell.

And under him thus to divide were chosen
   Francis, and Benedict, and Augustine,
   And down to us the rest from round to round.

Behold now the high providence divine;
   For one and other aspect of the Faith
   In equal measure shall this garden fill.

And know that downward from that rank which cleaves
   Midway the sequence of the two divisions,
   Not by their proper merit are they seated;

But by another's under fixed conditions;
   For these are spirits one and all assoiled
   Before they any true election had.

Well canst thou recognize it in their faces,
   And also in their voices puerile,
   If thou regard them well and hearken to them.

Now doubtest thou, and doubting thou art silent;
   But I will loosen for thee the strong bond
   In which thy subtile fancies hold thee fast.

Within the amplitude of this domain
   No casual point can possibly find place,
   No more than sadness can, or thirst, or hunger;

For by eternal law has been established
   Whatever thou beholdest, so that closely
   The ring is fitted to the finger here.

And therefore are these people, festinate
   Unto true life, not *sine causa* here
   More and less excellent among themselves.

The King, by means of whom this realm reposes
   In so great love and in so great delight
   That no will ventureth to ask for more,

In his own joyous aspect every mind
   Creating, at his pleasure dowers with grace
   Diversely; and let here the effect suffice.

And this is clearly and expressly noted
    For you in Holy Scripture, in those twins
    Who in their mother had their anger roused.

According to the color of the hair,
    Therefore, with such a grace the light supreme
    Consenteth that they worthily be crowned.

Without, then, any merit of their deeds,
    Stationed are they in different gradations,
    Differing only in their first acuteness.

'T is true that in the early centuries,
    With innocence, to work out their salvation
    Sufficient was the faith of parents only.

After the earlier ages were completed,
    Behoved it that the males by circumcision
    Unto their innocent wings should virtue add;

But after that the time of grace had come
    Without the baptism absolute of Christ,
    Such innocence below there was retained.

Look now into the face that unto Christ,
    Hath most resemblance; for its brightness only
    Is able to prepare thee to see Christ."

On her did I behold so great a gladness
    Rain down, borne onward in the holy minds
    Created through that altitude to fly,

That whatsoever I had seen before
    Did not suspend me in such admiration,
    Nor show me such similitude of God.

And the same Love that first descended there,
    "*Ave Maria, gratia plena*," singing,
    In front of her his wings expanded wide

Unto the canticle divine responded
    From every part the court beatified,
    So that each sight became serener for it.

"O holy father, who for me endurest
　To be below here, leaving the sweet place
　In which thou sittest by eternal lot,

Who is the Angel that with so much joy
　Into the eyes is looking of our Queen,
　Enamored so that he seems made of fire?"

Thus I again recourse had to the teaching
　Of that one who delighted him in Mary,
　As doth the star of morning in the sun.

And he to me: "Such gallantry and grace
　As there can be in Angel and in soul,
　All is in him; and thus we fain would have it;

Because he is the one who bore the palm
　Down unto Mary, when the Son of God
　To take our burden on himself decreed.

But now come onward with thine eyes, as I
　Speaking shall go, and note the great patricians
　Of this most just and merciful of empires.

Those two that sit above there most enraptured,
　As being very near unto Augusta,
　Are as it were the two roots of this Rose.

He who upon the left is near her placed
　The father is, by whose audacious taste
　The human species so much bitter tastes.

Upon the right thou seest that ancient father
　Of Holy Church, into whose keeping Christ
　The keys committed of this lovely flower.

And he who all the evil days beheld,
　Before his death, of her the beauteous bride
　Who with the spear and with the nails was won,

Beside him sits, and by the other rests
　That leader under whom on manna lived
　The people ingrate, fickle, and stiff-necked.

Opposite Peter seest thou Anna seated,
So well content to look upon her daughter,
Her eyes she moves not while she sings Hosanna.

And opposite the eldest household father
Lucìa sits, she who thy Lady moved
When to rush downward thou didst bend thy brows.

But since the moments of thy vision fly,
Here will we make full stop, as a good tailor
Who makes the gown according to his cloth,

And unto the first Love will turn our eyes,
That looking upon Him thou penetrate
As far as possible through his effulgence.

Truly, lest peradventure thou recede,
Moving thy wings believing to advance,
By prayer behoves it that grace be obtained;

Grace from that one who has the power to aid thee;
And thou shalt follow me with thy affection
That from my words thy heart turn not aside."

And he began this holy orison.

CANTO 33

"Thou Virgin Mother, daughter of thy Son,
Humble and high beyond all other creature,
The limit fixed of the eternal counsel,

Thou art the one who such nobility
To human nature gave, that its Creator
Did not disdain to make himself its creature.

Within thy womb rekindled was the love,
By heat of which in the eternal peace
After such wise this flower has germinated.

Here unto us thou art a noonday torch
Of charity, and below there among mortals
Thou art the living fountain-head of hope.

Lady, thou art so great, and so prevailing,
  That he who wishes grace, nor runs to thee,
  His aspirations without wings would fly.

Not only thy benignity gives succor
  To him who asketh it, but oftentimes
  Forerunneth of its own accord the asking.

In thee compassion is, in thee is pity,
  In thee magnificence; in thee unites
  Whate'er of goodness is in any creature.

Now doth this man, who from the lowest depth
  Of the universe as far as here has seen
  One after one the spiritual lives,

Supplicate thee through grace for so much power
  That with his eyes he may uplift himself
  Higher towards the uttermost salvation.

And I, who never burned for my own seeing
  More than I do for his, all of my prayers
  Proffer to thee, and pray they come not short,

That thou wouldst scatter from him every cloud
  Of his mortality so with thy prayers,
  That the Chief Pleasure be to him displayed.

Still farther do I pray thee, Queen, who canst
  Whate'er thou wilt, that sound thou mayst preserve
  After so great a vision his affections.

Let thy protection conquer human movements;
  See Beatrice and all the blessed ones
  My prayers to second clasp their hands to thee!

The eyes beloved and revered of God,
  Fastened upon the speaker, showed to us
  How grateful unto her are prayers devout;

Then unto the Eternal Light they turned,
  On which it is not credible could be
  By any creature bent an eye so clear.

And I, who to the end of all desires
  Was now approaching, even as I ought
  The ardor of desire within me ended.

Bernard was beckoning unto me, and smiling,
  That I should upward look; but I already
  Was of my own accord such as he wished;

Because my sight, becoming purified,
  Was entering more and more into the ray
  Of the High Light which of itself is true.

From that time forward what I saw was greater
  Than our discourse, that to such vision yields,
  And yields the memory unto such excess.

Even as he is who seeth in a dream,
  And after dreaming the imprinted passion
  Remains, and to his mind the rest returns not,

Even such am I, for almost utterly
  Ceases my vision, and distilleth yet
  Within my heart the sweetness born of it;

Even thus the snow is in the sun unsealed,
  Even thus upon the wind in the light leaves
  Were the soothsayings of the Sibyl lost.

O Light Supreme, that dost so far uplift thee
  From the conceits of mortals, to my mind
  Of what thou didst appear re-lend a little,

And make my tongue of so great puissance,
  That but a single sparkle of thy glory
  It may bequeath unto the future people;

For by returning to my memory somewhat,
  And by a little sounding in these verses,
  More of thy victory shall be conceived!

I think the keenness of the living ray
  Which I endured would have bewildered me,
  If but mine eyes had been averted from it;

And I remember that I was more bold
  On this account to bear, so that I joined
  My aspect with the Glory Infinite.

O grace abundant, by which I presumed
  To fix my sight upon the Light Eternal,
  So that the seeing I consumed therein!

I saw that in its depth far down is lying,
  Bound up with love together in one volume,
  What through the universe in leaves is scattered;

Substance, and accident, and their operations,
  All interfused together in such wise
  That what I speak of is one simple light.

The universal fashion of this knot
  Methinks I saw, since more abundantly
  In saying this I feel that I rejoice.

One moment is more lethargy to me,
  Than five and twenty centuries to the emprise
  That startled Neptune with the shade of Argo!

My mind in this wise wholly in suspense,
  Steadfast, immovable, attentive gazed.
  And evermore with gazing grew enkindled.

In presence of that light one such becomes,
  That to withdraw therefrom for other prospect
  It is impossible he e'er consent;

Because the good, which object is of will,
  Is gathered all in this, and out of it
  That is defective which is perfect there.

Shorter henceforward will my language fall
  Of what I yet remember, than an infant's
  Who still his tongue doth moisten at the breast.

Not because more than one unmingled semblance
  Was in the living light on which I looked.
  For it is always what it was before;

But through the sight, that fortified itself
   In me by looking, one appearance only
   To me was ever changing as I changed.

Within the deep and luminous subsistence
   Of the High Light appeared to me three circles,
   Of threefold color and of one dimension,

And by the second seemed the first reflected
   As Iris is by Iris, and the third
   Seemed fire that equally from both is breathed.

O how all speech is feeble and falls short
   Of my conceit, and this to what I saw
   Is such, 't is not enough to call it little!

O Light Eterne, sole in thyself that dwellest,
   Sole knowest thyself, and, known unto thyself
   And knowing, lovest and smilest on thyself!

That circulation, which being thus conceived
   Appeared in thee as a reflected light,
   When somewhat contemplated by mine eyes,

Within itself, of its own very color
   Seemed to me painted with our effigy,
   Wherefore my sight was all absorbed therein.

As the geometrician, who endeavors
   To square the circle, and discovers not,
   By taking thought, the principle he wants,

Even such was I at that new apparition;
   I wished to see how the image to the circle
   Conformed itself, and how it there finds place;

But my own wings were not enough for this,
   Had it not been that then my mind there smote
   A flash of lightning, wherein came its wish.

Here vigor failed the lofty fantasy:
   But now was turning my desire and will,
   Even as a wheel that equally is moved,

The Love which moves the sun and the other stars.

De Monarchia

The Need for Unity and Peace

CHAPTER 2

First principles: the goal of human civilization.

First, we must ascertain what temporal Monarchy is in its idea, as I may say, and in its purpose. Temporal Monarchy, called also the Empire, we define as a single Principality extending over all peoples in time, or in those things and over those things which are measured by time. Concerning it three main questions arise. First, we may ask and seek to prove whether it is necessary for the well-being of the world; secondly, whether the Roman people rightfully appropriated the office of Monarchy; and thirdly, whether the authority of Monarchy derives from God directly, or from another, a minister or vicar of God.

But as every truth which is not a first principle is manifested by the truth of some first principle, it is necessary in every investigation to know the first principle to which we may return, in analysis, for the proof of all propositions which are subsequently assumed. And as the present treatise is an investigation, we must before all else search out a basic principle, on the validity of which will depend whatever follows. Be it known, therefore, that certain things exist which are not at all subject to our control, and which we can merely speculate upon, but cannot cause to be or to do: such are mathematics, physics, and divinity. On the other hand, certain things exist which are subject to our control, and which are matter not only for speculation, but for execution. In these things the action is not performed for the sake of the speculation, but the latter for the sake of the former, because in them action is the end. Since the matter under consideration is governmental, nay, is the very source and first principle of right governments, and since everything governmental is subject to our control, it is clear that our present theme is primarily adapted for action rather than for speculation. Again, since the first principle and cause of all actions is their ultimate end, and since the ultimate end first puts the agent in motion, it follows that the entire procedure of the means toward an end must derive from the end itself. For the manner of cutting wood to build a house will be other than that of cutting wood to build a ship. So if there exists an end for universal government among men, that end will be the basic principle through which all things to be proved hereafter may be demonstrated satisfactorily. But to believe that there is an end for this government and for that government, and that there is no single end common to all, would indeed be irrational.

SOURCE: *The De Monarchia of Dante Alighieri*, translated by Aurelia Henry (Boston: Houghton Mifflin Co., 1904), pp. 5–8, 14–21, 40–46, 135–137, 140–156, 161–181, 183–187, 196–206.

CHAPTER 4

The best means toward this end is universal peace.

It has now been satisfactorily explained that the proper function of the human race, taken in the aggregate, is to actualize continually the entire capacity of the possible intellect, primarily in speculation, then, through its extension and for its sake, secondarily in action. And since it is true that whatever modifies a part modifies the whole, and that the individual man seated in quiet grows perfect in knowledge and wisdom, it is plain that amid the calm and tranquillity of peace the human race accomplishes most freely and easily its given work. How nearly divine this function is revealed in the words, "Thou hast made him a little lower than the angels." Whence it is manifest that universal peace is the best of those things which are ordained for our beatitude. And hence to the shepherds sounded from on high the message not of riches, nor pleasures, nor honors, nor length of life, nor health, nor beauty; but the message of peace. For the heavenly host said, "Glory to God in the highest, and on earth peace among men in whom he is well pleased." Likewise, "Peace be unto you" was the salutation of the Saviour of men. It befitted the supreme Saviour to utter the supreme salutation. It is evident to all that the disciples desired to preserve this custom; and Paul likewise in his words of greeting.

From these things which have been expounded we perceive through what better, nay, through what best means the human race may fulfill its proper office. Consequently we perceive the nearest way through which may be reached that universal peace toward which all our efforts are directed as their ultimate end, and which is to be assumed as the basic principle of subsequent reasoning. This principle was necessary, we have said, as a predetermined formula, into which, as into a most manifest truth, must be resolved all things needing to be proved.

CHAPTER 5

**To achieve this state of universal well-being, a single
world government is necessary.**

Resuming what was said in the beginning, I repeat, there are three main questions asked and debated in regard to temporal Monarchy, which is more commonly termed the Empire, and it is my purpose to make inquiry concerning these in the order cited, according to the principle now enunciated. And so let the first question be whether temporal Monarchy is necessary for the well-being of the world. The necessity of temporal Monarchy can be gainsaid with no force of reason or authority, and can be proved by the most powerful and patent arguments, of which the first is taken on the testimony of the Philosopher in the *Politics*. There this venerable authority asserts that when several things are ordained for one end, one of them must regulate or rule, and the others submit to regulation or rule. This, indeed, not only because of the author's glorious name, but because of inductive reasoning, demands credence.

If we consider the individual man, we shall see that this applies to him, for, when all his faculties are ordered for his happiness, the intellectual faculty itself is regulator and ruler of all others; in no way else can man attain to happiness. If we consider the household, whose end is to teach its members to live rightly, there is need for one called the *pater-familias*, or for some one holding his place, to direct and govern, according to the Philosopher when he says, "Every household is ruled by its eldest." It is for him, as Homer says, to guide and make laws for those dwelling with him. From this arises the proverbial curse, "May you have an equal in your house." If we consider the village, whose aim is adequate protection of persons and property, there is again needed for governing the rest either one chosen for them by another, or one risen to prëeminence from among themselves by their consent; otherwise, they not only obtain no mutual support, but sometimes the whole community is destroyed by many striving for first place. Again, if we consider the city, whose end is to insure comfort and sufficiency in life, there is need for undivided rule in rightly directed governments, and in those wrongly directed as well; else the end of civil life is missed, and the city ceases to be what it was. Finally, if we consider the individual kingdom, whose end is that of the city with greater promise of tranquillity, there must be one king to direct and govern. If not, not only the inhabitants of the kingdom fail of their end, but the kingdom lapses into ruin, in agreement with that word of infallible truth, "Every kingdom divided against itself is brought to desolation." If, then, this is true of these instances, and of all things ordained for a single end, it is true of the statement assumed above.

We are now agreed that the whole human race is ordered for one end, as already shown. It is meet, therefore, that the leader and lord be one, and that he be called Monarch, or Emperor. Thus it becomes obvious that for the well-being of the world there is needed a Monarchy, or Empire.

CHAPTER 12

Human freedom is only possible under world government.

If the principle of freedom is explained, it will be apparent that the human race is ordered for the best when it is most free. Observe, then, those words which are on the lips of many but in the minds of few, that the basic principle of our freedom is freedom of the will. Men come even to the point of saying that free will is free judgment in matters of will, and they say true; but the import of their words is far from them, as from our logicians who work daily with certain propositions used as examples in books of logic; for instance, that "a triangle has three angles equaling two right angles."

Judgment, I affirm, stands between apprehension and desire; for first a thing is apprehended; then the apprehension is adjudged good or bad; and finally he who so judges pursues or avoids it. So if judgment entirely controls desire, and is hindered by it in no way, judgment is free; but if desire influences judgment by hindering it in some manner, judgment cannot be free, for it acts not of itself, but is dragged captive by another. Thus brutes cannot have free judgment, for their judgments are always hindered by appetite. And thus intellectual substances whose wills are immutable, and disembodied souls who have departed in peace, do not lose freedom of the will by reason of this immutability, but retain it in greatest perfection and power.

With this in mind we may understand that this freedom, or basic principle of our freedom, is, as I said, the greatest gift bestowed by God upon human nature, for through it we attain to joy here as men, and to blessedness there as gods. If this is so, who will not admit that mankind is best ordered when able to use this principle most effectively? But the race is most free under a Monarch. Wherefore let us know that the Philosopher holds in his book *concerning simple Being*, that whatever exists for its own sake and not for the sake of another is free. For whatever exists for the sake of another is conditioned by that other, as a road by its terminus. Only if a Monarch rules can the human race exist for its own sake; only if a Monarch rules can the crooked policies be straightened, namely democracies, oligarchies, and tyrannies which force mankind into slavery, as he sees who goes among them, and under which kings, aristocrats called the best men, and zealots of popular libery play at politics. For since a Monarch loves men greatly, a point already touched upon, he desires all men to do good, which cannot be among players at crooked policies. Whence the Philosopher in his *Politics* says, "Under bad government the good man is a bad citizen; but under upright government 'good man' and 'good citizen' have the same meaning." Upright governments have liberty as their aim, that men may live for themselves; not citizens for the sake of the consuls, nor a people for a king, but conversely, consuls for the sake of the citizens, and a king for his people. As governments are not all established for the sake of laws, but laws for governments, so those living under the laws are not ordered for the sake of the legislator, but rather he for them, as the Philosopher maintains in what he has left us concerning the present matter. Wherefore it is also evident that although consul or king may be lord of others with respect to means of governing, they are servants with respect to the end of governing; and without doubt the Monarch must be held the chief servant of all. Now it becomes clear that a Monarch is conditioned in the making of laws by his previously determined end. Therefore the human race existing under a Monarch is best ordered, and from this it follows that a Monarchy is essential to the well-being of the world.

Temporal Rule Comes from God Not the Papacy

CHAPTER 1

The doctrine of this book is offensive to the papacy.

"He has shut the lions' mouths and they have not hurt me; inasmuch as before Him righteousness was found in me." In beginning this work I proposed to investigate three questions as far as the subject-matter would allow. For the first two questions this has been done satisfactorily in the foregoing books, I believe. We must now consider the third, the truth of which may, however, be a cause of indignation against me, since it cannot be brought forth without causing certain men to blush. But since Truth from her immutable throne demands it; and Solomon entering his forest of *Proverbs*, and marking out his own conduct, entreats that we "meditate upon truth and abhor wickedness;" and our teacher of morals, the Philosopher, admonishes us to sacrifice whatever is most precious for truth's sake: therefore, gaining assurance from the words of Daniel, wherein the power of God is shown as a shield for defenders of truth, and "putting on the breastplate of faith" according to the admonition of Paul, in the warmth of that coal taken from the heavenly altar by one of the Seraphim and touched to the lips of Isaiah, I will engage in the present conflict, and by the arm of Him who with His blood liberated us from the power of darkness, I will cast the ungodly and the liar from the arena, while the world looks on. Wherefore should I fear, when the Spirit, co-eternal with the Father and the Son, says by the mouth of David, "The righteous shall be in everlasting remembrance, he shall not be afraid of evil tidings"?

The question pending investigation, then, concerns two great luminaries, the Roman Pontiff and the Roman Prince: and the point at issue is whether the authority of the Roman Monarch, who, as proved in the second book, is rightful Monarch of the world, derives from God directly, or from some vicar or minister of God, by whom I mean the successor of Peter, veritable keeper of the keys of the kingdom of heaven.

CHAPTER 3

The authority of the church does not rest on tradition.

In entering on this third question, let us bear in mind that the truth of the first was made manifest in order to abolish ignorance rather than contention. But the investigation of the second had reference alike to ignorance and contention. Indeed, we are ignorant of many things concerning which we do not contend: the geometrician does not know the square of the circle, but he does not contend about it; the theologian does not know the number of the angels, but he renders it no cause for quarrel; the Egyptian knows naught of the civilization of Scythia, but does not therefore make the civilization a source of strife.

Now the truth of the third question has to do with so keen a contention that, whereas ignorance generally causes the discord, here the discord causes ignorance. For it always happens to men who will things before rationally considering them that, their desire being evil, they put behind them the light of reason; as blind men they are led about by their desire, and stubbornly deny their blindness. Whence it often occurs not only that falsehood has her own patrimony, but that many men going out from her boundaries run through strange camps, where, neither understanding nor being understood at all, they provoke some to wrath, some to disdain, and not a few to laughter.

Three classes of men struggle hardest against the truth which we would establish.

First the Chief Pontiff, Vicar of our Lord Jesus Christ and successor to Peter, he to whom we should render not what is due to Christ but what is due to Peter, he, perchance in his zeal for the keys, together with some pastors of Christian flocks, and others moved solely, I believe, by their zeal for Mother Church, contradict the truth I am about to declare. They contradict it, perchance, from zeal, I repeat, not from pride.

But others in their inveterate cupidity have quenched the light of reason, and call themselves sons of the Church, although they are of their father the devil. Not only do they arouse controversy in regard to this question, but, despising the very name of the most sacred Princehood, impudently deny the first principles of this and the previous questions.

The third class, called Decretalists, utterly ignorant and unregardful of Theology and Philosophy, depending entirely on the *Decretals* (which, I grant, are deserving of veneration), and I presume trusting in the ultimate supremacy of these, derogate from the imperial power. Nor is it to be wondered at, for I have heard one of them aver and insolently maintain that ecclesiastical traditions are the foundation of faith. Let those dispel this error of thought from mortal minds whom the world doubts not to have believed in Christ, the Son of God, ere ecclesiastical traditions were, believed in Him either to come, or present, or having already suffered, and believing hoped, and hoping burned with love, and burning with love were made co-heirs with Him.

And that such mistaken thinkers may be wholly shut out from the present discussion, it must be observed that some of the Scriptures take precedence of the Church, some are equivalent to the Church, and some subordinate to it.

Those taking precedence of the Church are the Old and New Testaments, which, as the Prophet says, "were commanded for ever," and to which the Church refers in saying to the Bridegroom, "Draw me after thee."

Equivalent to the Church are those Councils so worthy of reverence, and in the midst of which no believer doubts the presence of Christ; for we have, according to Matthew's testimony, the words spoken to His disciples at His ascension into heaven: "Lo, I am with you always, even unto the end of the world." In addition, there are the writings of the Doctors, Augustine, and others, and whosoever doubts the aid of the Holy Spirit therein has never seen their fruits, or if he has seen, has never tasted them.

Subordinate to the Church are the traditions called Decretals, which, while they must be revered for their apostolic authority, must nevertheless be held unquestionably inferior to the fundamental Scriptures, seeing that Christ rebuked the priests for not so doing. When they had inquired, "Why do thy disciples transgress the tradition of the elders?" (for they had omitted the washing of hands) Christ answered, as Matthew testifies, "Why do ye also transgress the commandment of God by your tradition?" Here the inferiority of tradition is clearly implied.

If, as we believe, traditions of the Church are subordinate to the Church, authority necessarily accrues not to the Church through traditions, but to traditions through the Church. And I repeat, those who have faith in traditions alone are excluded from this discussion. For they who would hunt down this truth must start in their search from those writings whence the authority of the Church emanates.

Others must likewise be excluded who, decked in the plumage of ravens, boast themselves white sheep of the Master's flock. In order to carry out their crimes, these sons of impiety defile their mother, banish their brethren, and scorn judgments brought against them. Why should reason be sought in behalf of these whose passions prevent them from understanding our basic principle?

There remains, then, the controversy with those only who, led by a certain zeal for their Mother the Church, are blind to the truth we are seeking. And with them, confident in that reverence which a loyal and loving son owes to father and mother, to Christ and the Church, to the Shepherd and all who profess the Christian religion, I enter in this book into combat for the preservation of truth.

CHAPTER 4

The analogy of sun and moon is not applicable to temporal authority.

Those men to whom the entire subsequent discussion is directed assert that the authority of the Empire depends on the authority of the Church, just as the inferior artisan depends on the architect. They are drawn to this by divers opposing arguments, some of which they take from Holy Scripture, and some from certain acts performed by the Chief Pontiff, and by the Emperor himself; and they endeavor to make their conviction reasonable.

For, first, they maintain that according to *Genesis* God made two mighty luminaries, a greater and a less, the former to hold supremacy by day and the latter by night. These they interpret allegorically to be the two rulers—spiritual and temporal. Whence they argue that as the lesser luminary, the moon, has no light but that gained from the sun, so the temporal ruler has no authority but that gained from the spiritual ruler.

Let it be noted for the refutation of this and their other arguments that, as the Philosopher holds in his writings *on Sophistry*, "the destruction of an argument is the exposure of error." And because error can occur in both the matter and the form of an argument, a two-fold fallacy is possible—that arising from a false assumption, and that from a failure to syllogize. The two objections brought by the Philosopher against Parmenides and Melissus were: "They accept what is false, and syllogize incorrectly." "False" I use here with large significance, embracing the improbable, which in matters of probability becomes the false element. He who would destroy a conclusion where there is error in the form of the argument must show a failure to comply with the rules of syllogizing. Where the error is material, he must show that an assumption has been made, either false in itself, or false in relation to something else. Absolute falsity may be destroyed by destroying the assumption, relative falsity by distinction of meanings.

Granting this, let us observe, in order to comprehend more clearly the fallacy of this and other arguments, that with regard to mystical interpretation a twofold error may arise, either by seeking one where it is not, or by explaining it other than it ought to be.

Of the first error Augustine says in *The City of God:* "Not all deeds recounted should be thought to have special significance, because for the sake of significant things insignificant details are interwoven. The plowshare by itself cuts the land into furrows, but that this may be accomplished the other parts of the plow are needed."

Of the second error he speaks in his *Christian Doctrine*, saying that the man who attempts to find in the Scriptures other things than the writer's meaning "is deceived as one who abandons a certain road, only by a long detour to reach the goal whither the road led directly." And he adds, "Such a man should be shown that a habit of leaving his path may lead him into cross-roads and tortuous ways." Then he gives the reason why this error should be avoided in the Scriptures, saying, "Shake the authority of the divine writings, and you shake all faith." However, I believe that when such errors are due to ignorance they should be pardoned after correction has been carefully administered, just as he should be pardoned who is terrified at a supposed lion in the clouds. But when such errors are due to design, the erring one should be treated like tyrants who never apply public laws for the general welfare, but endeavor to turn them to individual profit.

O unparalleled crime, though committed but in dreams, of turning into evil the intention of the Eternal Spirit! Such a sin would not be against Moses, or David, or Job, or Matthew, or Paul, but against the Holy Spirit that speaketh in them. For although the writers of the divine word are many, the dictator of the word is one, even God, who has deigned to make known his purpose to us through divers pens.

From these prefatory remarks I proceed to refute the above assumption that the two luminaries of the world typify its two ruling powers. The whole force of their argument lies in the interpretation; but this we can prove indefensible in two ways. First, since these ruling powers are as it were accidents necessitated by man himself, God would seem to have used a distorted order in creating first accidents, and then the subject necessitating them. It is absurd to speak thus of God, but it is evident from the Word that the two lights were created on the fourth day, and man on the sixth.

Secondly, the two ruling powers exist as the directors of men toward certain ends, as will be shown further on; but had man remained in the state of innocence in which God made him, he would have required no such direction. These ruling powers are therefore remedies against the infirmity of sin. Since on the fourth day man not only was not a sinner, but was not even existent, the creation of a remedy would have been purposeless, which is contrary to divine goodness. Foolish indeed would be the physician who should make ready a plaster for the future abscess of a man not yet born. Therefore it cannot be asserted that God made the two ruling powers on the fourth day; and consequently the meaning of Moses cannot have been what it is supposed to be.

Also, in order to be tolerant, we may refute this fallacy by distinction. Refutation by distinction deals more gently with an adversary, for it shows him to be not absolutely wrong, as does refutation by destruction. I say, then, that although the moon may have abundant light only as she receives it from the sun, it does not follow on that account that the moon herself owes her existence to the sun. It must be recognized that the essence of the moon, her strength, and her function are not one and the same thing. Neither in her essence, her strength, nor her function taken absolutely, does the moon owe her existence to the sun, for her movement is impelled by her own motor and her influence by her own rays. Besides, she has a certain light of her own, as is shown in eclipse. It is in order to fulfill her function better and more potently that she borrows from the sun abundance of light, and works thereby more efficaciously.

In like manner, I say, the temporal power receives from the spiritual neither its existence, nor its strength, which is its authority, nor even its function taken absolutely. But well for her does she receive therefrom, through the light of grace which the benediction of the Chief Pontiff sheds upon it in heaven and on earth, strength to fulfill her function more perfectly. So the argument was at fault in form, because the predicate of the conclusion is not a term of the major premise, as is evident. The syllogism runs thus: The moon receives light from the sun, which is the spiritual power; the temporal ruling power is the moon; therefore the temporal receives authority from the spiritual. They introduce "light" as the term of the major, but "authority" as predicate of the conclusion, which two things we have seen to be diverse in subject and significance.

CHAPTER 7

Refutation of papal claims.

From the book of Matthew they also cite the oblation of the Magi, claiming that Christ accepted both frankincense and gold, in order to signify that He was Lord and Governor of the spiritual and temporal domains. They draw as inference from this that the Vicar of Christ is lord and governor of these realms, and consequently has authority over both.

In answering this I grant the text of Matthew and their interpretation, but the inference they try to draw from it is false through deficiency in the terms. Their syllogism is this: God is Lord of the spiritual and temporal domains; the Pope is the Vicar of God; therefore he is lord of the spiritual and temporal domains. While each proposition is true, the middle term is changed to admit four terms to the argument, thereby impairing the syllogistic form. This is plain from the writings *on Syllogizing considered simply.* For one term is "God," the subject of the major premise, and the other term is "Vicar of God," the predicate of the minor.

And if any one insists on the equivalence of God and Vicar, his insistence is useless, for no vicar, divine or human, can be coördinate with His authority, as is easily seen. And we know that the successor of Peter is not coëqual with divine power, at least not in the operation of nature. He could not by virtue of the office committed to him make earth rise up, or fire fall. It is impossible that God should have intrusted all things to him, for God was in no way able to delegate the power of creation or of baptism, as is plainly proved despite the contrary statement of the Master in his fourth book.

We know, too, that a man's deputy, in so far as he is a deputy, is not of coördinate power with him, because no one can bestow what does not belong to him. Princely authority belongs to a prince only for his employment, since no prince can authorize himself; he has power to receive and to reject it, but no power to create it in another, seeing that the creation of a prince is not effected by a prince. If this is true, it is evident that no prince can substitute for himself a regent equal in all things to himself. Wherefore the protest is of no avail.

CHAPTER 8

From the same gospel they quote the saying of Christ to Peter, "Whatsoever thou shalt loose on earth shall be loosed in heaven," and understand this saying to refer alike to all the Apostles, according to the text of Matthew and John. They reason from this that the successor of Peter has been granted of God power to bind and loose all things, and then infer that he has power to loose the laws and decrees of the Empire, and to bind the laws and decrees of the temporal kingdom. Were this true, their inference would be correct.

But we must reply to it by making a distinction against the major premise of the syllogism which they employ. Their syllogism is this: Peter had power to bind and loose all things; the successor of Peter has like power with him; therefore the successor of Peter has power to loose and bind all things. From this they infer that he has power to loose and bind the laws and decrees of the Empire.

I concede the minor premise, but the major only with distinction. Wherefore I say that "all," the symbol of the universal, which is implied in "whatsoever," is never distributed beyond the scope of the distributed term. When I say, "All animals run," the distribution of "all" comprehends whatever comes under the genus "animal." But when I say, "All men run," the symbol of the universal only refers to whatever comes under the term "man." And when I say, "All grammarians run," the distribution is narrowed still further.

Therefore we must always determine what it is over which the symbol of the universal is distributed; then, from the recognized nature and scope of the distributed term, will be easily apparent the extent of the distribution. Now, were "whatsoever" to be understood absolutely when it is said, "Whatsoever thou shalt bind," he would certainly have the power they claim; nay, he would have even greater power, he would be able to loose a wife from her husband, and, while the man still lived, bind her to another—a thing he can in no wise do. He would be able to absolve me, while impenitent—a thing which God himself cannot do.

So it is evident that the distribution of the term under discussion is to be taken, not absolutely, but relatively to something else. A consideration of the concession to which the distribution is subjoined will make manifest this related something. Christ said to Peter, "I will give unto thee the keys of the kingdom of heaven;" that is, I will make thee doorkeeper of the kingdom of heaven. Then he adds, "and whatsoever," that is, "everything which," and He means thereby, "Everything which pertains to that office thou shalt have power to bind and loose." And thus the symbol of the universal which is implied in "whatsoever" is limited in its distribution to the prerogative of the keys of the kingdom of heaven. Understood thus, the proposition is true, but understood absolutely, it is obviously not. Therefore I conclude that although the successor of Peter has authority to bind and loose in accordance with the requirements of the prerogative granted to Peter, it does not follow, as they claim, that he has authority to bind and loose the decrees or statutes of Empire, unless they prove that this also belongs to the office of the keys. But we shall demonstrate farther on that the contrary is true.

CHAPTER 9

They quote also the words in Luke which Peter addressed to Christ, saying, "Behold, here are two swords," and they assert that the two ruling powers were predicted by those two swords, and because Peter declared they were "where he was," that is, "with him," they conclude that according to authority these two ruling powers abide with Peter's successor.

To refute this we must show the falsity of the interpretation on which the argument is based. Their assertion that the two swords which Peter designated signify the two ruling powers before spoken of, we deny outright, because such an answer would have been at variance with Christ's meaning, and because Peter replied in haste, as usual, with regard to the mere external significance of things.

A consideration of the words preceding it and of the cause of the words will show that such an answer would have been inconsistent with Christ's meaning. Let it be called to mind that this response was made on the day of the feast, which Luke mentions earlier, saying, "Then came the day of unleavened bread, when the passover must be killed." At this feast Christ had already foretold His impending passion, in which He must be parted from His disciples. Let it be remembered also that when these words were uttered, all the twelve disciples were together; wherefore a little after the words just quoted Luke says, "And when the hour was come, He sat down, and the twelve Apostles with him." Continuing the discourse from this place he reaches the words, "When I sent you without purse, and scrip, and shoes, lacked ye anything?" And they answered, "Nothing." Then said He unto them, "But now, he that hath a purse, let him take it, and likewise his scrip: and he that hath no sword, let him sell his garment, and buy one." The meaning of Christ is clear enough here. He did not say, "Buy or procure two swords," but "twelve;" for it was in order that each of the twelve disciples might have one that He said to them, "He that hath no sword, let him buy one." And He spake thus to forewarn them of the persecution and contempt the future should bring, as though he would say, "While I was with you ye were welcomed, now shall ye be turned away. It behooves you, therefore, to prepare for yourselves those things which before I denied to you, but for which there is present need." If Peter's reply to these words had carried the meaning ascribed to it, the meaning would have been at variance with that of Christ, and Christ would have censured Him, as he did oftentimes, for his witless answers. However, He did not do so, but assented, saying to him, "It is enough," meaning, "I speak because of necessity; but if each cannot have a sword, two will suffice."

And that Peter usually spoke of the external significance of things is shown in his quick and unthinking presumption, impelled, I believe, not only by the sincerity of his faith, but by the purity and simplicity of his nature. To this characteristic presumption all those who write of Christ bear witness.

First, Matthew records that when Jesus had inquired of the disciples: "Whom say ye that I am?" before all the others Peter replied, "Thou art Christ, the Son of the living God." He also records that when Christ was telling His disciples how He must go to Jerusalem and suffer many things, Peter took Him and began to rebuke Him, saying, "Be it far from thee, Lord: this shall not be unto thee." Then Christ, turning to him, said in reproof, "Get thee behind me, Satan." Matthew also writes that on the Mount of Transfiguration, in the presence of Christ, Moses, and Elias, and the two sons of Zebedee, Peter said, "Lord, it is good for us to be here. If thou wilt, let us make here three tabernacles, one for thee, one for Moses, and one for Elias." Matthew further writes that when the disciples were on the ship in the night, and Christ walked on the water, Peter said, "Lord, if it be thou, bid me come unto thee on the water." And that when Christ predicted how all His disciples should be offended because of Him, Peter answered, "Though all men shall be offended because of thee, yet will I never be offended." And afterwards, "Though I should die with thee, yet will I not deny thee." And this statement Mark confirms, while Luke writes that, just before the words we have quoted concerning the swords, Peter had said to Christ, "Lord, I am ready to go with thee, both into prison and to death."

John tells of him, that when Christ desired to wash his feet, Peter asked, "Lord, dost thou wash my feet?" and then said, "Thou shalt never wash my feet." He further relates how Peter smote with his sword the servant of the High Priest, an account in which the four Evangelists agree. And John tells how when Peter came to the sepulchre and saw the other disciples lingering at the door, he entered in straightway; and again when after the resurrection Jesus stood on the shore and

Peter "heard that it was the Lord, he girt his fisher's coat unto him (for he was naked), and did cast himself into the sea." Lastly, he recounts that when Peter saw John, he said to Jesus, "Lord, and what shall this man do?"

It is a source of joy to have summed up this evidence of our Head Shepherd, in praise of his singleness of purpose. From all this it is obvious that when he spoke of the two swords, his answer to Christ was unambiguous in meaning.

Even if the words of Christ and Peter are to be accepted typically, they cannot be interpreted in the sense these men claim, but rather as referring to the sword concerning which Matthew writes: "Think not that I am come to send peace on earth: I came not to send peace, but a sword. For I am come to set a man at variance against his father," and what follows. This He accomplished in word and deed, wherefore Luke tells Theophilus of all "that Jesus began to do and teach." Such was the sword Christ enjoined them to buy, and Peter made answer that already they had two with them. As we have shown, they were ready for words and for works to bring to pass those things which Christ proclaimed He had come to do by the sword.

CHAPTER 10

In addition, some persons affirm that the Emperor Constantine, healed of leprosy by the intercession of Sylvester, then the Supreme Pontiff, gave to the Church the very seat of Empire, Rome, together with many imperial dignities. Wherefore they argue that no one has power to assume these dignities except he receives them from the Church, to whom it is asserted they belong. And from this it would fairly follow, as they desire, that one authority is dependent on the other.

So having stated and refuted the arguments which seemed to be rooted in divine communications, it now remains to set forth and disprove those rooted in Roman deeds and human reason. We have just spoken of the first of these, whose syllogism runs thus: Those things which belong to the Church no one can rightly possess, unless granted them by the Church; and this we concede. The ruling power of Rome belongs to the Church; therefore no one can rightly possess it unless granted it by the Church. And the minor premise they prove by the facts mentioned above concerning Constantine.

This minor premise, then, I deny. Their proof is no proof, for Constantine had not the power to alienate the imperial dignity, nor had the Church power to receive it. Their insistent objection to what I say can be met thus. No one is free to do through an office assigned him anything contrary to the office, for thereby the same thing, in virtue of being the same, would be contrary to itself, which is impossible. But to divide the Empire would be contrary to the office assigned the Emperor, for as is easily seen from the first book of the treatise, his office is to hold the human race subject to one will in all things. Therefore, division of his Empire is not allowed an Emperor. If, as they claim, certain dignities were alienated by Constantine from the Empire and ceded to the power of the Church, the "seamless coat" would have been rent, which even they had not dared to mutilate who with their spears pierced Christ, the very God. Moreover, as the Church has its own foundation, so has the Empire its own. The foundation of the Church is Christ, as the Apostle writes to the Corinthians: "Other foundation can no man lay than that is laid, which is Jesus Christ." He is the rock on which the Church is founded, but the foundation of the Empire is human Right. Now I say that as the Church cannot act contrary to its foundation, but must be supported thereby, according to that verse of the *Canticles:* "Who is she that cometh up from the desert, abounding in delights, leaning on her beloved?" so the Empire cannot act in conflict with human Right. Therefore the Empire may not destroy itself, for, should it do so, it would act in conflict with human Right. Inasmuch as the Empire consists in the indivisibility of universal Monarchy, and inasmuch as an apportionment of the Empire would destroy it, it is evident that division is not allowed to him who discharges imperial duty. And it is proved, from what has been previously said, that to destroy the Empire would be contrary to human Right.

Besides, every jurisdiction exists prior to its judge, since the judge is ordained for the jurisdiction, and not conversely. As the Empire is a jurisdiction embracing in its circuit the administration of justice in all temporal things, so it is prior to its judge, who is Emperor; and the Emperor is ordained for it, and not conversely. Clearly the Emperor, as Emperor, cannot alter the Empire, for from it he receives his being and state. So I say, either he was Emperor when he made the concession they speak of to the Church, or he was not. If he was not, it is plain that he had no power to grant anything with regard to the Empire. And if he was, then as Emperor he could not have done this, for the concession would have narrowed his jurisdiction.

Further, if one Emperor has power to cut away one bit from the jurisdiction of the Empire, another may do the same for like reason. And since temporal jurisdiction is finite, and every finite thing may be consumed by finite losses, the possibility of annihilating primal jurisdiction would follow. But this is inconceivable.

And since he who confers a thing has the relation of agent, and he on whom it is conferred the relation of patient, according to the Philosopher in the fourth book *to Nicomachus*, then in order for a grant to be legal, proper qualification is essential not only in the giver, but in the recipient. Indeed, it seems that the acts of agents exist potentially in a properly qualified patient. But the Church was utterly disqualified for receiving temporal power by the express prohibitive command in Matthew: "Provide neither gold, nor silver, nor brass in your purses, nor scrip for your journey," etc. For although we learn from Luke of the mitigation of this order regarding certain things, yet I am unable to find that sanction was given the Church to possess gold and silver, subsequent to the prohibition. Wherefore if the Church had not power to receive, even had Constantine power to bestow, temporal authority, the action would nevertheless be impossible, because of the disqualification of the patient. It is demonstrated, then, that neither could the Church accept by way of possession, nor could Constantine confer by way of alienation. However, the Emperor did have power to depute to the protectorship of the Church a patrimony and other things, as long as his supreme command, the unity of which suffers no impairment, remained unchanged. And the Vicar of God had power to receive such things, not for possession, but for distribution on behalf of the Church of its fruits to the poor of Christ. We are not ignorant that thus the Apostles did.

CHAPTER 12

Papal and imperial powers cannot be represented by one man.

Their argument from reason, however, is this. They lay down the principle advanced in the tenth book of the *First Philosophy*, that "all things of one genus are reducible to a type which is the standard of measurement for all within the genus." Since all men are of one genus, they ought to be reducible to a type as a standard for all others. And since the Supreme Pontiff and the Emperor are men, they must therefore, if our conclusion is true, be reducible to one man. And since the Pope cannot be subordinated to another, it remains for the Emperor and all others to be subordinated to the Pope as their measure and rule; whence results the conclusion they desire.

That this reasoning may be invalidated, I agree that their statement is true that all things of one genus ought to be reduced to some one member of that genus as a standard of measurement. Likewise is it true that all men are of one genus. Also is true their conclusion drawn from these that all men ought to be subordinated to one standard for the genus. But when from this conclusion they draw the further inference concerning Pope and Emperor, they deceive themselves with the fallacy of accidental attributes.

To make this evident, be it known that it is one thing to be a man and another thing to be a Pope. And just so it is one thing to be a man and another thing to be an Emperor, as it is one thing to be a man and another to be a father or master. Man is man because of his substantial form, which is the determinant of his species and genus, and which places him under the category of substance. But a father is such because of an accidental form, that of relation, which is the determinant of a certain species and genus, and which places him under the category of relation. Otherwise everything would be reduced to the category of substance, since no accidental form exists in itself, apart from the basis of underlying substance. But this is false. Therefore since the Pope and Emperor are what they are because of certain relations, the former through the Papacy, a relation in the province of fatherhood, and the latter through the Empire, a relation in the province of government, it is manifest that the Pope and the Emperor, in so far as they are such, must have place under the category of relation, and consequently must be subordinated to something in that genus.

Whence, I repeat, they are to be measured by one standard in so far as they are men, and by another in so far as they are Pope and Emperor. Now, in so far as they are men, they have to be measured by the best man (whoever he may be), that is, by him who is the standard and ideal of all men, and who has the most perfect unity among his kind, as we may learn from the last book *to Nicomachus*. But in as far as they are relative, it is evident that one must be measured by the other, if one is subordinate; or they must unite in a common species from the nature of their relation; or they must be measured by a third something as their common ground of unity. But it cannot be maintained that one is subordinate to the other; that is, it is false to predicate one of the other, to call the Emperor the Pope, or to call the Pope the Emperor. Nor is it possible to maintain that they unite in a common species, for the relation of Pope, as such, is other than the relation of Emperor as Emperor. Therefore they must be measured by something beyond themselves in which they shall find a ground of unity.

At this point it must be understood that as relation stands to relation, so stands related thing to related thing. Hence if the Papacy and Empire, being relations of authority, must be measured with regard to the supreme authority from which they and their characteristic differences are derived, the Pope and Emperor, being relative, must be referred to some unity wherein may be found the supreme authority without these characteristic differences. And this will be either God Himself, in whom every relation is universally united, or in some substance inferior to God, in whom is found a supreme authority differentiated and derived from His perfect supremacy. And so it is evident that the Pope and Emperor, as men, are to be measured by one standard, but as Pope and Emperor by another. And this demonstration is from the argument according to reason.

CHAPTER 16

**God alone directs man towards his two-fold goal and
chooses rulers for each; the authority of the Empire
derives from God directly.**

Although by the method of reduction to absurdity it has been shown
in the foregoing chapter that the authority of Empire has not its source
in the Chief Pontiff, yet it has not been fully proved, save by an inference, that its immediate source is God, seeing that if the authority does
not depend on the Vicar of God, we conclude that it depends on God
Himself. For a perfect demonstration of the proposition we must prove
directly that the Emperor, or Monarch, of the world has immediate
relationship to the Prince of the universe, who is God.

In order to realize this, it must be understood that man alone of all
beings holds the middle place between corruptibility and incorruptibility, and is therefore rightly compared by philosophers to the horizon
which lies between the two hemispheres. Man may be considered with
regard to either of his essential parts, body or soul. If considered in
regard to the body alone, he is perishable; if in regard to the soul alone,
he is imperishable. So the Philosopher spoke well of its incorruptibility
when he said in the second book *on the Soul*, "And this only can be sepa-
rated as a thing eternal from that which perishes."

If man holds a middle place between the perishable and imperishable, then, inasmuch as every mean shares the nature of the extremes,
man must share both natures. And inasmuch as every nature is ordained for a certain ultimate end, it follows that there exists for man a
two-fold end, in order that as he alone of all beings partakes of the
perishable and the imperishable, so he alone of all beings should be
ordained for two ultimate ends. One end is for that in him which is
perishable, the other for that which is imperishable.

Ineffable Providence has thus designed two ends to be contemplated
of man: first, the happiness of this life, which consists in the activity of
his natural powers, and is prefigured by the terrestrial Paradise; and
then the blessedness of life everlasting, which consists in the enjoyment
of the countenance of God, to which man's natural powers may not
attain unless aided by divine light, and which may be symbolized by
the celestial Paradise.

To these states of blessedness, just as to diverse conclusions, man must
come by diverse means. To the former we come by the teachings of
philosophy, obeying them by acting in conformity with the moral and
intellectual virtues; to the latter through spiritual teachings which
transcend human reason, and which we obey by acting in conformity
with the theological virtues, Faith, Hope, and Charity. Now the former
end and means are made known to us by human reason, which the
philosophers have wholly explained to us; and the latter by the Holy

Spirit, which has revealed to us supernatural but essential truth through the Prophets and Sacred Writers, through Jesus Christ, the coeternal Son of God, and through His disciples. Nevertheless, human passion would cast all these behind, were not men, like horses astray in their brutishness, held to the road by bit and rein.

Wherefore a two-fold directive agent was necessary to man, in accordance with the twofold end; the Supreme Pontiff to lead the human race to life eternal by means of revelation, and the Emperor to guide it to temporal felicity by means of philosophic instruction. And since none or few—and these with exceeding difficulty—could attain this port, were not the waves of seductive desire calmed, and mankind made free to rest in the tranquillity of peace, therefore this is the goal which he whom we call the guardian of the earth and Roman Prince should most urgently seek; then would it be possible for life on this mortal threshing-floor to pass in freedom and peace. The order of the world follows the order inherent in the revolution of the heavens. To attain this order it is necessary that instruction productive of liberality and peace should be applied by the guardian of the realm, in due place and time, as dispensed by Him who is the ever present Watcher of the whole order of the heavens. And He alone foreordained this order, that by it in His providence He might link together all things, each in its own place.

If this is so, and there is none higher than He, only God elects and only God confirms. Whence we may further conclude that neither those who are now, nor those who in any way whatsoever have been, called Electors have the right to be so called; rather should they be entitled heralds of divine providence. Whence it is that those in whom is vested the dignity of proclamation suffer dissension among themselves at times, when, all or part of them being shadowed by the clouds of passion, they discern not the face of God's dispensation.

It is established, then, that the authority of temporal Monarchy descends without mediation from the fountain of universal authority. And this fountain, one in its purity of source, flows into multifarious channels out of the abundance of its excellence.

Methinks I have now approached close enough to the goal I had set myself, for I have taken the kernels of truth from the husks of falsehood, in that question which asked whether the office of Monarchy was essential to the welfare of the world, and in the next which made inquiry whether the Roman people rightfully appropriated the Empire, and in the last which sought whether the authority of the Monarch derived from God immediately, or from some other. But the truth of this final question must not be restricted to mean that the Roman Prince shall not be subject in some degree to the Roman Pontiff, for felicity that is mortal is ordered in a measure after felicity that is immortal. Wherefore let Caesar honor Peter as a first-born son should honor his father, so that, refulgent with the light of paternal grace, he may illumine with greater radiance the earthly sphere over which he has been set by Him who alone is Ruler of all things spiritual and temporal.

A STUDY GUIDE TO DANTE'S THOUGHT

1. What is the meaning of the first canto of the *Inferno*?
2. What are some of the symbols employed in this canto and what do they represent?
3. Why is Virgil Dante's guide in the *Inferno*?
4. Who are the Simoniacs?
5. Why is Boniface VIII in hell?
6. What is Dante's opinion of the papacy?
7. What is the punishment of Bertrand de Born?
8. What is Dante's theory of punishment?
9. What is the physical structure of the *Inferno*?
10. How does Dante's *Inferno* compare with the underworlds in Homer and Virgil?
11. What is Dante's theory of free will?
12. What is Dante's theory of love?
13. What function does Beatrice play in the poem?
14. Why can't Virgil continue as Dante's guide?
15. What is the theological purpose of Purgatory?
16. Why does St. Bernard replace Beatrice as Dante's guide?
17. According to Dante, how can man know God?
18. Is Dante a rationalist or a mystic?
19. On how many different levels does the *Divine Comedy* operate?
20. In what sense is the *Divine Comedy* a "comedy"?
21. What is the purpose of human government as discussed in *De Monarchia*?
22. Why is universal peace the ultimate object of government?
23. What is the best form of government?
24. What should the relationship be between monarchy and papacy?
25. What is the conclusion that Dante derives from the theory of two swords?
26. What is the Donation of Constantine?

4
SELECTIONS FROM MACHIAVELLI'S WORK

Principles and Ideals

Machiavellian Idealism

Machiavelli was a more diversified writer than is commonly realized; besides composing political and historical treatises, he wrote poetry and authored two bawdy comedies which modern critics recognize as monuments in Italian theatre. The following selections, presenting his theoretical and idealistic judgments, include: first, prose and poetic statements of his highest ideals; second, analyses of the nature of history, which for Machiavelli primarily entails a cyclical view of change and an unchanging view of humanity; third, reflections on the role of fortune in human events and the effect men can exercise on their fortune; and fourth, considerations on the nature of government, emphasizing the significance of degeneration and reform in political institutions.

Tercets on ambition.

> Luigi, though you marvel at this case
>   Which has occurred in Siena, you don't seem
>   To take this world of ours for what it is;
>
> And, if what you have heard seems strange indeed,
>   As you have written and confirmed to me,
>   Reflect some more on all our human greed:
>
> For from the Scythian to the Egyptian ground,
>   From England down to the opposite shore,
>   One sees this crime in blooming strength is found.

Source: *Lust and Liberty,* translated by Joseph Tusiani (New York: Ivan Obolensky, Inc., 1963), pp. 120–127. © 1963 by Joseph Tusiani. Reprinted with permission of Astor-Honor, Inc., New York.

What region or what town is free from it?
  What village or what hut? Wherever you go,
  Ambition follows, too, and Greed with it.

These two came to the world the very day
  Man was born; and if they were not down here
  Our human state would be most fair and gay.

Hardly had God created stars and light,
  Heaven and elements and man (the one
  He made lord over all such beauties bright);

And hardly had He thrown out of His home
  Proud Angels, out of Eden impious Adam
  Who with his mate had dared to taste the pome;

Than ah (it was the time Abel and Cain
  Lived with their father from their daily work,
  Happy indeed in their poor home's domain),

A hidden power which up above is nurtured,
  Among the stars rotating in the sky,
  And is not friendly to the human nature,

To give us war and strip us of sweet peace,
  To take all happiness and calm away,
  Unleashed two furies down to dwell with us.

Naked they are, and each of them goes by
  With such a gracefulness that many think
  They're grace itself and, oh, full, both, of joy.

On each of them four faces you discern,
  And eight hands; and because of this, therefore,
  You're caught and seen, if but one of them turn.

With these, Sloth, Hate, and Envy come and stride,
  Filling the world with their pestiferous being,
  And also Cruelty, Deceit, and Pride.

Concord is hurled by them down to the bottom
  And, just to show their infinite desire,
  They carry in their hands an urn without bottom.

Because of them life's sweet and quiet days,
  Which once filled Adam's dwelling on this earth,
  With Charity and Peace speed soon away.

And they were those who with a poisonous pest
  Armed Cain against his innocent, meek brother,
  Filling with hate his mind and soul and breast.

And it was they who showed their greatest art
  Since they were able, in those ancient times,
  To make a greedy and ambitious heart,

When men still lived neither with clothes nor with
  Fortune, and when they did not know at all
  Any example of poverty or wealth.

O human mind, insatiable and vain,
  Fraudulent, fickle, and, above all things,
  Impious, malignant, full of quick disdain!

It was because of your ambitious wish
  The first violent death came to the world,
  And the first grass was made to bleed and blush!

With the growth of this seed malevolent
  The cause of evil was, then, multiplied,
  And reasons for repentance soon were spent.

It comes from this that one descends, one climbs;
  And this is why with neither law nor pact
  All mortal states must vary at all times.

She prompted the French monarch more than once,
  And has destroyed, undone the state of Ludwig,
  And that of Saint Mark and of King Alphonso.

And not only the good his foe possesses
  Does man desire, but also (it has been
  And always will be so, as one can guess)

That which he feigns as good he tries to own
  More by removing this or that obstruction
  Than by whatever virtue of his own.

The good in others ever hurts us deep,
   And therefore ever with tormenting care
   We wish their evil and we lose our sleep.

By natural instinct we are led and trapped
   Into all this, and by our mobile passions,
   Unless by law or greater strength we're stopped.

But if you really want to know the cause
   That makes a people rule, another cry,
   While still Ambition reigns in every place;

And why can France remain victorious;
   Why, on the other hand, all Italy
   Crosses a stormy sea of aches and woes;

And why, in certain lands, appears less strong
   And painful the result of that bad seed
   Greed and Ambition sow, going along

The answer is that, when Ambition finds
   Ferocious hearts and valor armed to fight,
   Seldom does fear of harm afflict the mind.

When first a nation lives quite uncontrolled,
   By nature, and, by accident, is then
   Instructed by good laws and therefore molded

Into order, against external foes
   Ambition hurls that fury which, because
   Of kings and laws, at home cannot be used:

And nearly always one's own pain, therefore,
   Ends; but another's flock is sought and broken
   By pent-up fury that must find a war.

Thus, on the other hand, a servile place
   Remains exposed to injury and harm
   There where Ambition finds but cowardice.

When Cowardice and lack of order are
   Ambition's mates, you must expect disgrace
   And every ruin, every wound and scar.

If you perchance are tempted to accuse
   Nature if Italy, so weary and wounded,
   Does not produce so hard and bellicose

A people, this, I say, is not sufficient
   To erase our cowardice, for education
   Can supplement where nature is deficient.

Stern education made Italy bloom
   In ancient days, and made her rise and conquer
   The entire world and for herself make room.

But now she lives—if tears can be called life—
   Beneath that ruin and unhappy fate
   That she has reaped from her long lack of strife.

With all the rest this Cowardice belongs;
   And Ambition it was that killed the fair
   Italian provinces with wounds and wrongs.

So, forget Siena's fratricidal wounds,
   And to this place, Luigi, turn your eyes,
   Among these throngs, astounded and marooned.

Here you will see Ambition's double art:
   How one steals, how another weeps and sees
   All of his fortune snatched and fallen apart.

Let those who want to know what has been done
   By others come and look, and let them see if
   Ever such horrors were beneath the sun.

One mourns a father; one, a husband; one
   Is violently dragged out of his home,
   Naked and beaten, bleeding, sad, and dumb.

Alas, how many times, while one embraced
   His own dear son for the last time, a sword
   Suddenly pierced them both—from breast to breast!

His native soil another leaves meanwhile,
   Accusing all the cruel, thankless gods,
   With his dear ones following him to exile.

O tragic things that never were before!
  Every day we can see our women, ah,
  Give birth out of crushed wombs—in horrid gore.

Bemoaning, ah, her daughter, raped, defiled,
  A mother says: "For such a wretched wedding,
  For such a husband have I reared you, child!"

Ditches are stained with blood, rivers run blood,
  And all about lie skulls and legs and hands
  And maimed and putrid limbs left there to rot.

Ravenous birds and dogs and savage beasts
  Are their paternal burial, alas:
  O strange, fierce, horrid tombs in which to rest!

Their faces are forever dark and sad,
  For they are just as one who looks about
  Awaiting new disasters and new dread.

Wherever, ah, you turn your frightened eyes,
  You see the earth one pond of blood and tears,
  And the air sounds with shrieks and sobs and sighs.

If you now want to learn Ambition's nature,
  And how it should be used, let the distressing
  Example of these people be your teacher.

Since man with his sole strength cannot discard her,
  He must then use his wisdom to escort
  Ambition with ferociousness and order.

At his expense, and futilely—oh, look!—
  Too late Saint Mark now learns that he should hold
  Within his hand a sword, and not a book.

And nonetheless, in general, one's aim
  Is to reign; but the more we gain and conquer,
  The sooner, then, we lose—with greater shame.

Therefore, if something ever should appear
  With an importunate, impetuous birth,
  Such as to fill all hearts with sudden fear,

Do not be frightened, marvel not at all,
  For in the world the greatest part of men
  Soon into fortune's hands easily fall.

Alas, bemoaning other people's sorrow
  With these my words and thoughts, I am oppressed
  By a far greater fear—that of the morrow.

I hear and feel Ambition, with that train
  Of evils heaven gave her since time's birth,
  Flying above each Tuscan mount and plain;

And she has sown so many sparks around
  Already among that people full of envy,
  That lands and towns will soon be razed to the ground,

If grace or better order do not quench them.

The fallacy of disregarding the common good.

Those serious, though natural enmities, which occur between the popular classes and the nobility, arising from the desire of the latter to command, and the disinclination of the former to obey, are the causes of most of the troubles which take place in cities, and from this diversity of purpose, all the other evils which disturb republics derive their origin. This kept Rome disunited; and this, if it be allowable to compare small things with great, held Florence in disunion; although in each city it produced a different result; for animosities were only beginning when the people and nobility of Rome contended, while ours were brought to a conclusion by the contentions of our citizens. A new law settled the disputes of Rome, those of Florence were only terminated by the death and banishment of many of her best people. Those of Rome increased her military virtue, while that of Florence was quite extinguished by her divisions. The quarrels of Rome established different ranks of society, those of Florence abolished the distinctions which had previously existed. This diversity of effects must have been occasioned by the different purposes which the two peoples had in view. While the people of Rome endeavored to associate with the nobility in the supreme honors, those of Florence strove to exclude the nobility from all participation in them: as the desire of the Roman people was more reasonable, no particular offence was given to the nobility; they therefore consented to it without having recourse to arms; so that, after some disputes concerning particular points, both parties agreed to the

SOURCE: *History of Florence* (New York: Colonial Press, 1901), pp. 121–131.

enactment of a law which, while it satisfied the people, preserved the nobility in the enjoyment of their dignity.

On the other hand, the demands of the people of Florence being insolent and unjust, the nobility, became desperate, prepared for their defence, with their utmost energy, and thus bloodshed and the exile of citizens followed. The laws which were afterward made, did not provide for the common good, but were framed wholly in favor of the conquerors. This too must be observed, that from the acquisition of power made by the people of Rome, their minds were very much improved; for all the offices of state being attainable as well by the people as the nobility, the peculiar excellencies of the latter exercised a most beneficial influence upon the former; and as the city increased in virtue she attained a more exalted greatness.

But in Florence, the people being conquerors, the nobility were deprived of all participation in the government; and, in order to regain a portion of it, it became necessary for them not only to seem like the people, but to be like them in behavior, mind, and mode of living. Hence arose those changes in armorial bearings, and in the titles of families, which the nobility adopted, in order that they might seem to be of the people; military virtue and generosity of feeling became extinguished in them; the people not possessing these qualities, they could not appreciate them, and Florence became by degrees more and more depressed and humiliated. The virtue of the Roman nobility degenerating into pride, the citizens soon found that the business of the state could not be carried on without a prince. Florence had now come to such a point, that with a comprehensive mind at the head of affairs she would easily have been made to take any form that he might have been disposed to give her; as may be partly observed by a perusal of the preceding book.

Having given an account of the origin of Florence, the commencement of her liberty, with the causes of her divisions, and shown how the factions of the nobility and the people ceased with the tyranny of the Duke of Athens, and the ruin of the former, we have now to speak of the animosities between the citizens and the plebeians, and the various circumstances which they produced.

The nobility being overcome, and the war with the Archbishop of Milan concluded, there did not appear any cause of dissension in Florence. But the evil fortune of the city, and the defective nature of her laws, gave rise to enmities between the family of the Albizzi and that of the Ricci, which divided the citizens as completely as those of the Buondelmonti and the Uberti, or the Donati and the Cerchi had formerly done. The pontiffs, who at this time resided in France, and the emperors, who abode in Germany, in order to maintain their influence in Italy, sent among us multitudes of soldiers of many countries, as English, Dutch, and Bretons. As these, upon the conclusion of a war, were thrown out of pay, though still in the country, they, under the standard of some soldier of fortune, plundered such people as were least prepared to defend themselves. In the year 1353 one of these companies came into Tuscany under the command of Monsignor Reale, of Provence, and his approach terrified all the cities of Italy. The Florentines not only provided themselves forces, but many citizens, among whom were the Albizzi and the Ricci, armed themselves in their own defence. These families were at the time full of hatred against each other, and each thought to obtain the sovereignty of the republic by overcoming his enemy. They had not yet proceeded to open violence, but only contended in the magistracies and councils. The city being all in arms, a quarrel arose in the old market-place, and, as it frequently happens in similar cases, a great number of people was drawn together. The disturbance spreading, it was told the Ricci that the Albizzi had assailed their partisans, and to the Albizzi that the Ricci were in quest of them. Upon this the whole city arose, and it was all the magistrates could do to restrain these families, and prevent the actual occurrence of a disaster which, without being the fault of either of them, had been wilfully though falsely reported as having already taken place. This apparently trifling circumstance served to inflame the minds of the parties, and make each the more resolved to increase the number of their followers. And as the citizens, since the ruin of the nobility, were on such an equality that the magistrates were more respected now than they had previously been, they designed to proceed toward the suppression of this disorder with civil authority alone.

We have before related, that after the victory of Charles I the government was formed by the Guelfic party, and that it thus acquired great authority over the Ghibellines. But time, a variety of circumstances, and new divisions had so contributed to sink this party feeling into oblivion, that many of Ghibelline descent now filled the highest offices. Observing this, Uguccione, the head of the family of the Ricci, contrived that the law against the Ghibellines should be again brought into operation; many imagining the Albizzi to be of that faction, they having arisen in Arezzo, and come long ago to Florence. Uguccione by this means hoped to deprive the Albizzi of participation in the government, for all of Ghibelline blood who were found to hold offices, would be condemned in the penalties which this law provided. The design of Uguccione was discovered to Piero, son of Filippo degli Albizzi, and he resolved to favor it; for he saw that to oppose it would at once declare him a Ghibelline; and thus the law which was renewed by the ambition of the Ricci for his destruction, instead of robbing Piero degli Albizzi of reputation, contributed to increase his influence, although it laid the foundation of many evils. Nor is it possible for a republic to enact a law more pernicious than one relating to matters which have long transpired. Piero having favored this law, which had been contrived by his enemies for his stumbling-block, it became the stepping-stone to his greatness; for, making himself the leader of this new order of things, his authority went on increasing, and he was in greater favor with the Guelfs than any other man.

As there could not be found a magistrate willing to search out who were Ghibellines, and as this renewed enactment against them was therefore of small value, it was provided that authority should be given to the Capitani to find who were of this faction; and, having discovered, to signify and admonish them that they were not to take upon themselves any office of government; to which admonitions, if they were disobedient, they became condemned in the penalties. Hence, all those who in Florence are deprived of the power to hold offices are called "Ammoniti," or "Admonished."

The Capitani in time acquiring greater audacity, admonished not only those to whom the admonition was applicable, but any others at the suggestion of their own avarice or ambition; and from 1356, when this law was made, to 1366, there had been admonished above 200 citizens. The Captains of Parts and the sect of the Guelfs were thus become powerful; for everyone honored them for fear of being admonished; and most particularly the leaders, who were Piero degli Albizzi, Lapo da Castiglionchio, and Carlo Strozzi. This insolent mode of proceeding was offensive to many; but none felt so particularly injured with it as the Ricci; for they knew themselves to have occasioned it, they saw it involved the ruin of the republic, and their enemies, the Albizzi, contrary to their intention, become great in consequence.

On this account Uguccione de' Ricci, being one of the Signory, resolved to put an end to the evil which he and his friends had originated, and with a new law provided that to the six Captains of Parts an additional three should be appointed, of whom two should be chosen from the companies of minor artificers, and that before any party could be considered Ghibelline, the declaration of the Capitani must be confirmed by twenty-four Guelfic citizens, appointed for the purpose. This provision tempered for the time the power of the Capitani, so that the admonitions were greatly diminished, if not wholly laid aside. Still the parties of the Albizzi and the Ricci were continually on the alert to oppose each other's laws, deliberations, and enterprises, not from a conviction of their inexpediency, but from hatred of their promoters.

In such distractions the time passed from 1366 to 1371, when the Guelfs again regained the ascendant. There was in the family of the Buondelmonti a gentleman named Benchi, who, as an acknowledgment of his merit in a war against the Pisans, though one of the nobility, had been admitted among the people, and thus became eligible to office among the Signory; but when about to take his seat with them, a law was made that no nobleman who had become of the popular class should be allowed to assume that office. This gave great offence to Benchi, who, in union with Piero degli Albizzi, determined to depress the less powerful of the popular party with admonitions, and obtain the government for themselves. By the interest which Benchi possessed with the ancient nobility, and that of Piero with most of the influential citizens, the Guelfic party resumed their ascendancy, and by new reforms among the Parts, so remodelled the administration as to be able to dispose of the offices of the captains and the twenty-four citizens at pleasure. They then returned to the admonitions with greater audacity than ever, and the house of the Albizzi became powerful as the head of this faction.

On the other hand, the Ricci made the most strenuous exertions against their designs; so that anxiety universally prevailed, and ruin was apprehended alike from both parties. In consequence of this, a great number of citizens, out of love to their country, assembled in the Church of St. Piero Scarraggio, and after a long consideration of the existing disorders, presented themselves before the Signors, whom one of the principal among them addressed in the following terms:

"Many of us, Magnificent Signors! were afraid of meeting even for consideration of public business, without being publicly called together, lest we should be noted as presumptuous or condemned as ambitious. But seeing that many citizens daily assemble in the lodges and halls of the palace, not for any public utility, but only for the gratification of their own ambition, we have thought that as those who assemble for the ruin of the republic are fearless, so still less ought they to be apprehensive who meet together only for its advantage; nor ought we to be anxious respecting the opinion they may form of our assembling, since they are so utterly indifferent to the opinion of others. Our affection for our country, Magnificent Signors! caused us to assemble first, and now brings us before you, to speak of grievances already great and daily increasing in our republic, and to offer our assistance for their removal; and we doubt not that, though a difficult undertaking, it will still be attended with success, if you will lay aside all private regards, and authoritatively use the public force.

"The common corruption of all the cities of Italy, Magnificent Signors! has infested and still vitiates your own; for when this province had shaken off the imperial yoke, her cities not being subject to any powerful influence that might restrain them, administered affairs, not as free men do, but as a factious populace; and hence have arisen all the other evils and disorders that have appeared. In the first place, there cannot be found among the citizens either unity or friendship, except with those whose common guilt, either against their country or against private individuals, is a bond of union. And as the knowledge of religion and the fear of God seem to be alike extinct, oaths and promises have lost their validity, and are kept as long as it is found expedient; they are adopted only as a means of deception, and he is most applauded and respected whose cunning is most efficient and secure. On this account bad men are received with the approbation due to virtue, and good ones are regarded only in the light of fools.

"And certainly in the cities of Italy all that is corruptible and corrupting is assembled. The young are idle, the old lascivious, and each sex and every age abounds with debasing habits, which the good laws, by misapplication, have lost the power to correct. Hence arise the avarice so observable among the citizens, and that greediness, not for true glory, but for unworthy honors; from which follow hatred, animosities, quarrels, and factions; resulting in deaths, banishments, affliction to all good men, and the advancement of the most unprincipled; for the good, confiding in their innocence, seek neither safety nor advancement by illegal methods as the wicked do, and thus unhonored and undefended they sink into oblivion.

"From proceedings such as these, arise at once the attachment for and influence of parties; bad men follow them through ambition and avarice, and necessity compels the good to pursue the same course. And most lamentable is it to observe how the leaders and movers of parties sanctify their base designs with words that are all piety and virtue; they have the name of liberty constantly in their mouths, though their actions prove them her greatest enemies. The reward which they desire from victory is not the glory of having give liberty to the city, but the satisfaction of having vanquished others, and of making themselves rulers; and to attain their end, there is nothing too unjust, too cruel, too avaricious for them to attempt. Thus laws and ordinances, peace, wars, and treaties are adopted and pursued, not for the public good, nor for the common glory of the state, but for the convenience or advantage of a few individuals.

"And if other cities abound in these disorders, ours is more than any infected with them; for her laws, statutes, and civil ordinances are not, nor have they ever been, established for the benefit of men in a state of freedom, but according to the wish of the faction that has been uppermost at the time. Hence it follows, that when one party is expelled, or faction extinguished, another immediately arises; for, in a city that is governed by parties rather than by laws, as soon as one becomes dominant and unopposed, it must of necessity soon divide against itself; for the private methods at first adopted for its defence, will now no longer keep it united. The truth of this, both the ancient and modern dissensions of our city, prove. Everyone thought that when the Ghibellines were destroyed, the Guelfs would long continue happy and honored; yet after a short time they divided into Bianchi and Neri, the black faction and the white. When the Bianchi were overcome, the city was not long free from factions; for either, in favor of the emigrants, or on account of the animosity between the nobility and the people, we were still constantly at war. And as if resolved to give up to others, what in mutual harmony we either would not or were unable to retain, we confided the care of our precious liberty first to King Robert, then to his brother, next to his son, and at last to the Duke of Athens. Still we have never in any condition found repose, but seem like men who can neither agree to live in freedom nor be content with slavery. Nor did we hesitate (so greatly does the nature of our ordinances dispose us to division), while yet under allegiance to the king, to substitute for his majesty, one of the vilest of men born at Agobbio.

"For the credit of the city, the name of the Duke of Athens ought to be consigned to oblivion. His cruel and tyrannical disposition, however, might have taught us wisdom and instructed us how to live; but no sooner was he expelled than we handled our arms, and fought with more hatred, and greater fury than we had ever done on any former occasion; so that the ancient nobility were vanquished and the city was left at the disposal of the people. It was generally supposed that no further occasion of quarrel or of party animosity could arise, since those whose pride and insupportable ambition had been regarded as the causes of them were depressed; however, experience proves how liable human judgment is to error, and what false impressions men imbibe, even in regard to the things that most intimately concern them; for we find the pride and ambition of the nobility are not extinct, but only transferred from them to the people who at this moment, according to the usual practice of ambitious men, are endeavoring to render themselves masters of the republic; and knowing they have no chance of success but what is offered by discord, they have again divided the city, and the names of Guelf and Ghibelline, which were beginning to be forgotten (and it would have been well if they had never been heard among us), are repeated anew in our ears.

"It seems almost necessarily ordained, in order that in human affairs there may be nothing either settled or permanent, that in all republics there are what may be called fatal families, born for the ruin of their country. Of this kind of pest our city has produced a more copious brood than any other; for not one, but many, have disturbed and harassed her: first the Buondelmonti and the Uberti; then the Donati and the Cerchi; and now, oh, ridiculous! oh, disgraceful thought! the Ricci and the Albizzi have caused a diversion of her citizens.

"We have not dwelt upon our corrupt habits or our old and continual dissensions to occasion you alarm, but to remind you of their causes;

to show that as you, doubtless, are aware of them, we also keep them in view, and to remind you that their results ought not to make you diffident of your power to repress the disorders of the present time. The ancient families possessed so much influence, and were held in such high esteem, that civil force was insufficient to restrain them; but now, when the empire has lost its ascendancy, the Pope is no longer formidable, and the whole of Italy is reduced to a state of the most complete equality, there can be no difficulty. Our republic might, more especially than any other (although at first our former practices seem to present a reason to the contrary), not only keep itself united but be improved by good laws and civil regulations, if you, the Signory, would once resolve to undertake the matter; and to this, we, induced by no other motive than the love of our country, would most strongly urge you. It is true the corruption of the country is great, and much discretion will be requisite to correct it; but do not impute the past disorders to the nature of the men, but to the times, which, being changed, give reasonable ground to hope that, with better government, our city will be attended with better fortune; for the malignity of the people will be overcome by restraining the ambition and annulling the ordinances of those who have encouraged faction, and adopting in their stead only such principles as are comfortable to true civil liberty. And be assured, that these desirable ends will be more certainly attained by the benign influence of the laws, than by a delay which will compel the people to effect them by force and arms."

The Signory, induced by the necessity of the case, of which they were previously aware, and further encouraged by the advice of those who now addressed them, gave authority to fifty-six citizens to provide for the safety of the republic. It is usually found that most men are better adapted to pursue a good course already begun, than to discover one applicable to immediate circumstances. These citizens thought rather of extinguishing existing factions than of preventing the formation of new ones, and effected neither of these objects. The facilities for the establishment of new parties were not removed; and out of those which they guarded against, another more powerful, arose, which brought the republic into still greater danger. They, however, deprived three of the family of the Albizzi, and three of that of the Ricci, of all the offices of government, except those of the Guelfic party, for three years; and among the deprived were Piero degli Albizzi and Uguccione de' Ricci. They forbade the citizens to assemble in the palace, except during the sittings of the Signory. They provided that if anyone were beaten, or possession of his property detained from him, he might bring his case before the council and denounce the offender, even if he were one of the nobility; and that if it were proved, the accused should be subject to the usual penalties. This provision abated the boldness of the Ricci, and increased that of the Albizzi; since, although it applied equally to both, the Ricci suffered from it by far the most; for if Piero was excluded from the palace of the Signory, the chamber of the Guelfs, in which he possessed the greatest authority, remained open to him; and if he and his followers had previously been ready to admonish, they became after this injury, doubly so. To this pre-disposition for evil, new excitements were added.

Love of city.

16 April 1527, Forlì
To Francesco Vettori, in Florence
Magnificent, etc.:

Monseigneur de la Motte has been today in the camp of the imperials with the final form of the agreement made there. If Bourbon accepts, he must halt his army; if he moves, it is a sign that he does not wish any agreement. So tomorrow will be the judge of our affairs. Therefore the decision here, if tomorrow he moves, is to think on war completely, without having a hair that thinks further of peace; if he does not move, it is to think of peace and to lay aside all thought of war. With this north wind we too must sail and, if we decide on war, we must cut off all the affairs of peace, and in such a way that the allies will come on without any hesitation, because now we cannot hobble any more but must go like mad; often desperation finds remedies that choice has been unable to find.

They are coming without artillery into a difficult region. Hence if, with what little life remains to us, we unite with the forces of the League that are ready, either they will leave this province with shame or they will come down to reasonable terms.

I love Messer Francesco Guicciardini; I love my native city more than my soul; and I tell you this through the experience which sixty years have given me, namely, that I do not believe that ever more difficult articles than these were struggled with, where peace is necessary and war cannot be abandoned; and to have on our hands a prince who scarcely is able to deal with peace alone or with war alone.

I send you my regards.

Niccolò Machiavelli, in Forlì.

The greatest good is that which one does to one's country.

I believe that the greatest honor men can have is that which is willingly given them by their native lands. I believe that the greatest good that can be done, and the most pleasing to God, is that which is done

Source: *Machiavelli: The Chief Works*, translated by A. Gilbert (Durham, N.C.; Duke University Press, 1965), 2, p. 1010.

Source: *Machiavelli: The Chief Works*, translated by A. Gilbert (Durham, N.C.; Duke University Press, 1965), 7, p. 91.

to one's country. In addition to this, no man is so much raised on high by any of his acts as are those who have reformed republics and kingdoms with new laws and institutions. After those who have been gods, such men get the first praises; and because there have been few who have had the opportunity to do it, and still fewer who have known how to do it, the number of those who have done it is small. This sort of glory has been so highly esteemed by men, who have never sought anything except glory, that those who have not been able to set up a state in reality have done it in writing; for Aristotle, Plato, and many others have desired to show the world that if they have not been able to found a commonwealth as did Solon and Lycurgus, they have not failed from ignorance but from lack of opportunity to put their ideas into practice.

History

The continuity of human nature.

Prudent men are wont to say—and this not rashly or without good ground—that he who would foresee what has to be, should reflect on what has been, for everything that happens in the world at any time has a genuine resemblance to what happened in ancient times. This is due to the fact that the agents who bring such things about are men, and that men have, and always have had, the same passions, whence it necessarily comes about that the same effects are produced. It is true that men's deeds are sometimes more virtuous in this country than in that, and in that than in some other, according to the type of education from which their inhabitants have derived their mode of life.

Knowledge of the future based on the past is also facilitated when we find a nation which for a long time has had the same customs, which has been, for instance, consistently grasping or consistently deceitful, or which has had any other such vice or virtue. Thus, whoever studies the past history of this our city of Florence and compares what happened then with what has happened in quite recent times will find the German and French peoples imbued with avarice, pride, ferocity and unreliability, for all these four characteristics of theirs have at different times done much harm to our city. In regard to untrustworthiness, for instance, everybody knows how often money was given to King Charles VIII, and how he promised to restore the citadel of Pisa and never did so; whereby this king displayed alike his untrustworthiness and no small avarice.

But let us pass over these recent events. Everybody will have heard of what happened in the war which the Florentines waged against the

---

SOURCE: *The Discourses of Machiavelli*, translated by L. J. Walker (New Haven: Yale University Press, 1950), pp. 575–577. Reprinted with permission of Routledge & Kegan Paul, Ltd., London.

Visconti, Dukes of Milan. Since the Florentines had no other expedient available, they considered bringing the Emperor into Italy that his standing and his forces might be of avail in the attack on Lombardy. The Emperor promised to come with a strong army to join them in their war with the Visconti, and to protect Florence against that power, on condition that the Florentines gave him a hundred thousand ducats on his starting out and another hundred thousand when he should arrive in Italy; to which terms the Florentines agreed. Having been paid the first instalment, and then the second, when he got to Verona he turned back without doing anything, pleading that he was held up by those who had not fulfilled the agreements he had made with them. So that, had Florence neither been driven to it by necessity nor overcome by passion, but had read about and become acquainted with the habits of barbarians in ancient times, she would not have been misled by them on this occasion and on many others, since they have always been the same and have behaved everywhere and to everybody in the same way.

This may be seen from what they did of old to the Tuscans. The latter were much harassed by the Romans by whom they had often been put to flight and routed. It became clear to them that with their own forces they could not resist such attacks, so they made an agreement with the Gauls who had settled on the Italian side of the Alps whereby in return for a sum of money they were to join forces with them and to march against the Romans. The result was that, having accepted the money, the Gauls refused to take up arms on their behalf, alleging that they had accepted it not on the understanding that they should make war on the enemies of Tuscany but that they should abstain from pillaging Tuscan territory. So that, owing to the avarice and untrustworthiness of the Gauls, the Tuscan peoples at once lost their money and the help they had hoped to get from them.

Thus we see that in the case of the ancient Tuscans and in that of the Florentines, the Gauls adopted the same policy; from which it is easy to judge how much reliance rulers can place in them.

The cycle of human affairs.

It may be observed, that provinces amid the vicissitudes to which they are subject, pass from order into confusion, and afterward recur to a state of order again; for the nature of mundane affairs not allowing them to continue in an even course, when they have arrived at their greatest perfection, they soon begin to decline. In the same manner, having been reduced to disorder, and sunk to their utmost state of depression, unable to descend lower, they, of necessity, reascend; and thus from

SOURCE: *History of Florence* (New York: Colonial Press, 1901), p. 225.

good they gradually decline to evil, and from evil again return to good. The reason is, that valor produces peace; peace, repose; repose, disorder; disorder, ruin; so from disorder, order springs; from order, virtue, and from this, glory and good-fortune. Hence, wise men have observed, that the age of literary excellence is subsequent to that of distinction in arms; and that in cities and provinces, great warriors are produced before philosophers. Arms having secured victory, and victory peace, the buoyant vigor of the martial mind cannot be enfeebled by a more excusable indulgence than that of letters; nor can indolence, with any greater or more dangerous deceit, enter a well-regulated community.

The continuity of world and purpose of studying history.

Men always, but not always with good reason, praise bygone days and criticise the present, and so partial are they to the past that they not only admire past ages the knowledge of which has come down to them in written records, but also, when they grow old, what they remember having seen in their youth. And, when this view is wrong, as it usually is, there are, I am convinced, various causes to which the mistake may be due.

The first of them is, I think, this. This whole truth about olden times is not grasped, since what redounds to their discredit is often passed over in silence, whereas what is likely to make them appear glorious is pompously recounted in all its details. For so obsequious are most writers to the fortune of conquerors that, in order to make their victories seem glorious, they not only exaggerate their own valorous deeds, but also magnify the exploits of the enemy, so that anyone born afterwards either in the conquering or in the conquered province may find cause to marvel at such men and such times, and is bound, in short, to admire them and to feel affection for them.

Another reason is that, since it is either through fear or through envy that men come to hate things, in the case of the past the two most powerful incentives for hating it are lacking, since the past cannot hurt you nor give you cause for envy. Whereas it is otherwise with events in which you play a part and which you see with your own eyes, for of these you have an intimate knowledge, are in touch with every detail, and in them find, mingled with much good, also that which displeases you; so that you cannot help thinking them far inferior to the remote past, even though in fact the present is much more deserving of praise and renown. I am not here referring to what pertains to the arts, for in themselves they have so much lustre that time can scarce take away or add much to the glory which they themselves deserve. I am speaking

SOURCE: *The Discourses of Machiavelli*, translated by L. J. Walker (New Haven: Yale University Press, 1950), pp. 353–356. Reprinted with permission of Routledge & Kegan Paul, Ltd., London.

of things appertaining to human life and human customs, the evidence for whose merit is not so clear to one's eyes.

My answer is, then, that it is true there exists this habit of praising the past and criticising the present, and not always true that to do so is a mistake, for it must be admitted that sometimes such a judgment is valid because, since human affairs are ever in a state of flux, they move either upwards or downwards. Thus one sees a city or a province that has been endowed with a sound political constitution by some eminent man, thanks to its founder's virtue for a time go on steadily improving. Anyone born in such a state at such a time, is wrong if he gives more praise to the past than to the present, and his mistake will be due to the causes we have mentioned above. But those who are born in this city or province later on, when there has come a time in which it is on the decline and is deteriorating, will not then be in error.

When I reflect that it is in this way that events pursue their course it seems to me that the world has always been in the same condition, and that in it there has been just as much good as there is evil, but that this evil and this good has varied from province to province. This may be seen from the knowledge we have of ancient kingdoms, in which the balance of good and evil has changed from one to the other owing to changes in their customs, whereas the world as a whole has remained the same. The only difference is that the world's virtue first found a home in Assyria, then flourished in Media and later in Persia, and at length arrived in Italy and Rome. And, if since the Roman empire there has been no other which has lasted, and in which the world's virtue has been centred, one none the less finds it distributed amongst many nations where men lead virtuous lives. There was, for instance, the kingdom of the Franks; the kingdom of the Turks, [i.e.] that of the Sultan; and today all the peoples of Germany. Earlier still there were the Saracens, who performed such great exploits and occupied so much of the world, since they broke up the Roman empire in the East. Hence, after ruin had overtaken the Romans, there continued to exist in all these provinces and in all these separate units, and still exists in some of them, that virtue which is desired and quite rightly praised. If, then, anyone born there praises the past over and above the present, he may well be mistaken; but anyone born in Italy who is not an ultramontane at heart, or anyone born in Greece who is not at heart a Turk, has good reason to criticise his own times and to praise others, since in the latter there are plenty of things to evoke his admiration, whereas in the former he comes across nothing but extreme misery, infamy and contempt, for there is no observance either of religion or of the laws, or of military traditions, but all is besmirched with filth of every kind. And so much the more are these vices detestable when they are more prevalent amongst those who sit on the judgment seat, prescribe rules for others, and expect from them adoration.

But to return to our main point, I maintain that if man's judgment is biased when he tries to decide which is the better, the present age, or some past age of which he cannot have so perfect a knowledge as he has of his own times precisely because it is long since past, this ought not to bias the judgment of old men when they compare the days of their youth with those of their old age, for of both they have had the same knowledge and experience. Nor would it in point of fact, if during the various phases of their lives men judged always in the same way and had the same appetites. But, as men's appetites change, even though their circumstances remain the same, it is impossible that things should look the same to them seeing that they have other appetites, other interests, other standpoints, from what they had in their youth. For, since, when men grow old, they lack energy but increase in judgment and prudence, it is inevitable that what in their youth appeared to be tolerable and good, in their old age should become intolerable and bad; so that, instead of blaming the times, they should lay the blame on their own judgment.

Furthermore, human appetites are insatiable, for by nature we are so constituted that there is nothing we cannot long for, but by fortune we are such that of these things we can attain but few. The result is that the human mind is perpetually discontented, and of its possessions is apt to grow weary. This makes it find fault with the present, praise the past, and long for the future; though for its doing so no rational cause can be assigned. Hence I am not sure but that I deserve to be reckoned amongst those who thus deceive themselves if in these my discourses I have praised too much the days of the ancient Romans and have found fault with our own. Indeed, if the virtue which then prevailed and the vices which are prevalent today were not as clear as the sun, I should be more reserved in my statements lest I should fall into the very fault for which I am blaming others. But as the facts are there for any one to see, I shall make so bold as to declare plainly what I think of those days and of our own, so that the minds of young men who read what I have written may turn from the one and prepare to imitate the other whenever fortune provides them with occasion for so doing. For it is the duty of a good man to point out to others what is well done, even though the malignity of the times or of fortune has not permitted you to do it for yourself, to the end that, of the many who have the capacity, some one, more beloved of heaven, may be able to do it.

Having, therefore, in the discourses of the last book spoken of the decisions the Romans came to in regard to the internal affairs of the city, in this we shall speak of the measures the Roman people took to increase their empire.

Fortune

The end, alas, was near of that cold night
    As one by one the stars were fading fast,
    And the whole sky was turning, turning white.

The moon was being vanquished by the sun
    When thus my lady spoke: "I must now leave,
    And do the things that must indeed be done

"To please our fate forever, lest I should
    Be shamed: I have to take all my flocks out
    Where they can find their long-awaited food.

"But in the meantime you alone shall be
    Here in this room, and when tonight I'm back,
    All this big place I will take you to see.

"Do not go out—and my advice now take:
    If people call, answer no one: for many
    Were fully ruined by this one mistake."

And so she went; and I, who had now turned
    All of my thoughts to her beautiful face
    That more than any other shone and burned,

Seeing myself in that room all alone,
    Jumped out of bed, so as to quench a bit
    The fire that in my heart had quickly grown.

And as soon as I was far from her side,
    The wound that she alone had fully healed,
    By my old, piercing thoughts was opened wide.

I was just like a person who suspects
    Many a thing, and but deceives himself
    By wanting something he does not expect:

And since one thought follows another thought,
    My mind flew back to all the past events
    Which, though time passes, we cannot forget.

SOURCE: *Lust and Liberty*, translated by Joseph Tusiani (New York: Ivan Obolensky, Inc., 1963), pp. 76–81. © 1963 by Joseph Tusiani. Reprinted with permission of Astor-Honor, Inc., New York.

Thinking now this, now that, in my unrest,
　　All nations great and famous I recalled,
　　Which fortune oft had bitten, or caressed;

And they all seemed to me so very high
　　That I decided, then, to meditate
　　On how all things change in this world, and why.

The most precipitous ill to ruin states
　　Is always this: all rulers here on earth
　　With wealth and power never feel replete.

And of their greed this is the main result:
　　Those who have lost are not content, and start
　　To think of ruining those who now exult.

One rises, then, and one must lose his life;
　　And he who now has risen is devoured
　　By sudden doubt and thirst for some new strife.

This is the appetite that ruins all
　　States: and the wonder of all this is that
　　Men know this trap and yet into it fall.

Saint Mark, importunate and eager to run,
　　Hoping forever for propitious winds,
　　Did not think twice to ruin everyone;

Nor did he see how too much power and pomp
　　Was hurting him, and it would have been better
　　To keep beneath the water tail and rump.

Often with tears one occupies the throne
　　And, as soon as he gets it, realizes
　　It is to his own ruin, his own moan.

Athens and Sparta, whose renown and sound
　　Spread through the world, into oblivion sank
　　The day they seized and tamed the states around.

In Germany, as is at present found,
　　Each city lives secure and safe from harm,
　　Barely encompassing six miles of ground.

And our own city was not scared at all
   By Henry and his whole tremendous might
   While her own boundaries ended with her walls;

But now that all her power has greatly spread,
   And she has gained in greatness and in ground,
   Not only armies, but all things she dreads:

For, as you know, man has sufficient vigor
   To lift one body, but his strength can fail
   To lift a weight that has become much bigger.

One whose ambition is to reach both poles,
   Like Icarus after his foolish flight,
   Upon the ground in ruination falls.

True, more or less a state will last as long
   As all its laws are quite efficient, and
   The order of its life is felt and strong.

That kingdom or that empire will not stop
   Which is by constant valor forced to act,
   And is forever destined to go up;

But, on the contrary, a city sour
   With savage thorns and disorderly bushes
   Will soon become, if she will alter power

Between summer and winter, thus deceiving
   Herself by aiming always at low goals
   When laws are good, yet bad the ways of living.

Who ancient history well understands,
   He knows each empire starts with Ninyas
   And with Sardanapalus sadly ends.

Just as a god the first one was renowned;
   The second among maidens, handling flax,
   Just like a maiden was once seen and found.

Valor it is that quiets regions down:
   And then from quiet, laziness derives,
   And laziness soon burns both land and town.

Then, once a nation has long had its share
   Of disorder and war, valor again
   Is born and back it goes to dwell right there.

This is the way Order is told to run
   By Him who governs us, so that no thing
   May ever find a pause beneath the sun.

And it is, and will always be, and was
   Always so: evil follows good; good, evil;
   And each is of the other the sole cause.

True, there are those who think that greed has been
   Fatal to kingdoms, and that these may be
   Destroyed by usury or carnal sin;

They believe also that their greatness comes,
   And both their height and power thus derive,
   From prayers and from fastings and from alms.

But those who are more wise and prudent claim
   That all such things can neither ruin states
   Nor keep on earth their power and their fame.

To think that without *you* for *you* God fights,
   While you are on your knees and nothing do,
   Has ruined many kingdoms, many states.

Prayers are necessary as a rule,
   And he who from his people snatches rites
   And orisons is utterly a fool.

Perfect control and union they keep,
   And if you have all this, it is quite true
   You will good fortune ultimately reap.

But let your brain prove not so small and short
   By thinking that, should your house fall and crumble,
   God would soon save it with no man's support:

You would soon die beneath its very stones.

Men and fortune.

If one ponders well the course of human affairs, it will be seen that many events happen and many misfortunes come about, against which the heavens have not been willing that any provision at all should be made. Since this statement holds good in the case of Rome, which was conspicuous alike for virtue, religion, and orderly conduct, it is no wonder that the same thing happens yet more often in cities and provinces which are lacking in these respects. There is a well-known passage in which Titus Livy shows at length and with great force the power that heaven exercises over human affairs. He says that, with a view to making the Romans recognise its power, heaven first caused the Fabii to act wrongly when sent as ambassadors to the Gauls, and by means of what they did excited the Gauls to make war on Rome; then ordained that in Rome nothing worthy of the Roman people should be done to meet their attack; for first it brought about that Camillus, who was the only hope they had in those evil days, should be sent as an exile to Ardea; then that, when the Gauls were marching on Rome, they did not appoint a dictator, as they had done to meet the attack of the Volsci and other enemies in the neighbourhood. It also caused them to be weak and to take no particular care in calling up troops, who were so slow in taking up arms that they scarce had time to confront the Gauls on the banks of the Allia, which was but ten miles from Rome. There the tribunes set up their camp without their accustomed diligence, since they did not inspect the site beforehand, nor surround it with trenches and stockades, nor take any other precautions, either human or divine; while in preparing for battle they made their ranks thin and weak, and neither troops nor officers behaved as Roman discipline required. No blood was shed during the battle because at the first onslaught the Romans ran away, the greater number going to Veii, and the rest retiring on Rome, where they sought refuge in the Capitol without first going home; whereupon the senate took so little thought for Rome's defence that, for one thing, they omitted to close the gates; and some of its members fled, while others went with the rest into the Capitol. Granted, in their defence of the Capitol they used some sort of discipline, for they did not pack all the useless people inside, and they got in all the corn they could, so as to be able to stand the siege; while of the useless crowd of old men, women and children, most fled to the country round about, and the rest stayed in Rome at the mercy of the Gauls. So that no one who had read of what was done so often in years gone by and were to read what was now being done, would think they were one and the same people.

SOURCE: *The Discourses of Machiavelli*, translated by L. J. Walker (New Haven: Yale University Press, 1950), pp. 444–446, 549–552. Reprinted with permission of Routledge & Kegan Paul, Ltd., London.

Having described all the disorders mentioned above, Titus Livy concludes with the remark: 'To such an extent does fortune blind the minds of men when she does not want them to oppose the force she is using.'

Nor can anything be more true than the conclusion Livy draws. Hence men who in this life normally either suffer great adversity or enjoy great prosperity, deserve neither praise nor blame, for one usually finds that they have been driven either to ruin or to greatness by the prospect of some great advantage which the heavens have held out, whereby they have been given the chance, or have been deprived of the chance, of being able to act virtuously. Fortune arranges this quite nicely. For, when it wants a man to take the lead in doing great things, it chooses a man of high spirits and great virtue who will seize the occasion it offers him. And in like manner, when it wants a man to bring about a great disaster, it gives precedence to men who will help to promote it; and, if anyone gets in the way, it either kills him off or deprives him of all power of doing good.

It plainly appears from Livy's evidence that, in order to make Rome greater and to lead it on to its future greatness, fortune decided it was necessary first to chastise it in a way that will be described at length in the beginning of the next book, but did not want to ruin it altogether. Hence we see that it made an exile of Camillus, but did not cause him to die; that it caused Rome to be taken, but not the Capitol; that it arranged matters so that nothing useful was thought of to help Rome, nor anything overlooked that could help in the defence of the Capitol. It brought it about that, since Rome was to be taken, the greater part of the troops which were routed at Allia, should go on to Veii, thus leaving the city without any men to defend it. But in arranging things thus, it also prepared the way for Rome's recovery; for since there was a Roman army at Veii, and Camillus was at Ardea, it became possible to make a more vigorous attempt to deliver the fatherland under a general whose career was free from the stain of defeat and whose reputation was untarnished.

In confirmation of this one might adduce further examples from modern times, but I do not think this necessary, so pass them over, since that I have given should be enough to satisfy anybody. I assert once again as a truth to which history as a whole bears witness that men may second their fortune, but cannot oppose it; that they may act in accordance with, but cannot infringe, its ordinances. Yet they should never give up, because there is always hope, though they know not the end and move towards it along roads which cross one another and as yet are unexplored; and since there is hope, they should not despair, no matter what fortune brings or in what travail they find themselves. . . .

Amongst the other splendid things which our historian makes

Camillus say and do in order to show how an outstanding man should behave he puts into Camillus' mouth these words: 'The dictatorship did not elate me, nor did exile depress me. One sees here how great men remain the same whatever befalls. If fortune changes, sometimes raising them, sometimes casting them down, they do not change, but remain ever resolute, so resolute in mind and in conduct throughout life that it is easy for anyone to see that fortune holds no sway over them. Not so do weak men behave; for by good fortune they are buoyed up and intoxicated, and ascribe such success as they meet with, to a virtue they never possessed, so that they become insupportable and odious to all who have anything to do with them. This then brings about a sudden change in their lot, the prospect of which causes them to go to the other extreme and to become base and abject. Hence it comes about that rulers so built prefer to run away rather than to defend themselves in adversity, just as do men who find themselves defenceless because they have misused the good fortune they had.

These virtues and these vices, which are found as I have been saying in a particular man, are found in a republic; of which the Romans and the Venetians provide us with examples. No bad luck ever made the first become abject, nor did good fortune ever make them arrogant. This is manifest from their behaviour after the defeat at Cannae, and after the victory they gained over Antiochus. For though the defeat was very serious since it was their third, they never became disheartened, but kept their armies in the field; declined to redeem those who had allowed themselves to be taken prisoners, contrary to their practice, did not send emissaries to Hannibal or to Carthage to sue for peace, but, dispensing with any such abject steps as these, devoted their whole attention to the war, and, owing to shortage of men, armed both the old and the slaves. When Hanno, the Carthaginian, came to hear of this, he pointed out to the Carthaginian senate—as we have remarked above, what small account the Romans made of the defeat at Cannae. Hence it is clear that in trying times the Romans were not despondent, nor were they humbled. Nor, on the other hand, did prosperous times make them arrogant; for when Antiochus sent envoys to Scipio to ask for terms prior to the battle in which he was finally defeated, Scipio laid down the following as his conditions for peace: that Antiochus should withdraw into Syria and that the rest should be left to the decision of the Roman people. These terms Antiochus having rejected, a battle took place, and having lost it, he sent to Scipio envoys commissioned to accept all the conditions which the victors should lay down. Whereupon Scipio proposed precisely the same terms as those he had offered before he won, and then remarked 'that the Romans, when beaten, do not lose courage, nor, when they win, do they become arrogant'.

The Venetians we find doing just the opposite of this. To them it seemed that their good fortune was due to a virtue which they did not in fact possess. Moreover, so arrogant did they become that they called the king of France a 'son of St. Mark', showed no respect for the Church, had their eye by no means on Italy alone, but had already made up their minds to set up a monarchy similar to that of Rome. Then, when good luck deserted them and a partial defeat was inflicted on them at Vaila by the king of France, they lost the whole of their dominions, not merely through rebellions, but a goodly portion of them they gave to the Pope and to the king of Spain out of sheer dejection and despondency of mind. So dispirited, indeed, were they that they sent ambassadors to the Emperor offering to become his tributaries, and wrote grovelling and abject letters to the Pope to stir up his compassion. To reach which unhappy state it took them four days, and yet it was but a partial defeat they had suffered; for, after the engagement, in the fighting which took place during the retreat of their army only about half their forces were engaged, so that one of their commissioners who escaped, reached Verona with more than twenty thousand troops, comprising both foot and cavalry. Hence, if in Venice and in Venetian institutions there had been any sort of virtue they could easily have pulled themselves together and tried their luck again, this time either to win or to lose with greater glory, or to come to an agreement on more honourable terms. But their pusillanimity, which arose from their institutions being ill adapted for war, made them lose at one stroke alike their dominions and their courage.

It will always happen thus to any state governed as was theirs. For this arrogance in prosperity and dejection in adversity is due to the way you behave and to the education you have received; which, if it be feeble and futile, makes you the same, and if it be of the other kind, makes you another sort of person, i.e. makes you know the world better and so be less exhilarated in good times and less depressed in bad. And what I say of the individual here may be said also of the many who live together in one and the same republic, for they are fashioned to the same state of perfection as characterises that republic's mode of life.

Although I have said elsewhere that the security of all states is based on good military discipline, and that where it does not exist, there can neither be good laws nor anything else that is good, to repeat this does not seem to me superfluous; for the need for this discipline is apparent on every page in Livy's history, where one sees that the soldiery cannot be good unless they are in training, and that it is impossible to train them unless they are your own subjects. For, since no soldiery is always at war, nor yet can be, it is important to train it in time of peace; but this training is impossible on account of the cost except in the case of subjects.

When Camillus led forth an army to fight the Tuscans, as we have said above, and his soldiers saw how large was the army of the enemy, they were terrified, for so inferior did they feel themselves to be that it looked to them as if they could not possibly withstand their attack. When it came to the ears of Camillus that the men in camp were so ill disposed to fight, he appeared amongst them and, going about the camp talking to this group of soldiers and that, drove this notion out of their heads. Finally, without issuing any further orders to those in camp, he merely said: 'Let each man do what he has been taught to do or has been accustomed to do.' If we consider carefully this restraint and the words used to encourage the men to go and fight the enemy, it is clear that neither could such words have been used nor the army have been induced to do any such thing unless that army had already been trained and drilled both in peace-time and in war. For on soldiers who have not learned how to do anything, no general can rely, confident that anything they may do will be well done. Even should a second Hannibal command such troops he would in that case go under. For, since during a battle a general cannot be everywhere, he will inevitably meet with disaster unless he has already so drilled every unit that it has imbibed his spirit and is well acquainted with his practice and mode of procedure.

If then a city be armed and disciplined as Rome was, and all its citizens, alike in their private and official capacity, have a chance to put alike their virtue and the power of fortune to the test of experience, it will be found that always and in all circumstances they will be of the same mind and will maintain their dignity in the same way. But, when they are not familiar with arms and trust merely to the whim of fortune, not to their own virtue, they will change with the changes of fortune and will display in all cases the characteristics exemplified by the Venetians.

Government

Kinds, origin, and cycle of government.

I propose to dispense with a discussion of cities which from the outset have been subject to another power, and shall speak only of those which have from the outset been far removed from any kind of external servitude, but, instead, have from the start been governed in accordance with their wishes, whether as republics or principalities. As such cities have had diverse origins, so too they have had diverse laws and institutions. For either at the outset, or before very long, to some of them laws have been given by some one person at some one time, as laws were

Source: *The Discourses of Machiavelli*, translated by L. J. Walker (New Haven: Yale University Press, 1950), pp. 211–216. Reprinted with permission of Routledge & Kegan Paul, Ltd., London.

given to the Spartans by Lycurgus; whereas others have acquired them by chance and at different times as occasion arose. This was the case in Rome.

Happy indeed should we call that commonwealth which produces a man so prudent that men can live securely under the laws which he prescribes without having to emend them. Sparta, for instance, observed its laws for more than eight hundred years without corrupting them and without any dangerous disturbance. Unhappy, on the other hand, in some degree is that city to be deemed which, not having chanced to meet with a prudent organiser, has to reorganise itself. And, of such, that is the more unhappy which is the more remote from order; and, of these, that is the more remote from order whose institutions have missed altogether the straight road which leads it to its perfect and true destiny. For it is almost impossible that states of this type should by any eventuality be set on the right road again; whereas those which, if their order is not perfect, have made a good beginning and are capable of improvement, may become perfect should something happen which provides the opportunity. It should, however, be noted that they will never introduce order without incurring danger, because few men ever welcome new laws setting up a new order in the state unless necessity makes it clear to them that there is need for such laws; and since such a necessity cannot arise without danger, the state may easily be ruined before the new order has been brought to completion. The republic of Florence bears this out, for owing to what happened at Arezzo in '02 it was reconstituted, and owing to what happened at Prato in '12 its constitution was destroyed.

It being now my intention to discuss what were the institutions of the city of Rome and what events conducted to its perfection, I would remark that those who have written about states say that there are to be found in them one of three forms of government, called by them *Principality*, *Aristocracy*, and *Democracy*, and that those who set up a government in any particular state must adopt one of them, as best suits their purpose.

Others—and with better judgment many think—say that there are six types of government, of which three are very bad, and three are good in themselves but easily become corrupt, so that they too must be classed as pernicious. Those that are good are the three above mentioned. Those that are bad are the other three, which depend on them, and each of them is so like the one associated with it that it easily passes from one form to the other. For *Principality* easily becomes *Tyranny*. From *Aristocracy* the transition to *Oligarchy* is an easy one. *Democracy* is without difficulty converted into *Anarchy*. So that if anyone who is organising a commonwealth sets up one of the three first forms of government, he sets up what will last but for a while, since there are no means whereby to prevent it passing into its contrary, on account of the likeness which in such a case virtue has to vice.

These variations of government amongst men are due to chance. For in the beginning of the world, when its inhabitants were few, they lived for a time scattered like the beasts. Then, with the multiplication of their offspring, they drew together and, in order the better to be able to defend themselves, began to look about for a man stronger and more courageous than the rest, made him their head, and obeyed him.

It was thus that men learned how to distinguish what is honest and good from what is pernicious and wicked, for the sight of someone injuring his benefactor evoked in them hatred and sympathy and they blamed the ungrateful and respected those who showed gratitude, well aware that the same injuries might have been done to themselves. Hence to prevent evil of this kind they took to making laws and to assigning punishments to those who contravened them. The notion of justice thus came into being.

In this way it came about that, when later on they had to choose a prince, they did not have recourse to the boldest as formerly, but to one who excelled in prudence and justice.

But when at a yet later stage they began to make the prince hereditary instead of electing him, his heirs soon began to degenerate as compared with their ancestors, and, forsaking virtuous deeds, considered that princes have nought else to do but to surpass other men in extravagance, lasciviousness, and every other form of licentiousness. With the result that the prince came to be hated, and, since he was hated, came to be afraid, and from fear soon passed to offensive action, which quickly brought about a tyranny.

From which, before long, was begotten the source of their downfall; for tyranny gave rise to conspiracies and plots against princes, organised not by timid and weak men, but by men conspicuous for their liberality, magnanimity, wealth and ability, for such men could not stand the dishonourable life the prince was leading. The masses, therefore, at the instigation of these powerful leaders, took up arms against the prince, and, when he had been liquidated, submitted to the authority of those whom they looked upon as their liberators. Hence the latter, to whom the very term 'sole head' had become odious, formed themselves into a government. Moreover, in the beginning, mindful of what they had suffered under a tyranny, they ruled in accordance with the laws which they had made, subordinated their own convenience to the common advantage, and, both in private matters and public affairs, governed and preserved order with the utmost diligence.

But when the administration passed to their descendants who had no experience of the changeability of fortune, had not been through bad times, and instead of remaining content with the civic equality then prevailing, reverted to avarice, ambition, and to seizing other men's womenfolk, they caused government by an aristocracy to become government by an oligarchy in which civic rights were entirely disregarded; so that in a short time there came to pass in their case the same thing as happened to the tyrant, for the masses, sick of their government, were ready to help anyone who had any sort of plan for attacking their rulers; and so there soon arose someone who with the aid of the masses liquidated them.

Then, since the memory of the prince and of the injuries inflicted by him was still fresh, and since, having got rid of government by the few, they had no desire to return to that of a prince, they turned to a democratic form of government, which they organised in such a way that no sort of authority was vested either in a few powerful men or in a prince.

And, since all forms of government are to some extent respected at the outset, this democratic form of government maintained itself for a while but not for long, especially when the generation that had organised it had passed away. For anarchy quickly supervened, in which no respect was shown either for the individual or for the official, and which was such that, as everyone did what he liked, all sorts of outrages were constantly committed. The outcome was inevitable. Either at the suggestion of some good man or because this anarchy had to be got rid of somehow, principality was once again restored. And from this there was, stage by stage, a return to anarchy, by way of the transitions and for the reasons assigned.

This, then, is the cycle through which all commonwealths pass, whether they govern themselves or are governed. But rarely do they return to the same form of government, for there can scarce be a commonwealth of such vitality that it can undergo often such changes and yet remain in being. What usually happens is that, while in a state of commotion in which it lacks both counsel and strength, a commonwealth becomes subject to a neighbouring and better organised state. Were it not so, a commonwealth might go on for ever passing through these governmental transitions.

I maintain then, that all the forms of government mentioned above are far from satisfactory, the three good ones because their life is so short, the three bad ones because of their inherent malignity. Hence prudent legislators, aware of their defects, refrained from adopting as such any one of these forms, and chose instead one that shared in them all, since they thought such a government would be stronger and more stable, for if in one and the same state there was principality, aristocracy and democracy each would keep watch over the other.

Lycurgus is one of those who have earned no small measure of praise for constitutions of this kind. For in the laws which he gave to Sparta, he assigned to the kings, to the aristocracy, and to the populace each its own function, and thus introduced a form of government which lasted for more than eight hundred years to his very great credit and to the tranquillity of that city.

It was not so in the case of Solon, who drew up laws for Athens, for he set up merely a democratic form of government, which was so short lived that he saw before his death the birth of a tyranny under Pisistratus; and though, forty years later, Pisistratus' heirs were expelled, and Athens returned to liberty because it again adopted a democratic form of government in accordance with Solon's laws, it did not retain its liberty for more than a hundred years. For, in spite of the fact that many constitutions were made whereby to restrain the arrogance of the upper class and the licentiousness of the general public, for which Solon had made no provision, none the less Athens had a very short life as compared with that of Sparta because with democracy Solon had not blended either princely power or that of the aristocracy.

But let us come to Rome. In spite of the fact that Rome had no Lycurgus to give it at the outset such a constitution as would ensure to it a long life of freedom, yet, owing to friction between the plebs and the senate, so many things happened that chance effected what had not been provided by a lawgiver. So that, if Rome did not get fortune's first gift, it got its second. For her early institutions, though defective, were not on wrong lines and so might pave the way to perfection. For Romulus and the rest of the kings made many good laws quite compatible with freedom; but, because their aim was to found a kingdom, not a republic, when the city became free, it lacked many institutions essential to the preservation of liberty, which had to be provided, since they had not been provided by the kings. So, when it came to pass that its kings lost their sovereignty, for reasons and in the manner described earlier in this discourse, those who had expelled them at once appointed two consuls to take the place of the king, so that what they expelled was the title of king, not the royal power. In the republic, then, at this stage there were the consuls and the senate, so that as yet it comprised but two of the aforesaid estates, namely, Principality and Aristocracy. It remained to find a place for Democracy. This came about when the Roman nobility became so overbearing for reasons which will be given later—that the populace rose against them, and they were constrained by the fear that they might lose all, to grant the populace a share in the government; the senate and the consuls retaining, however, sufficient authority for them to be able to maintain their position in the commonwealth.

It was in this way that tribunes of the plebs came to be appointed, and their appointment did much to stabilise the form of government in this commonwealth, for in its government all three estates now had a share. And so favoured was it by fortune that, though the transition from Monarchy to Aristocracy and thence to Democracy, took place by the very stages and for the very reasons laid down earlier in this discourse, none the less the granting of authority to the aristocracy did not abolish altogether the royal estate, nor was the authority of the aristocracy wholly removed when the populace was granted a share in it. On the contrary, the blending of these estates made a perfect commonwealth; and since it was friction between the plebs and the senate that brought this perfection about, in the next two chapters we shall show more fully how this came to be. . . .

People versus prince.

Nothing is more futile and more inconstant than are the masses. So says our author, Titus Livy, and so say all other historians. For in the records of the actions men have performed one often finds the masses condemning someone to death, and then lamenting him and ardently wishing he were alive. The Roman people did this in Manlius Capitolinus's case: first they condemned him to death, then urgently wished him back. Of this our author says that 'soon after he had ceased to be a danger, the desire for him took hold of the people'. And again, when describing the events which happened in Syracuse after the death of Hieronymus, the nephew of Hiero, he says: 'It is of the nature of the masses either servilely to obey or arrogantly to domineer.'

I know not whether the view I am about to adopt will prove so hard to uphold and so full of difficulties that I shall have either shamefully to abandon it or laboriously to maintain it; for I propose to defend a position which all writers attack, as I have said. But, however that may be, I think, and always shall think there can be no harm in defending an opinion by arguments so long as one has no intention of appealing either to authority or force.

I claim, then, that for the failing for which writers blame the masses, any body of men one cares to select may be blamed, and especially princes; for anyone who does not regulate his conduct by laws will make the same mistakes as the masses are guilty of. This is easily seen, for there are and have been any number of princes, but of good and wise ones there have been but few. I am speaking of princes who have succeeded in breaking the bonds which might have held them in check; amongst which I do not include those kings who were born in Egypt when that most ancient of ancient realms was governed in accordance with the law, nor those born in Sparta, nor those born in France in our

SOURCE: *The Discourses of Machiavelli*, translated by L. J. Walker (New Haven: Yale University Press, 1950), pp. 341–345. Reprinted with permission of Routledge & Kegan Paul, Ltd., London.

own times, for the kingdom of France is better regulated by laws than is any other of which at present we have knowledge. Kings who are born under such conditions are not to be classed amongst those whose nature we have to consider in each individual case to see whether it resembles that of the masses; for, should there be masses regulated by laws in the same way as they are, there will be found in them the same goodness as we find in kings, and it will be seen that they neither 'arrogantly dominate nor servilely obey'. Such was the Roman populace which, so long as the republic remained uncorrupt, was never servilely obsequious, nor yet did it ever dominate with arrogance: on the contrary, it had its own institutions and magistrates and honourably kept its own place. But when it was necessary to take action against some powerful person, it did so, as is seen in the case of Manlius, of the Ten, and in the case of others who sought to oppress it. Also, when it had to obey dictators or consuls in the public interest, it did so. Nor is it any wonder that the Roman populace wanted Manlius Capitolinus back when he was dead, for what they wanted was his virtues, which had been such that his memory evoked everyone's sympathy, and would have had power to produce the same effect in a prince, for all writers are of opinion that virtue is praised and admired even in one's enemies. Again, had Manlius, in response to this desire, been raised from the dead, the Roman populace would have passed on him the same sentence as it did, have had him arrested and, shortly after, have condemned him to death: though, for that matter, one also finds that reputedly wise princes have put people to death and then wished them alive again; Alexander, for instance, in the case of Cleitus and other of his friends, and Herod in the case of Mariamne. But the truth is that what our historian says of the nature of the masses is not said of the masses when disciplined by laws, as were the Romans, but of undisciplined masses, like those of Syracuse, i.e. of masses which make the same kind of mistakes as do men when infuriated and undisciplined, just as did Alexander the Great and Herod in the cases cited.

The nature of the masses, then, is no more reprehensible than is the nature of princes, for all do wrong and to the same extent when there is nothing to prevent them doing wrong. Of this there are plenty of examples besides those given, both amongst the Roman emperors and amongst other tyrants and princes; and in them we find a degree of inconstancy and changeability in behaviour such as is never found in the masses.

I arrive, then, at a conclusion contrary to the common opinion which asserts that populaces, when in power, are variable, fickle and ungrateful, and affirm that in them these faults are in no wise different from those to be found in certain princes. Were the accusation made against both the masses and princes, it would be true; but, if princes be excepted, it is false. For when the populace is in power and is well-ordered, it will be stable, prudent, and grateful, in much the same way, or in a better way, than is a prince, however wise he be thought. And, on the other hand, a prince who contemns the laws, will be more ungrateful, fickle, and imprudent than is the populace. Nor is inconstancy of behaviour due to a difference in nature, for they are pretty much the same, or, if one be better than the other, it is the populace: it is due to the greater or less respect which they have for the laws under which both alike are living.

If we consider the Roman populace it will be found that for four hundred years they were enemies to the very name of king and lovers of glory and of the common good of their country. Of both characteristics the Roman populace affords numerous and striking examples. And, should anyone bring up against me the ingratitude the populace displayed toward Scipio, my answer is that I have already discussed this question at length and have there shown the ingratitude of the populace to be less than that of princes. While in the matter of prudence and stability I claim that the populace is more prudent, more stable, and of sounder judgment than the prince. Not without good reason is the voice of the populace likened to that of God; for public opinion is remarkably accurate in its prognostications, so much so that it seems as if the populace by some hidden power discerned the evil and the good that was to befall it. With regard to its judgment, when two speakers of equal skill are heard advocating different alternatives, very rarely does one find the populace failing to adopt the better view or incapable of appreciating the truth of what it hears. While, if in bold actions and such as appear advantageous it errs, as I have said above, so does a prince often err where his passions are involved, and these are much stronger than those of the populace.

It is found, too, that in the election of magistrates the populace makes a far better choice than does the prince; nor can the populace ever be persuaded that it is good to appoint to such an office a man of infamous life or corrupt habits, whereas a prince may easily and in a vast variety of ways be persuaded to do this. Again, one finds that when the populace begins to have a horror of something it remains of the same mind for many centuries; a thing that is never observed in the case of a prince. For both these characteristics I shall content myself with the evidence afforded by the Roman populace, which in the course of so many hundreds of years and so many elections of consuls and tribunes did not make four elections of which it had to repent. So much, too, as I have said, was the title of king hated that no service rendered by one of its citizens who ambitioned it, could render him immune from the penalties prescribed. Besides this, one finds that cities in which the populace is the prince, in a very short time extend vastly their dominions much more than do those which have always been under a prince; as Rome did after the expulsion of the kings, and Athens after it was free of Pisistratus.

This can only be due to one thing: government by the populace is better than government by princes. Nor do I care whether to this opinion of mine all that our historian has said in the aforesaid passage or what others have said, be objected; because if account be taken of all the disorders due to populaces and of all those due to princes, and of all the glories won by populaces and all those won by princes, it will be found that alike in goodness and in glory the populace is far superior. And if princes are superior to populaces in drawing up laws, codes of civic life, statutes and new institutions, the populace is so superior in sustaining what has been instituted, that it indubitably adds to the glory of those who have instituted them.

In short, to bring this topic to a conclusion, I say that, just as princely forms of government have endured for quite a long time, so, too, have republican forms of government; and that in both cases it has been essential for them to be regulated by laws. For a prince who does what he likes is a lunatic, and a populace which does what it likes is unwise. If, therefore, it be a question of a prince subservient to the laws and of a populace chained up by laws, more virtue will be found in the populace than in the prince; and if it be a question of either of them loosed from control by the law, there will be found fewer errors in the populace than in the prince, and these of less moment and much easier to put right. For a licentious and turbulent populace, when a good man can obtain a hearing, can easily be brought to behave itself; but there is no one to talk to a bad prince, nor is there any remedy except the sword. From which an important inference may be drawn in regard to their respective maladies; for, if to cure the malady of the populace a word suffices and the sword is needed to cure that of a prince, no one will fail to see that the greater the cure, the greater the fault.

When the populace has thrown off all restraint, it is not the mad things it does that are terrifying, nor is it of present evils that one is afraid, but of what may come of them, for amidst such confusion there may come to be a tyrant. In the case of bad princes it is just the opposite: it is present evils that are terrifying, but for the future there is hope, since men are convinced that the evil ways of a bad prince may make for freedom in the end. Thus one sees the difference between the two cases amounts to the same thing as the difference between what is and what must come to be. The brutalities of the masses are directed against those whom they suspect of conspiring against the common good; the brutalities of a prince against those whom he suspects of conspiring against his own good. The reason why people are prejudiced against the populace is because of the populace anyone may speak ill without fear and openly, even when the populace is ruling. But of princes people speak with the utmost trepidation and the utmost reserve.

Nor does it seem to me foreign to my purpose, since I find the topic attractive, to discuss in the next chapter on which more reliance can be placed, on confederations made by a republic or on confederations formed by a prince.

Reform in government: government and religion are naturally degenerate.

It is a well-established fact that the life of all mundane things is of finite duration. But things which complete the whole of the course appointed them by heaven are in general those whose bodies do not disintegrate, but maintain themselves in orderly fashion either without change; or, if there be change, it tends rather to their conservation than to their destruction. Here I am concerned with composite bodies, such as are states and religious institutions, and in their regard I affirm that those changes make for their conservation which lead them back to their start. Hence those are better constituted and have a longer life whose institutions make frequent renovations possible, or which can be brought to such a renovation by some event which has nothing to do with their constitution. For it is clearer than daylight that, without renovation, these bodies do not last.

The way to renovate them, as has been said, is to reduce them to their starting-points. For at the start religious institutions, republics and kingdoms have in all cases some good in them, to which their early reputation and progress is due. But since in process of time this goodness is corrupted, such a body must of necessity die unless something happens which brings it up to the mark. Thus, our medical men, speaking of the human body, say that 'every day it absorbs something which from time to time requires treatment'.

This return to its starting point in the case of a republic, is brought about either by some external event or by its own intrinsic good sense. Thus, as an example of the former, we see how it was necessary that Rome should be taken by the Gauls in order that it should be re-born and in its re-birth take on alike a new vitality and a new virtue, and also take up again the observance of religion and justice, both of which had begun to show blemishes. This plainly appears from Livy's account where he shows how, when the Romans led out their army against the Gauls and created tribunes with consular power, they observed no religious ceremony. And, in like manner, not only did they not punish the three Fabii who had attacked the Gauls 'in contravention of the

SOURCE: *The Discourses of Machiavelli*, translated by L. J. Walker (New Haven: Yale University Press, 1950), pp. 459–463. Reprinted with permission of Routledge & Kegan Paul, Ltd., London.

Law of Nations', but they made them tribunes. Whence it is easy to infer that of the good constitutions established by Romulus and by those other wise princes they had begun to take less account than was reasonable and necessary for the maintenance of a free state. This defeat in a war with outsiders, therefore, came about so that the institutions of this city should be renovated and to show this people that not only is it essential to uphold religion and justice, but also to hold in high esteem good citizens and to look upon their virtue as of greater value than those comforts of which there appeared to them to be a lack owing to what these men had done. This actually came about. For as soon as Rome had been recovered they renewed all the ordinances of their ancient religion and punished the Fabii who had fought 'in contravention of the Law of Nations'. They also set such esteem on the virtue and goodness of Camillus that the senate and the rest, putting envy aside, laid on his shoulders the whole burden of this republic.

It is, therefore, as I have said, essential that men who live together under any constitution should frequently have their attention called to it either by some external or by some internal occurrence. When internal, such occurrences are usually due to some law which from time to time causes the members of this body to review their position; or again to some good man who arises in their midst and by his example and his virtuous deeds produces the same effect as does the constitution.

Such benefits, therefore, are conferred on a republic either by the virtue of some individual or by the virtue of an institution. In regard to the latter, the institutions which caused the Roman republic to return to its start were the introduction of plebeian tribunes, of the censorship, and of all the other laws which put a check on human ambition and arrogance; to which institutions life must needs be given by some virtuous citizen who co-operates strenuously in giving them effect despite the power of those who contravene them. Notable amongst such drastic actions, before the taking of Rome by the Gauls, were the death of Brutus's sons, the death of the ten citizens, and that of Maelius, the corn-dealer. After the taking of Rome there was the death of Manlius Capitolinus, the death of Manlius Torquatus's son, the action taken by Papirius Cursor against Fabius, his master of horse, and the charge brought against the Scipios. Such events, because of their unwonted severity and their notoriety, brought men back to the mark every time one of them happened; and when they began to occur less frequently, they also began to provide occasion for men to practise corruption, and were attended with more danger and more commotion. For between one case of disciplinary action of this type and the next there ought to elapse at most ten years, because by this time men begin to change their habits and to break the laws; and, unless something happens which recalls to their minds the penalty involved and reawakens fear in them, there will soon be so many delinquents that it will be impossible to punish them without danger.

In regard to this, those who governed the state of Florence from 1434 to 1494 used to say that it was necessary to reconstitute the government every five years; otherwise it was difficult to maintain it; where by 'reconstituting the government' they meant instilling men with that terror and that fear with which they had instilled them when instituting it in that at this time they had chastised those who, viewed from the standpoint of this regime, had misbehaved. As, however, the remembrance of this chastisement disappears, men are emboldened to try something fresh and to talk sedition. Hence provision has of necessity to be made against this by restoring that government to what it was at the start.

Such a return to their starting-point in republics is sometimes due to the simple virtue of one man alone, independently of any laws spurring you to action. For of such effect is a good reputation and good example that men seek to imitate it, and the bad are ashamed to lead lives which go contrary to it. Those who in Rome are outstanding examples of this good influence, are Horatius Cocles, Scaevola, Fabricius, the two Decii, Regulus Attilius, and several others, whose rare and virtuous examples wrought the same effects in Rome as laws and institutions would have done. If then effective action of the kind described above, together with this setting of good example, had occurred in that city at least every ten years, it necessarily follows that it would never have become corrupt. But when both the one and the other began to occur more rarely, corruption began to spread. For, after the time of Marcus Regulus, there appeared no examples of this kind, and, though in Rome there arose the two Catos, between them and any prior instance there was so great an interval, and again between the Catos themselves, that they stood alone and their good example could have no good effect; especially in the case of the younger Cato who found the greater part of the city so corrupt that he could not by his example effect any improvement amongst the citizens. So much then for republics.

As to religious institutions one sees here again how necessary these renovations are from the example of our own religion, which, if it had not been restored to its starting-point by St. Francis and St. Dominic, would have become quite extinct. For these men by their poverty and by their exemplification of the life of Christ revived religion in the minds of men in whom it was already dead, and so powerful were these new religious orders that they prevented the depravity of prelates and of religious heads from bringing ruin on religion. They also lived so frugally and had such prestige with the populace as confessors and preachers that they convinced them it is an evil thing to talk evilly of evil doing, and a good thing to live under obedience to such prelates, and that, if they did wrong, it must be left to God to chastise them. And, this being so, the latter behave as badly as they can, because they are not afraid of punishments which they do not see and in which they do not believe. It is, then, this revival which has maintained and continues to maintain this religion.

Kingdoms also need to be renovated and to have their laws brought back to their starting-points. The salutary effect this produces is seen in the kingdom of France, for the conduct of affairs in this kingdom is controlled by more laws and more institutions than it is in any other. These laws and these institutions are maintained by *parlements*, notably by that of Paris, and by it they are renovated whenever it takes action against a prince of this realm or in its judgments condemns the king. Up to now it has maintained its position by the pertinacity with which it has withstood the nobility of this realm. But should it at any time let an offence remain unpunished and should offences begin to multiply, the result would unquestionably be either that they would have to be corrected to the accompaniment of grievous disorders or that the kingdom would disintegrate.

The conclusion we reach, then, is that there is nothing more necessary to a community, whether it be a religious establishment, a kingdom, or a republic, than to restore to it the prestige it had at the outset, and to take care that either good institutions or good men shall bring this about rather than that external force should give rise to it. For though this on occasion may be the best remedy, as it was in Rome's case, it is so dangerous that in no case is it what one should desire.

In order to make it clear to all how much the action of particular men contributed to the greatness of Rome and produced in that city so many beneficial results, I shall proceed to narrate and to discuss their doings, and shall confine myself to this topic in this third and last book on this first Decad [of Livy's history]. And, though the actions of the kings were great and noteworthy, since history deals with them at length I shall not mention them here, except where they may have done things with a view to their personal advantage. . . .

Reform in government: liberty and license in cities.

Republican governments, more especially those imperfectly organized, frequently change their rulers and the form of their institutions; not by the influence of liberty or subjection, as many suppose, but by that of slavery and license; for with the nobility or the people, the ministers respectively of slavery or licentiousness, only the name of liberty is in

SOURCE: *History of Florence* (New York: Colonial Press, 1901), pp. 175–180.

any estimation, neither of them choosing to be subject either to magistrates or laws. When, however, a good, wise, and powerful citizen
appears (which is but seldom), who establishes ordinances capable of
appeasing or restraining these contending dispositions, so as to prevent
them from doing mischief, then the government may be called free,
and its institutions firm and secure; for having good laws for its basis,
and good regulations for carrying them into effect, it needs not, like
others, the virtue of one man for its maintenance. With such excellent
laws and institutions, many of those ancient republics, which were of
long duration, were endowed. But these advantages are, and always
have been, denied to those which frequently change from tyranny to
license, or the reverse; because, from the powerful enemies which each
condition creates itself, they neither have, nor can possess, any stability;
for tyranny cannot please the good, and license is offensive to the wise:
the former may easily be productive of mischief, while the latter can
scarcely be beneficial; in the former, the insolent have too much
authority, and in the latter, the foolish; so that each requires for their
welfare the virtue and the good fortune of some individual who may be
removed by death, or become unserviceable by misfortune.

Hence, it appears, that the government which commenced in
Florence at the death of Giorgio Scali, in 1381, was first sustained by
the talents of Maso degli Albizzi, and then by those of Niccolo da
Uzzano. The city remained tranquil from 1414 to 1422; for King
Ladislaus was dead, and Lombardy divided into several parts; so that
there was nothing either internal or external to occasion uneasiness.
Next to Niccolo da Uzzano in authority, were Bartolomeo Valori,
Neroni di Nigi, Rinaldo degli Albizzi, Neri di Gino, and Lapo Nic-
colini. The factions that arose from the quarrels of the Albizzi and the
Ricci, and which were afterwards so unhappily revived by Salvestro
de' Medici, were never extinguished; for though the party most favored
by the rabble only continued three years, and in 1381 was put down,
still, as it comprehended the greatest numerical proportion, it was
never entirely extinct, though the frequent Balias and persecutions of
its leaders from 1381 to 1400, reduced it almost to nothing. The first
families that suffered in this way were the Alberti, the Ricci, and the
Medici, which were frequently deprived both of men and money; and
if any of them remained in the city, they were deprived of the honors
of government. These oft-repeated acts of oppression humiliated the
faction, and almost annihilated it. Still, many retained the remembrance of the injuries they had received, and a desire of vengeance remained pent in their bosoms, ungratified and unquenched. Those
nobles of the people, or new nobility, who peaceably governed the
city, committed two errors, which eventually caused the ruin of their
party; the first was, that by long continuance in power they became

insolent; the second, that the envy they entertained toward each other, and their uninterrupted possession of power, destroyed that vigilance over those who might injure them, which they ought to have exercised. Thus daily renewing the hatred of the mass of the people by their sinister proceedings, and either negligent of the threatened dangers, because rendered fearless by prosperity, or encouraging them through mutual envy, they gave an opportunity to the family of the Medici to recover their influence.

The first to do so was Giovanni di Bicci de' Medici, who having become one of the richest men, and being of a humane and benevolent disposition, obtained the supreme magistracy by consent of those in power. This circumstance gave so much gratification to the mass of the people (the multitude thinking they had now found a defender), that not without occasion the judicious of the party observed it with jealousy, for they perceived all the former feelings of the city revived. Niccolo da Uzzano did not fail to acquaint the other citizens with the matter, explaining to them how dangerous it was to aggrandize one who possessed so much influence; that it was easy to remedy an evil at its commencement, but exceedingly difficult after having allowed it to gather strength; and that Giovanni possessed several qualities far surpassing those of Salvestro. The associates of Niccolo were uninfluenced by his remarks; for they were jealous of his reputation, and desired to exalt some person, by means of whom he might be humbled.

This was the state of Florence, in which opposing feelings began to be observable, when Filippo Visconti, second son of Giovanni Galeazzo, having, by the death of his brother, become master of all Lombardy, and thinking he might undertake almost anything, greatly desired to recover Genoa, which enjoyed freedom under the Dogiate of Tommaso da Campo Fregoso. He did not think it advisable to attempt this, or any other enterprise, till he had renewed amicable relations with the Florentines, and made his good understanding with them known; but with the aid of their reputation he trusted he should attain his wishes. He therefore sent ambassadors to Florence to signify his desires. Many citizens were opposed to his design, but did not wish to interrupt the peace with Milan, which had now continued for many years. They were fully aware of the advantages he would derive from a war with Genoa, and the little use it would be to Florence. Many others were inclined to accede to it, but would set a limit to his proceedings, which if he were to exceed, all would perceive his base design, and thus they might, when the treaty was broken, more justifiably make war against him. The question having been strongly debated, an amicable arrangement was at length effected, by which Filippo engaged not to interfere with anything on the Florentine side of the rivers Magra and Panaro.

Soon after the treaty was concluded, the duke took possession of Brescia, and shortly afterward of Genoa, contrary to the expectation of those who had advocated peace; for they thought Brescia would be defended by the Venetians, and Genoa would be able to defend herself. And as in the treaty which Filippo made with the Doge of Genoa, he had acquired Serezana and other places situated on this side the Magra, upon condition that, if he wished to alienate them, they should be given to the Genoese, it was quite palpable that he had broken the treaty; and he had beside, entered into another treaty with the legate of Bologna, in opposition to his engagement respecting the Panaro. These things disturbed the minds of the citizens, and made them, apprehensive of new troubles, consider the means to be adopted for their defence.

The dissatisfaction of the Florentines coming to the knowledge of Filippo, he, either to justify himself, or to become acquainted with their prevailing feelings, or to lull them to repose, sent ambassadors to the city, to intimate that he was greatly surprised at the suspicions they entertained, and offer to revoke whatever he had done that could be thought a ground of jealousy. This embassy produced no other effect than that of dividing the citizens; one party, that in greatest reputation, judged it best to arm, and prepare to frustrate the enemy's designs; and if he were to remain quiet, it would not be necessary to go to war with him, but an endeavor might be made to preserve peace. Many others, either envious of those in power, or fearing a rupture with the duke, considered it unadvisable so lightly to entertain suspicions of an ally, and thought his proceedings need not have excited so much distrust; that appointing the Ten and hiring forces was in itself a manifest declaration of war, which, if undertaken against so great a prince, would bring certain ruin upon the city without the hope of any advantage; for possession could never be retained of the conquests that might be made, because Romagna lay between, and the vicinity of the Church ought to prevent any attempt against Romagna itself. However, the views of those who were in favor of war prevailed, the Council of Ten were appointed, forces were hired, and new taxes levied, which, as they were more burdensome upon the lower than the upper ranks, filled the city with complaints, and all condemned the ambition and avarice of the great, declaring that, to gratify themselves and oppress the people, they would go to war without any justifiable motive.

They had not yet come to an open rupture with the duke, but everything tended to excite suspicion; for Filippo had, at the request of the legate of Bologna (who was in fear of Antonio Bentivogli, an exile of Bologna at Castel Bolognese), sent forces to that city, which, being close upon the Florentine territory, filled the citizens with apprehension; but what gave every one greater alarm, and offered sufficient occasion for the declaration of war, was the expedition made by the duke against Furli. Giorgio Ordelaffi was Lord of Furli, who dying, left Tibaldo, his son, under the guardianship of Filippo. The boy's mother, suspicious of his guardian, sent him to Ludovico Alidossi, her father, who was Lord of Imola, but she was compelled by the people of Furli to obey the will of her deceased husband, to withdraw him from his natural guardian, and place him in the hands of the duke. Upon this Filippo, the better to conceal his purpose, caused the Marquis of Ferrara to send Guido Torello as his agent, with forces, to seize the government of Furli, and thus the territory fell into the duke's hands. When this was known at Florence, together with the arrival of forces at Bologna, the arguments in favor of war were greatly strengthened, but there were still many opposed to it, and among the rest Giovanni de' Medici, who publicly endeavored to show, that even if the ill designs of the duke were perfectly manifest, it would still be better to wait and let him commence the attack, than to assail him; for in the former case they would be justified in the view of the princes of Italy as well as in their own; but if they were to strike the first blow at the duke, public opinion would be as favorable to him as to themselves; and besides, they could not so confidently demand assistance as assailants, as they might do if assailed; and that men always defend themselves more vigorously when they attack others. The advocates of war considered it improper to await the enemy in their houses, and better to go and seek him; that fortune is always more favorable to assailants than to such as merely act on the defensive, and that it is less injurious, even when attended with greater immediate expense, to make war at another's door than at our own. These views prevailed, and it was resolved that the Ten should provide all the means in their power for rescuing Furli from the hands of the duke.

Filippo, finding the Florentines resolved to occupy the places he had undertaken to defend, postponed all personal considerations against Imola, that Ludovico, having to provide for the defence of his own possessions, might be unable to protect the interests of his grandson. Agnolo approached Imola while the forces of the Florentines were at Modigliana, and an intense frost having rendered the ditches of the city passable, he crossed them during the night, captured the place, and sent Ludovico a prisoner to Milan. The Florentines finding Imola in the hands of the enemy, and the war publicly known, sent their forces to Furli and besieged it on all sides. That the duke's people might not relieve it, they hired Count Alberigo, who from Zangonara, his own domain, overran the country daily, up to the gates of Imola. Agnolo della Pergola, finding the strong position which the Florentines had taken prevented him from relieving Furli, determined to attempt the capture of Zangonara, thinking they would not allow that place to be lost, and that in the endeavor to relieve it they would be compelled to give up their design against Furli, and come to an engagement under great disadvantage. Thus the duke's people compelled Alberigo to sue for terms, which he obtained on condition of giving up Zangonara, if the Florentines did not relieve him within fifteen days. This misfortune being known in the Florentine camp and in the city, and all being anxious that the enemy should not obtain the expected advantage, they enabled him to secure a greater; for having abandoned the siege of Furli to go to the relief of Zangonara, on encountering the enemy they were soon routed, not so much by the bravery of their adversaries as by the severity of the season; for, having marched many hours through deep mud and heavy rain, they found the enemy quite fresh, and were therefore easily vanquished. Nevertheless, in this great defeat, famous throughout all Italy, no death occurred except those of Ludovico degli Obizzi and two of his people, who having fallen from their horses were drowned in the morass.

Reform in government: difficult reform demands a prince.

It will not, I think, be foreign to my purpose nor contrary to the plan of my previous discourse to consider whether in a corrupt state it is possible to maintain a free government where it exists, and whether, when there has been none, it can be set up. In regard to this question I maintain that in either case it will be a very difficult thing to do. It is, moreover, almost impossible to lay down rules, for the method to be adopted will of necessity depend upon the degree of corruption. None the less, since it is well to take account of all cases, I do not propose to shelve the question. I suppose then an exceedingly corrupt state, whereby the difficulty will clearly be intensified, since in it there will be found neither laws nor institutions which will suffice to check widespread corruption. Because, just as for the maintenance of good customs laws are required, so if laws are to be observed, there is need of good customs. Furthermore, institutions and laws made in the early days of a republic when men were good, no longer serve their purpose when men have become bad. And, if by any chance the laws of the state are changed, there will never, or but rarely, be a change in its institutions. The result is that new laws are ineffectual, because the institutions, which remain constant, corrupt them.

In order to make this point more clear I would point out that in Rome there was a constitution regulating its government, or rather its form of government, and then laws enabling the magistrates to keep the citizens in order. To the constitution determining its form of gov-

SOURCE: *The Discourses of Machiavelli*, translated by L. J. Walker (New Haven: Yale University Press, 1950), pp. 258–262. Reprinted with permission of Routledge & Kegan Paul, Ltd., London.

ernment pertained the authority vested in the people, the senate, the tribunes, and in the consuls, the method of applying for and of appointing to magisterial posts, and its legislative procedure. These institutions underwent little or no change in the course of events, whereas there were changes in the laws which kept the citizens in order. There was, for instance, the law concerning adultery, the sumptuary law, a law concerning ambition, and many others. These laws were introduced step by step as the citizens became corrupt. But since the institutions determining its form of government remained unchanged and, when corruption had set in, were no longer good, these modifications of the laws did not suffice to keep men good, though they might have helped had the introduction of new laws been accompanied by a modification of the institutions.

That it is true to say that such institutions would not be good in a corrupted state is clearly seen in two important cases, in the appointing of magistrates and in the making of laws. The Roman people had never given the consulate or any other important office in the city except to such as had applied for the post. This institution was at the outset good, because only such citizens applied for posts as judged themselves worthy to fill them, and to be rejected was looked upon as ignominious; so that everybody who was judged worthy, behaved well. This procedure, when the city became corrupt, was extremely harmful; because not those who had more virtue, but those who had more power, applied for magistracies, and the powerless, though virtuous, refrained from applying through fear. This inconvenience did not come about all at once, but by stages, as is the case with all inconveniences. For when the Romans had conquered Africa and Asia, and had reduced the greater part of Greece to subjection, they had become secure as to their liberty nor had they any more enemies whom there was ground to fear. This sense of security and this weakness on the part of their enemies caused the Roman people in appointing to the consulate to consider not a man's virtue, but his popularity. This drew to that office men who knew better how to get round men, not those who knew better how to conquer enemies. They then turned from those who had more popularity and gave it to those who had more power. Thus owing to the defectiveness of this institution it came about that good men were wholly excluded from consular rank.

Again, a tribune or any other citizen could propose to the people a law, in regard to which every citizen was entitled to speak either in favour of it or against, prior to a decision being reached. This institution was good so long as the citizens were good, because it is always a good thing that anyone anxious to serve the public should be able to propose his plan. It is also a good thing that everyone should be at liberty to express his opinion on it, so that when the people have heard what each has to say they may choose the best plan. But when the citizens had become perverse, this institution became a nuisance; because only the powerful proposed laws, and this for the sake, not of their common liberties, but to augment their own power. And against such projects no one durst speak for fear of such folk; with the result that the people were induced, either by deceit or by force, to adopt measures which spelt their own ruin.

In order to maintain Rome's liberty, therefore, when corruption had set in, it was necessary in the course of its development to introduce new institutions just as there had been made new laws; for different institutions and a different procedure should be prescribed for the governed according as they are good or bad, since similar forms cannot subsist in matter which is disposed in a contrary manner. Now defective institutions must either be renovated all at once as soon as the decline from goodness is noticed, or little by little before they become known to everybody. Neither of which courses is possible, I maintain. For if the renovation is to take place little by little, there is need of someone who shall see the inconvenience coming while yet it is far off and in its infancy. But it may quite easily happen in a state that no such person will ever arise, or, should he arise in point of fact, that he will never be able to persuade others to see things as he does himself, for men accustomed to a certain mode of life are reluctant to change it, especially when they have not themselves noticed the evil in question, but have had their attention called to it by conjectures. While with regard to modifying institutions all at once when everybody realises that they are no good, I would point out that, though it is easy to recognise their futility, it is not easy to correct it; for, to do this, normal methods will not suffice now that normal methods are bad. Hence it is necessary to resort to extraordinary methods, such as the use of force and an appeal to arms, and, before doing anything, to become a prince in the state, so that one can dispose it as one thinks fit.

But, to reconstitute political life in a state presupposes a good man, whereas to have recourse to violence in order to make oneself prince in a republic supposes a bad man. Hence very rarely will there be found a good man ready to use bad methods in order to make himself prince, though with a good end in view, nor yet a bad man who, having become a prince, is ready to do the right thing and to whose mind it will occur to use well that authority which he has acquired by bad means.

It is on account of all this that it is difficult, or rather impossible, either to maintain a republican form of government in states which have become corrupt or to create such a form afresh. Should a republic simply have to be created or to be maintained, it would be necessary to introduce into it a form of government akin rather to a monarchy than to a democracy, so that those men whose arrogance is such that they cannot be corrected by legal processes, may yet be restrained to some extent by a quasi-regal power. To try to make them become good in any other way would be either a most brutal or an impossible undertaking—the kind of thing that Cleomenes did, as I said above; for that he might rule alone, he killed the ephors, and for the same reasons Romulus killed his brother and Titus Tatius the Sabine, and afterwards both of them made good use of their authority. It should, however, be noted that neither the one nor the other had subjects steeped in corruption, which in this chapter we have taken as the basis of our argument; so that both were able to resolve on such steps, and, having done so, to camouflage their plan.

Machiavellian Realism: The Dictates of the Times

Warfare

Unstable conditions in early sixteenth-century Italy precluded the possibility of establishing Machiavelli's beloved Republican government in Florence; however, Machiavelli recognized that changing conditions demand different solutions. Two of the most pressing problems facing Florence concerned its inability to organize and maintain an efficient army and to preserve a stable and effective government. With regard to the first of these problems, Machiavelli advised that the contemporary system of mercenary warfare was the source of military inefficiency and argued for the reestablishment of the citizen army that had been abandoned in Dante's day. As for government, he concluded that only a strong prince could effectively rule in such turbulent times. The following selections present his ideas on both of these subjects.

Italian wars enrich mercenaries and impoverish people.

Those who make war have always and very naturally designed to enrich themselves and impoverish the enemy; neither is victory sought or conquest desirable, excepting to strengthen themselves and weaken the enemy. Hence it follows that those who are impoverished by victory or debilitated by conquest must either have gone beyond or fallen short of the end for which wars are made. A republic or a prince is enriched by the victories he obtains, when the enemy is crushed and possession is retained of the plunder and ransom. Victory is injurious when the foe escapes, or when the soldiers appropriate the booty and ransom. In such a case, losses are unfortunate, and conquests still more so; for the vanquished suffers the injuries inflicted by the enemy, and the victor those occasioned by his friends, which being less justifiable, must

SOURCE: *History of Florence* (New York: Colonial Press, 1901), pp. 283–284.

cause the greater pain, particularly from a consideration of his being thus compelled to oppress his people by an increased burden of taxation. A ruler possessing any degree of humanity cannot rejoice in a victory that afflicts his subjects. The victories of the ancient and well-organized republics, enabled them to fill their treasuries with gold and silver won from their enemies, to distribute gratuities to the people, reduce taxation, and by games and solemn festivals, disseminate universal joy. But the victories obtained in the times of which we speak, first emptied the treasury, and then impoverished the people, without giving the victorious party security from the enemy. This arose entirely from the disorders inherent in their mode of warfare; for the vanquished soldiery, divesting themselves of their accoutrements, and being neither slain nor detained prisoners, only deferred a renewed attack on the conqueror, till their leader had furnished them with arms and horses. Besides this, both ransom and booty being appropriated by the troops, the victorious princes could not make use of them for raising fresh forces, but were compelled to draw the necessary means from their subjects' purses, and this was the only result of victory experienced by the people, except that it diminished the ruler's reluctance to such a course, and made him less particular about his mode of oppressing them. To such a state had the practice of war been brought by the sort of soldiery then on foot, that the victor and the vanquished, when desirous of their services, alike needed fresh supplies of money; for the one had to re-equip them, and the other to bribe them; the vanquished could not fight without being remounted, and the conquerors would not take the field without a new gratuity. Hence it followed that the one derived little advantage from the victory, and the other was the less injured by defeat; for the routed party had to be re-equipped, and the victorious could not pursue his advantage.

Men, not riches, are the sinews of war.

Since it is open to anyone having the requisite authority to begin a war but not to end it, a ruler before committing himself to such an undertaking should calculate what forces he has at his disposal and act accordingly. Moreover, he should also take good care not to make any mistake about such forces, as he will do every time he bases his calculations on money or on the terrain or on the goodwill of men, but, on the other hand, lacks troops of his own. For though such things undoubtedly add to your strength, they certainly do not provide you with it; and, as such, are nought and of no avail without faithful

SOURCE: *The Discourses of Machiavelli*, translated by L. J. Walker (New Haven: Yale University Press, 1950), pp. 383–386. Reprinted with permission of Routledge & Kegan Paul, Ltd., London.

troops. For, without these no amount of money will suffice you: the
natural strength of the country will not help you; nor will the goodwill
of men last, since they cannot remain faithful to you unless you are
able to protect them. Every mountain, every lake, every inaccessible
fastness, becomes but as a plain, when strong defenders are lacking.
Money, too, not only affords you no protection, but makes you the
sooner fall a prey. Nor can any opinion be more false than that which
asserts that money is the sinews of war.

This view was advocated by Quintus Curtius in connection with
the war which took place between Antipater, the Macedonian, and
the king of Sparta; where he tells how, for want of money, the king of
Sparta of necessity had to join battle, and was beaten; whereas, had he
postponed the battle for a few days, he would have had news from
Greece of the death of Alexander, and so would have remained the
victor without putting up a fight. But, since he was without funds and
feared lest for lack of them his army might desert, he was forced to try
his luck in battle. On which ground Quintus Curtius maintains that
money is the sinews of war.

The view adopted by Quintus Curtius is put forward daily, and is
followed by rulers whose prudence is not up to the mark. Taking this
as their basic principle, they think they can defend themselves if they
have a well-filled treasury, and do not consider that, if treasures guaran-
teed victory, Darius would have conquered Alexander, the Greeks
would have conquered the Romans, in our day Duke Charles would
have conquered the Swiss, nor yet, but a few days ago, would the combined forces of the Pope and the Florentines have had any difficulty in
overcoming Francesco Maria, the nephew of Julius II, in the war of
Urbino. Yet all those mentioned were overcome by those who held
that the sinews of war lay not in money, but in good soldiers.

Amongst the other things that Croesus, king of Lydia, showed to
Solon, the Athenian, was a treasure too great to count. Solon was then
asked what opinion he had formed of the king's power, to which he
replied that he did not think him more powerful on this account, for
war is made with steel, not with gold, and, if anyone came along who
had more steel than he had, he could deprive him of his power.

Again, when, after the death of Alexander the Great, a host of Gauls
crossed into Greece, and then to Asia, and sent ambassadors to arrange
a treaty with the king of Macedonia, the king, in order to display his
power and to frighten them, showed them a lot of gold and silver;
whereupon the Gauls who up till then had been intent on peace, broke
off negotiations, so eager were they to relieve him of that gold. So the
king was despoiled on account of the very thing he had accumulated
for his defence.

The Venetians, a few years ago, also had a well-filled treasury, yet lost all their dominions without being able to use their treasures to defend them.

I assert, then, that it is not gold, as is acclaimed by common opinion, that constitutes the sinews of war, but good soldiers; for gold does not find good soldiers, but good soldiers are quite capable of finding gold. If the Romans had chosen to wage war rather by means of money than by the sword, not all the treasure in the world would have sufficed in view of the great enterprises they undertook and the difficulties they had to encounter in them. But, since they made war with the sword, they did not suffer for want of gold, because those who were afraid of them brought it right into their camps. And if that Spartan king for lack of money had to try his luck in battle, what happened to him on the score of money has very often happened for other reasons; for it is obvious that, when an army is short of provisions and must needs either die of hunger or fight, it always chooses to fight, since this is the more honourable course, and one that gives fortune some chance to show you favour. Again, it often happens that when a general sees that the enemy's army is about to be reinforced, he must either engage it and try his fortune in battle, or wait till the enemy's force has increased, and then have to fight it anyhow to his own great disadvantage. One sees, too—as happened to Hasdrubal when he was attacked jointly by Claudius Nero and the other Roman consul in the March—how a general who is obliged either to run away or to fight, always chooses to fight, since it seems to him that this course, even should the issue be extremely doubtful, gives him a chance to win, whereas the other would mean losing in any case. There are, then, many situations which compel a general to prefer the alternative of fighting even though he had no intention of so doing, of which lack of money may sometimes be one. But one ought not for this reason to infer that money is the sinews of war, any more than are other situations which place men in a like predicament.

I repeat, therefore: gold is not the sinews of war, but good soldiers are. Gold is necessary, but is of secondary importance, and good soldiers can get it for themselves; for it is as impossible for good soldiers to fail to find gold as it is for gold to find good soldiers. That in this we are speaking the truth history shows again and again, in spite of the fact that Pericles advised the Athenians to wage war with the whole of the Peloponnese on the ground that their industry and their pecuniary resources should enable them to win it. And, though during the war the Athenians sometimes prospered, in the end they lost, so that Sparta's wisdom and good soldiery was worth more than Athens' industry and money. On this point Titus Livy is a better witness than anybody else. I refer to the passage in which he discusses whether, if Alexander the Great had come to Italy, he would have beaten the Romans. In it he points out that three things are necessary for war; plenty of good soldiers, wise generals, and good luck; and then, having enquired whether the Romans or Alexander was the better off in these things, he draws his conclusion without any mention of money. The Capuans, at that time the richest of the Sidicines who took up arms against the Samnites, must have calculated their strength on a monetary basis, and not on the basis of troops, for, when they decided to help them, after being twice routed, they were forced to become Rome's tributaries if they wished to survive.

The Prince

CHAPTER 7

Concerning new principalities which are acquired either by the arms of others or by good fortune.

Those who solely by good fortune become princes from being private citizens have little trouble in rising, but much in keeping atop; they have not any difficulties on the way up, because they fly, but they have many when they reach the summit. Such are those to whom some state is given either for money or by the favour of him who bestows it; as happened to many in Greece, in the cities of Ionia and of the Hellespont, where princes were made by Darius, in order that they might hold the cities both for his security and his glory; as also were those emperors who, by the corruption of the soldiers, from being citizens came to empire. Such stand simply upon the goodwill and the fortune of him who has elevated them—two most inconstant and unstable things. Neither have they the knowledge requisite for the position; because, unless they are men of great worth and ability, it is not reasonable to expect that they should know how to command, having always lived in a private condition; besides, they cannot hold it because they have not forces which they can keep friendly and faithful.

States that rise unexpectedly, then, like all other things in nature which are born and grow rapidly, cannot have their foundations and correspondencies fixed in such a way that the first storm will not overthrow them; unless, as is said, those who unexpectedly become princes are men of so much ability that they know they have to be prepared at once to hold that which fortune has thrown into their laps, and that those foundations, which others have laid *before* they became princes, they must lay *afterwards*.

Concerning these two methods of rising to be a prince by ability or fortune, I wish to adduce two examples within our own recollection, and

SOURCE: *The Prince*, translated by W. K. Marriott. Everyman's Library edition, 1908, pp. 53–63, 97–154, 185–216. Reprinted by permission of E. P. Dutton & Co., Inc., New York, and J. M. Dent & Sons, Ltd., London.

these are Francesco Sforza and Cesare Borgia. Francesco, by proper means and with great ability, from being a private person rose to be Duke of Milan, and that which he had acquired with a thousand anxieties he kept with little trouble. On the other hand, Cesare Borgia, called by the people Duke Valentino, acquired his State during the ascendency of his father, and on its decline he lost it, notwithstanding that he had taken every measure and done all that ought to be done by a wise and able man to fix firmly his roots in the states which the arms and fortunes of others had bestowed on him.

Because, as is stated above, he who has not first laid his foundations may be able with great ability to lay them afterwards, but they will be laid with trouble to the architect and danger to the building. If, therefore, all the steps taken by the duke be considered, it will be seen that he laid solid foundations for his future power, and I do not consider it superfluous to discuss them, because I do not know what better precepts to give a new prince than the example of his actions; and if his dispositions were of no avail, that was not his fault, but the extraordinary and extreme malignity of fortune.

Alexander the Sixth, in wishing to aggrandise the duke, his son, had many immediate and prospective difficulties. Firstly, he did not see his way to make him master of any state that was not a state of the Church; and if he was willing to rob the Church he knew that the Duke of Milan and the Venetians would not consent, because Faenza and Rimini were already under the protection of the Venetians. Besides this, he saw the arms of Italy, especially those by which he might have been assisted, in hands that would fear the aggrandisement of the Pope, namely, the Orsini and the Colonnesi and their following. It behoved him, therefore, to upset this state of affairs and embroil the powers, so as to make himself securely master of part of their states. This was easy for him to do, because he found the Venetians, moved by other reasons, inclined to bring back the French into Italy; he would not only not oppose this, but he would render it more easy by dissolving the former marriage of King Louis. Therefore the king came into Italy with the assistance of the Venetians and the consent of Alexander. He was no sooner in Milan than the Pope had soldiers from him for the attempt on the Romagna, which yielded to him on the reputation of the king. The duke, therefore, having acquired the Romagna and beaten the Colonnesi, while wishing to hold that and to advance further, was hindered by two things: the one, his forces did not appear loyal to him, the other, the goodwill of France: that is to say, he feared that the forces of the Orsini, which he was using, would not stand to him, that not only might they hinder him from winning more, but might themselves seize what he had won, and that the king might also do the same. Of the Orsini he had a warning when, after taking Faenza and attacking Bologna, he saw them go very unwillingly to that attack. And as to the king, he learned his mind when he himself, after taking the Duchy of Urbino, attacked Tuscany, and the king made him desist from that undertaking; hence the duke decided to depend no more upon the arms and the luck of others.

For the first thing he weakened the Orsini and Colonnesi parties in Rome, by gaining to himself all their adherents who were gentlemen, making them his gentlemen, giving them good pay, and, according to their rank, honouring them with office and command in such a way that in a few months all attachment to the factions was destroyed and turned entirely to the duke. After this he awaited an opportunity to crush the Orsini, having scattered the adherents of the Colonna house. This came to him soon and he used it well; for the Orsini, perceiving at length that the aggrandisement of the duke and the Church was ruin to them, called a meeting at Magione in Perugia. From this sprung the rebellion at Urbino and the tumults in the Romagna, with endless dangers to the duke, all of which he overcame with the help of the French. Having restored his authority, not to leave it at risk by trusting either to the French or other outside forces, he had recourse to his wiles, and he knew so well how to conceal his mind that, by the mediation of Signor Pagolo—whom the duke did not fail to secure with all kinds of attentions, giving him money, apparel, and horses—the Orsini were reconciled, so that their simplicity brought them into his power at Sinigalia. Having exterminated the leaders, and turned their partisans into his friends, the duke had laid sufficiently good foundations to his power, having all the Romagna and the Duchy of Urbino; and the people now beginning to appreciate their prosperity, he gained them all over to himself. And as this point is worthy of notice, and to be imitated by others, I am not willing to leave it out.

When the duke occupied the Romagna he found it under the rule of weak masters, who rather plundered their subjects than ruled them, and gave them more cause for disunion than for union, so that the country was full of robbery, quarrels, and every kind of violence; and so, wishing to bring back peace and obedience to authority, he considered it necessary to give it a good governor. Thereupon he promoted Messer Ramiro d'Orco, a swift and cruel man, to whom he gave the fullest power. This man in a short time restored peace and unity with the greatest success. Afterwards the duke considered that it was not advisable to confer such excessive authority, for he had no doubt but that he would become odious, so he set up a court of judgment in the country, under a most excellent president, wherein all cities had their advocates. And because he knew that the past severity had caused some hatred against himself, so, to clear himself in the minds of the people, and gain them entirely to himself, he desired to show that, if any cruelty had been practised, it had not originated with him, but in the natural sternness of the minister. Under this pretence he took Ramiro, and one morning caused him to be executed and left on the piazza at Cesena with the block and a bloody knife at his side. The barbarity of this spectacle caused the people to be at once satisfied and dismayed.

But let us return whence we started. I say that the duke, finding himself now sufficiently powerful and partly secured from immediate dangers by having armed himself in his own way, and having in a great measure crushed those forces in his vicinity that could injure him if he wished to proceed with his conquest, had next to consider France, for he knew that the king, who too late was aware of his mistake, would not support him. And from this time he began to seek new alliances and to temporise with France in the expedition which she was making towards the kingdom of Naples against the Spaniards who were besieging Gaeta. It was his intention to secure himself against them, and this he would have quickly accomplished had Alexander lived.

Such was his line of action as to present affairs. But as to the future he had to fear, in the first place, that a new successor to the Church might not be friendly to him and might seek to take from him that which Alexander had given him, so he decided to act in four ways. Firstly, by exterminating the families of those lords whom he had despoiled, so as to take away that pretext from the Pope. Secondly, by winning to himself all the gentlemen of Rome, so as to be able to curb the Pope with their aid, as has been observed. Thirdly, by converting the college more to himself. Fourthly, by acquiring so much power before the Pope should die that he could by his own measures resist the first shock. Of these four things, at the death of Alexander, he had accomplished three. For he had killed as many of the dispossessed lords as he could lay hands on, and few had escaped; he had won over the Roman gentlemen, and he had the most numerous party in the college. And as to any fresh acquisition, he intended to become master of Tuscany, for he already possessed Perugia and Piombino, and Pisa was under his protection. And as he had no longer to study France (for the French were already driven out of the kingdom of Naples by the Spaniards, and in this way both were compelled to buy his goodwill), he pounced down upon Pisa. After this, Lucca and Siena yielded at once, partly through hatred and partly through fear of the Florentines; and the Florentines would have had no remedy had he continued to prosper, as he was prospering the year that Alexander died, for he had acquired so much power and reputation that he would have stood by himself, and no longer have depended on the luck and the forces of others, but solely on his own power and ability.

But Alexander died five years after he had first drawn the sword. He left the duke with the state of Romagna alone consolidated, with the rest in the air, between two most powerful hostile armies, and sick unto death. Yet there were in the duke such boldness and ability, and he knew so well how men are to be won or lost, and so firm were the foundations which in so short a time he had laid, that if he had not had those armies on his back, or if he had been in good health, he would have overcome all difficulties. And it is seen that his foundations were good, for the Romagna awaited him for more than a month. In Rome, although but half alive, he remained secure; and whilst the Baglioni, the Vitelli, and the Orsini might come to Rome, they could not effect anything against him. If he could not have made Pope him whom he wished, at least the one whom he did not wish would not have been elected. But if he had been in sound health at the death of Alexander, everything would have been easy to him. On the day that Julius the Second was elected, he told me that he had thought of everything that might occur at the death of his father, and had provided a remedy for all, except that he had never anticipated that, when the death did happen, he himself would be on the point to die.

When all the actions of the duke are recalled, I do not know how to blame him, but rather it appears to me, as I have said, that I ought to offer him for imitation to all those who, by the fortune or the arms of others, are raised to government. Because he, having a lofty spirit and far-reaching aims, could not have regulated his conduct otherwise, and only the shortness of the life of Alexander and his own sickness frustrated his designs. Therefore, he who considers it necessary to secure himself in his new principality, to win friends, to overcome either by force or fraud, to make himself beloved and feared by the people, to be followed and revered by the soldiers, to exterminate those who had power or reason to hurt him, to change the old order of things for new, to be severe and gracious, magnanimous and liberal, to destroy a disloyal soldiery and to create new, to maintain friendship with kings and princes in such a way that they must help him with zeal and offend with caution, cannot find a more lively example than the actions of this man.

Only can he be blamed for the election of Julius the Second, in whom he made a bad choice, because, as is said, not being able to elect a Pope to his own mind, he could have hindered any other from being elected Pope; and he ought never to have consented to the election of any cardinal whom he had injured or who had cause to fear him if they became pontiffs. For men injure either from fear or hatred. Those whom he had injured, amongst others, were San Pietro ad Vincula, Colonna, San Giorgio, and Ascanio. The rest, in becoming Pope, had to fear him, Rouen and the Spaniards excepted; the latter from their relationship and obligations, the former from his influence, the kingdom of France having relations with him. Therefore, above everything, the duke ought to have created a Spaniard Pope, and, failing him, he ought to have consented to Rouen and not San Pietro ad Vincula. He who believes that new benefits will cause great personages to forget old injuries is deceived. Therefore, the duke erred in his choice, and it was the cause of his ultimate ruin.

CHAPTER 12

How many kinds of soldiery there are, and concerning mercenaries.

Having discoursed particularly on the characteristics of such principalities as in the beginning I proposed to discuss, and having considered in some degree the causes of their being good or bad, and having shown the methods by which many have sought to acquire them and to hold them, it now remains for me to discuss generally the means of offence and defence which belong to each of them.

We have seen above how necessary it is for a prince to have his foundations well laid, otherwise it follows of necessity he will go to ruin. The chief foundations of all states, new as well as old or composite, are good laws and good arms; and as there cannot be good laws where the state is not well armed, it follows that where they are well armed they have good laws. I shall leave the laws out of the discussion and shall speak of the arms.

I say, therefore, that the arms with which a prince defends his state are either his own, or they are mercenaries, auxiliaries, or mixed. Mercenaries and auxiliaries are useless and dangerous; and if one holds his state based on these arms, he will stand neither firm nor safe; for they are disunited, ambitious and without discipline, unfaithful, valiant before friends, cowardly before enemies; they have neither the fear of God nor fidelity to men, and destruction is deferred only so long as the attack is; for in peace one is robbed by them, and in war by the enemy. The fact is, they have no other attraction or reason for keeping the field than a trifle of stipend, which is not sufficient to make them willing to die for you. They are ready enough to be your soldiers whilst you do not make war, but if war comes they take themselves off or run from the foe; which I should have little trouble to prove, for the ruin of Italy has been caused by nothing else than by resting all her hopes for many years on mercenaries, and although they formerly made some display and appeared valiant amongst themselves, yet when the foreigners came they showed what they were. Thus it was that Charles, King of France, was allowed to seize Italy with chalk in hand; and he who told us that our sins were the cause of it told the truth, but they were not the sins he imagined, but those which I have related. And as they were the sins of princes, it is the princes who have also suffered the penalty.

I wish to demonstrate further the infelicity of these arms. The mercenary captains are either capable men or they are not; if they are, you cannot trust them, because they always aspire to their own greatness, either by oppressing you, who are their master, or others contrary to your intentions; but if the captain is not skilful, you are ruined in the usual way.

And if it be urged that whoever is armed will act in the same way, whether mercenary or not, I reply that when arms have to be resorted to, either by a prince or a republic, then the prince ought to go in person and perform the duty of captain; the republic has to send its citizens, and when one is sent who does not turn out satisfactorily, it ought to recall him, and when one is worthy, to hold him by the laws so that he does not leave the command. And experience has shown princes and republics, single-handed, making the greatest progress, and mercenaries doing nothing except damage; and it is more difficult to bring a republic, armed with its own arms, under the sway of one of its citizens than it is to bring one armed with foreign arms. Rome and Sparta stood for many ages armed and free. The Switzers are completely armed and quite free.

Of ancient mercenaries, for example, there are the Carthaginians, who were oppressed by their mercenary soldiers after the first war with the Romans, although the Carthaginians had their own citizens for captains. After the death of Epaminondas, Philip of Macedon was made captain of their soldiers by the Thebans, and after victory he took away their liberty.

Duke Filippo being dead, the Milanese enlisted Francesco Sforza against the Venetians, and he, having overcome the enemy at Caravaggio, allied himself with them to crush the Milanese, his masters. His father, Sforza, having been engaged by Queen Johanna of Naples, left her unprotected, so that she was forced to throw herself into the arms of the King of Aragon, in order to save her kingdom. And if the Venetians and Florentines formerly extended their dominions by these arms, and yet their captains did not make themselves princes, but have defended them, I reply that the Florentines in this case have been favoured by chance, for of the able captains, of whom they might have stood in fear, some have not conquered, some have been opposed, and others have turned their ambitions elsewhere. One who did not conquer was Giovanni Acuto, and since he did not conquer his fidelity cannot be proved; but every one will acknowledge that, had he conquered, the Florentines would have stood at his discretion. Sforza had the Bracceschi always against him, so they watched each other. Francesco turned his ambition to Lombardy; Braccio against the Church and the kingdom of Naples. But let us come to that which happened a short while ago. The Florentines appointed as their captain Pagolo Vitelli, a most prudent man, who from a private position had risen to the greatest renown. If this man had taken Pisa, nobody can deny that it would have been proper for the Florentines to keep in with him, for if he became the soldier of their enemies they had no means of resisting, and if they held to him they must obey him. The Venetians, if their achievements are considered, will be seen to have acted safely and gloriously so long as they sent to war their own men, when with armed gentlemen and plebeians they did valiantly. This was before they turned to enterprises on land, but when they began to fight on land they forsook this virtue and followed the custom of Italy. And in the beginning of their expansion on land, through not having much territory, and because of their great reputation, they had not much to fear from their captains; but when they expanded, as under Carmignuola, they had a taste of this mistake; for, having found him a most valiant man (they beat the Duke of Milan under his leadership), and, on the other hand, knowing how lukewarm he was in the war, they feared they would no longer conquer under him, and for this reason they were not willing, nor were they able, to let him go; and so, not to lose again that which they had acquired, they were compelled, in order to secure themselves, to murder him. They had afterwards for their captains Bartolomeo da Bergamo, Roberto da San Severino, the Count of Pitigliano, and the like, under whom they had to dread loss and not gain, as happened afterwards at Vaila, where in one battle they lost that which in eight hundred years they had acquired with so much trouble. Because from such arms conquests come but slowly, long delayed and inconsiderable, but the losses sudden and portentous.

And as with these examples I have reached Italy, which has been ruled for many years by mercenaries, I wish to discuss them more seriously, in order that, having seen their rise and progress, one may be better prepared to counteract them. You must understand that the empire has recently come to be repudiated in Italy, that the Pope has acquired more temporal power, and that Italy has been divided up into more states, for the reason that many of the great cities took up arms against their nobles, who, formerly favoured by the emperor, were oppressing them, whilst the Church was favouring them so as to gain authority in temporal power: in many others their citizens became princes. From this it came to pass that Italy fell partly into the hands of the Church and of republics, and, the Church consisting of priests and the republic of citizens unaccustomed to arms, both commenced to enlist foreigners.

The first who gave renown to this soldiery was Alberigo da Conio, the Romagnian. From the school of this man sprang, among others, Braccio and Sforza, who in their time were the arbiters of Italy. After these came all the other captains who till now have directed the arms of Italy; and the end of all their valour has been, that she has been over-run by Charles, robbed by Louis, ravaged by Ferdinand, and insulted by the Switzers. The principle that has guided them has been, first, to lower the credit of infantry so that they might increase their own. They did this because, subsisting on their pay and without territory, they were unable to support many soldiers, and a few infantry did not give them any authority; so they were led to employ cavalry, with a moderate force of which they were maintained and honoured; and affairs were brought to such a pass that, in an army of twenty thousand soldiers, there were not to be found two thousand foot soldiers. They had, besides this, used every art to lessen fatigue and danger to themselves and their soldiers, not killing in the fray, but taking prisoners and liberating without ransom. They did not attack towns at night, nor did the garrisons of the towns attack encampments at night; they did not surround the camp either with stockade or ditch, nor did they campaign in the winter. All these things were permitted by their military rules, and devised by them to avoid, as I have said, both fatigue and dangers; thus they have brought Italy to slavery and contempt.

CHAPTER 13

Concerning auxiliaries, mixed soldiery, and one's own.

Auxiliaries, which are the other useless arm, are employed when a prince is called in with his forces to aid and defend, as was done by Pope Julius in the most recent times; for he, having, in the enterprise against Ferrara, had poor proof of his mercenaries, turned to auxiliaries, and stipulated with Ferdinand, King of Spain, for his assistance with men and arms. These arms may be useful and good in themselves, but for him who calls them in they are always disadvantageous; for losing, one is undone, and winning, one is their captive.

And although ancient histories may be full of examples, I do not wish to leave this recent one of Pope Julius the Second, the peril of which cannot fail to be perceived; for he, wishing to get Ferrara, threw himself entirely into the hands of the foreigner. But his good fortune brought about a third event, so that he did not reap the fruit of his rash choice; because, having his auxiliaries routed at Ravenna, and the Switzers having risen and driven out the conquerors (against all expectation, both his and others), it so came to pass that he did not become prisoner to his enemies, they having fled, nor to his auxiliaries, he having conquered by other arms than theirs.

The Florentines, being entirely without arms, sent ten thousand

Frenchmen to take Pisa, whereby they ran more danger than at any other time of their troubles.

The Emperor of Constantinople, to oppose his neighbours, sent ten thousand Turks into Greece, who, on the war being finished, were not willing to quit; this was the beginning of the servitude of Greece to the infidels.

Therefore, let him who has no desire to conquer make use of these arms, for they are much more hazardous than mercenaries, because with them the ruin is ready made; they are all united, all yield obedience to others; but with mercenaries, when they have conquered, more time and better opportunities are needed to injure you; they are not all of one community, they are found and paid by you, and a third party, which you have made their head, is not able all at once to assume enough authority to injure you. In conclusion, in mercenaries dastardy is most dangerous; in auxiliaries, valour. The wise prince, therefore, has always avoided these arms and turned to his own; and has been willing rather to lose with them than to conquer with others, not deeming that a real victory which is gained with the arms of others.

I shall never hesitate to cite Cesare Borgia and his actions. This duke entered the Romagna with auxiliaries, taking there only French soldiers, and with them he captured Imola and Forli; but afterwards, such forces not appearing to him reliable, he turned to mercenaries, discerning less danger in them, and enlisted the Orsini and Vitelli; whom presently, on handling and finding them doubtful; unfaithful, and dangerous, he destroyed and turned to his own men. And the difference between one and the other of these forces can easily be seen when one considers the difference there was in the reputation of the duke, when he had the French, when he had the Orsini and Vitelli, and when he relied on his own soldiers, on whose fidelity he could always count and found it ever increasing; he was never esteemed more highly than when every one saw that he was complete master of his own forces.

I was not intending to go beyond Italian and recent examples, but I am unwilling to leave out Hiero, the Syracusan, he being one of those I have named above. This man, as I have said, made head of the army by the Syracusans, soon found out that a mercenary soldiery, constituted like our Italian condottieri, was of no use; and it appearing to him that he could neither keep them nor let them go, he had them all cut to pieces, and afterwards made war with his own forces and not with aliens.

I wish also to recall to memory an instance from the Old Testament applicable to this subject. David offered himself to Saul to fight with Goliath, the Philistine champion, and, to give him courage, Saul armed him with his own weapons; which David rejected as soon as he had them on his back, saying he could make no use of them, and that he wished to meet the enemy with his sling and his knife. In conclusion, the arms of others either fall from your back, or they weigh you down, or they bind you fast.

Charles the Seventh, the father of King Louis the Eleventh, having by good fortune and valour liberated France from the English, recognised the necessity of being armed with forces of his own, and he established in his kingdom ordinances concerning men-at-arms and infantry. Afterwards his son, King Louis, abolished the infantry and began to enlist the Switzers, which mistake, followed by others, is, as is now seen, a source of peril to that kingdom; because, having raised the reputation of the Switzers, he has entirely diminished the value of his own arms, for he has destroyed the infantry altogether; and his men-at-arms he has subordinated to others, for, being as they are so accustomed to fight along with Switzers, it does not appear that they can now conquer without them. Hence it arises that the French cannot stand against the Switzers, and without the Switzers they do not come off well against others. The armies of the French have thus become mixed, partly mercenary and partly national, both of which arms together are much better than mercenaries alone or auxiliaries alone, yet much inferior to one's own forces. And this example proves it, for the kingdom of France would be unconquerable if the ordinance of Charles had been enlarged or maintained.

But the scanty wisdom of man, on entering into an affair which looks well at first, cannot discern the poison that is hidden in it, as I have said above of hectic fevers. Therefore, if he who rules a principality cannot recognise evils until they are upon him, he is not truly wise; and this insight is given to few. And if the first disaster to the Roman Empire should be examined, it will be found to have commenced only with the enlisting of the Goths; because from that time the vigour of the Roman Empire began to decline, and all that valour which had raised it passed away to others.

I conclude, therefore, that no principality is secure without having its own forces; on the contrary, it is entirely dependent on good fortune, not having the valour which in adversity would defend it. And it has always been the opinion and judgment of wise men that nothing can be so uncertain or unstable as fame or power not founded on its own strength. And one's own forces are those which are composed either of subjects, citizens, or dependents; all others are mercenaries or auxiliaries. And the way to make ready one's own forces will be easily found if the rules suggested by me shall be reflected upon, and if one will consider how Philip, the father of Alexander the Great, and many republics and princes have armed and organised themselves, to which rules I entirely commit myself.

CHAPTER 14

That which concerns a prince on the subject of the art of war.

A prince ought to have no other aim or thought, nor select anything else for his study, than war and its rules and discipline; for this is the sole art that belongs to him who rules, and it is of such force that it not only upholds those who are born princes, but it often enables men to rise from a private station to that rank. And, on the contrary, it is seen that when princes have thought more of ease than of arms they have lost their states. And the first cause of your losing it is to neglect this art; and what enables you to acquire a state is to be master of the art. Francesco Sforza, through being martial, from a private person became Duke of Milan; and the sons, through avoiding the hardships and troubles of arms, from dukes became private persons. For among other evils which being unarmed brings you, it causes you to be despised, and this is one of those ignominies against which a prince ought to guard himself, as is shown later on. Because there is nothing proportionate between the armed and the unarmed; and it is not reasonable that he who is armed should yield obedience willingly to him who is unarmed, or that the unarmed man should be secure among armed servants. Because, there being in the one disdain and in the other suspicion, it is not possible for them to work well together. And therefore a prince who does not understand the art of war, over and above the other misfortunes already mentioned, cannot be respected by his soldiers, nor can he rely on them. He ought never, therefore, to have out of his thoughts this subject of war, and in peace he should addict himself more to its exercise than in war; this he can do in two ways, the one by action, the other by study.

As regards action, he ought above all things to keep his men well organised and drilled, to follow incessantly the chase, by which he accustoms his body to hardships, and learns something of the nature of localities, and gets to find out how the mountains rise, how the valleys open out, how the plains lie, and to understand the nature of rivers and marshes, and in all this to take the greatest care. Which knowledge is useful in two ways. Firstly, he learns to know his country, and is better able to undertake its defence; afterwards, by means of the knowledge and observation of that locality, he understands with ease any other which it may be necessary for him to study hereafter; because the hills, valleys, and plains, and rivers and marshes that are, for instance, in Tuscany, have a certain resemblance to those of other countries, so that with a knowledge of the aspect of one country one can easily arrive at a knowledge of others. And the prince that lacks this skill lacks the essential which it is desirable that a captain should possess, for it teaches him to surprise his enemy, to select quarters, to lead armies, to array the battle, to besiege towns to advantage.

Philopoemen, Prince of the Acheans, among other praises which writers have bestowed on him, is commended because in time of peace he never had anything in his mind but the rules of war; and when he was in the country with friends, he often stopped and reasoned with them: "If the enemy should be upon that hill, and we should find ourselves here with our army, with whom would be the advantage? How should one best advance to meet him, keeping the ranks? If we should wish to retreat, how ought we to set about it? If they should retreat, how ought we to pursue?" And he would set forth to them, as he went, all the chances that could befall an army; he would listen to their opinion and state his, confirming it with reasons, so that by these continual discussions there could never arise, in time of war, any unexpected circumstances that he could not deal with.

But to exercise the intellect the prince should read histories, and study there the actions of illustrious men, to see how they have borne themselves in war, to examine the causes of their victories and defeat, so as to avoid the latter and imitate the former; and above all do as an illustrious man did, who took as an exemplar one who had been praised and famous before him, and whose achievements and deeds he always kept in his mind, as it is said Alexander the Great imitated Achilles, Caesar Alexander, Scipio Cyrus. And whoever reads the life of Cyrus, written by Xenophon, will recognise afterwards in the life of Scipio how that imitation was his glory, and how in chastity, affability, humanity, and liberality Scipio conformed to those things which have been written of Cyrus by Xenophon. A wise prince ought to observe some such rules, and never in peaceful times stand idle, but increase his resources with industry in such a way that they may be available to him in adversity, so that if fortune changes it may find him prepared to resist her blows.

CHAPTER 15

Concerning things for which men, and especially princes, are praised or blamed.

It remains now to see what ought to be the rules of conduct for a prince towards subject and friends. And as I know that many have written on this point, I expect I shall be considered presumptuous in mentioning it again, especially as in discussing it I shall depart from the methods of other people. But, it being my intention to write a thing which shall be useful to him who apprehends it, it appears to me more appropriate to follow up the real truth of a matter than the imagination of it; for many have pictured republics and principalities which in fact have never been known or seen, because how one lives is so far distant from how one ought to live, that he who neglects what is done for what ought to be done, sooner effects his ruin than his preservation;

for a man who wishes to act entirely up to his professions of virtue soon meets with what destroys him among so much that is evil.

Hence it is necessary for a prince wishing to hold his own to know how to do wrong, and to make use of it or not according to necessity. Therefore, putting on one side imaginary things concerning a prince, and discussing those which are real, I say that all men when they are spoken of, and chiefly princes for being more highly placed, are remarkable for some of those qualities which bring them either blame or praise; and thus it is that one is reputed liberal, another miserly, using a Tuscan term (because an avaricious person in our language is still he who desires to possess by robbery, whilst we call one miserly who deprives himself too much of the use of his own); one is reputed generous, one rapacious; one cruel, one compassionate; one faithless, another faithful; one effeminate and cowardly, another bold and brave; one affable, another haughty; one lascivious, another chaste; one sincere, another cunning; one hard, another easy; one grave, another frivolous; one religious, another unbelieving, and the like. And I know that every one will confess that it would be most praiseworthy in a prince to exhibit all the above qualities that are considered good; but because they can neither be entirely possessed nor observed, for human conditions do not permit it, it is necessary for him to be sufficiently prudent that he may know how to avoid the reproach of those vices which would lose him his state; and also to keep himself, if it be possible, from those which would not lose him it; but this not being possible, he may with less hesitation abandon himself to them. And again, he need not make himself uneasy at incurring a reproach for those vices without which the state can only be saved with difficulty, for if everything is considered carefully, it will be found that something which looks like virtue, if followed, would be his ruin; whilst something else, which looks like vice, yet followed brings him security and prosperity.

CHAPTER 16

Concerning liberality and meanness.

Commencing then with the first of the above-named characteristics, I say that it would be well to be reputed liberal. Nevertheless, liberality exercised in a way that does not bring you the reputation for it, injures you; for if one exercises it honestly and as it should be exercised, it may not become known, and you will not avoid the reproach of its opposite. Therefore, any one wishing to maintain among men the name of liberal is obliged to avoid no attribute of magnificence; so that a prince thus inclined will consume in such acts all his property, and will be compelled in the end, if he wish to maintain the name of liberal, to unduly weigh down his people, and tax them, and do everything he can to get money. This will soon make him odious to his subjects, and becoming poor he will be little valued by any one; thus, with his liberality, having offended many and rewarded few, he is affected by the very first trouble and imperilled by whatever may be the first danger; recognising this himself, and wishing to draw back from it, he runs at once into the reproach of being miserly.

Therefore, a prince, not being able to exercise this virtue of liberality in such a way that it is recognised, except to his cost, if he is wise he ought not to fear the reputation of being mean, for in time he will come to be more considered than if liberal, seeing that with his economy his revenues are enough, that he can defend himself against all attacks, and is able to engage in enterprises without burdening his people; thus it comes to pass that he exercises liberality towards all from whom he does not take, who are numberless, and meanness towards those to whom he does not give, who are few.

We have not seen great things done in our time except by those who have been considered mean; the rest have failed. Pope Julius the Second was assisted in reaching the papacy by a reputation for liberality, yet he did not strive afterwards to keep it up, when he made war on the King of France; and he made many wars without imposing any extraordinary tax on his subjects, for he supplied his additional expenses out of his long thriftiness. The present King of Spain would not have undertaken or conquered in so many enterprises if he had been reputed liberal. A prince, therefore, provided that he has not to rob his subjects, that he can defend himself, that he does not become poor and abject, that he is not forced to become rapacious, ought to hold of little account a reputation for being mean, for it is one of those vices which will enable him to govern.

And if any one should say: Caesar obtained empire by liberality, and many others have reached the highest positions by having been liberal, and by being considered so, I answer: Either you are a prince in fact, or in a way to become one. In the first case this liberality is dangerous, in the second it is very necessary to be considered liberal; and Caesar was one of those who wished to become pre-eminent in Rome; but if he had survived after becoming so, and had not moderated his expenses, he would have destroyed his government. And if any one should reply: Many have been princes, and have done great things with armies, who have been considered very liberal, I reply: Either a prince spends that which is his own or his subjects' or else that of others. In the first case he ought to be sparing, in the second he ought not to neglect any opportunity for liberality. And to the prince who goes forth with his army, supporting it by pillage, sack, and extortion, handling that which belongs to others, this liberality is necessary, otherwise he would not be followed by soldiers. And of that which is neither yours nor your subjects' you can be a ready giver, as were Cyrus, Caesar, and Alexander; because it does not take away your reputation if you squander that of others, but adds to it; it is only squandering your own that injures you.

And there is nothing wastes so rapidly as liberality, for even whilst you exercise it you lose the power to do so, and so become either poor or despised, or else, in avoiding poverty, rapacious and hated. And a prince should guard himself, above all things, against being despised and hated; and liberality leads you to both. Therefore it is wiser to have a reputation for meanness which brings reproach without hatred, than to be compelled through seeking a reputation for liberality to incur a name for rapacity which begets reproach with hatred.

CHAPTER 17

Concerning cruelty and clemency, and whether it is better to be loved than feared.

Coming now to the other qualities mentioned above, I say that every prince ought to desire to be considered clement and not cruel. Nevertheless he ought to take care not to misuse this clemency. Cesare Borgia was considered cruel; notwithstanding, his cruelty reconciled the Romagna, unified it, and restored it to peace and loyalty. And if this be rightly considered, he will be seen to have been much more merciful than the Florentine people, who, to avoid a reputation for cruelty, permitted Pistoia to be destroyed. Therefore a prince, so long as he keeps his subjects united and loyal, ought not to mind the reproach of cruelty; because with a few examples he will be more merciful than those who, through too much mercy, allow disorders to arise, from which follow murder or robbery; for these are wont to injure the whole people, whilst those executions which originate with a prince offend the individual only.

And of all princes, it is impossible for the new prince to avoid the imputation of cruelty, owing to new states being full of dangers. Hence Virgil, through the mouth of Dido, excuses the inhumanity of her reign owing to its being new, saying:

> Res dura, et regni novitas me talia cogunt
> Moliri, et late fines custode tueri.

Nevertheless he ought to be slow to believe and to act, nor should he himself show fear, but proceed in a temperate manner with prudence and humanity, so that too much confidence may not make him incautious and too much distrust render him intolerable.

Upon this a question arises: whether it be better to be loved than feared or feared than loved? It may be answered that one should wish to be both, but, because it is difficult to unite them in one person, it is much safer to be feared than loved, when, of the two, either must be dispensed with. Because this is to be asserted in general of men, that they are ungrateful, fickle, false, cowards, covetous, and as long as you succeed they are yours entirely; they will offer you their blood, property, life, and children, as is said above, when the need is far distant; but when it approaches they turn against you. And that prince who, relying entirely on their promises, has neglected other precautions, is ruined; because friendships that are obtained by payments, and not by greatness or nobility of mind, may indeed be earned, but they are not secured, and in time of need cannot be relied upon; and men have less scruple in offending one who is beloved than one who is feared, for love is preserved by the link of obligation which, owing to the baseness of men, is broken at every opportunity for their advantage; but fear preserves you by a dread of punishment which never fails.

Nevertheless a prince ought to inspire fear in such a way that, if he does not win love, he avoids hatred; because he can endure very well being feared whilst he is not hated, which will always be as long as he abstains from the property of his citizens and subjects and from their women. But when it is necessary for him to proceed against the life of some one, he must do it on proper justification and for manifest cause, but above all things he must keep his hands off the property of others, because men more quickly forget the death of their father than the loss of their patrimony. Besides, pretexts for taking away the property are never wanting; for he who has once begun to live by robbery will always find pretexts for seizing what belongs to others; but reasons for taking life, on the contrary, are more difficult to find and sooner lapse. But when a prince is with his army, and has under control a multitude of soldiers, then it is quite necessary for him to disregard the reputation of cruelty, for without it he would never hold his army united or disposed to its duties.

Among the wonderful deeds of Hannibal this one is enumerated: that having led an enormous army, composed of many various races of men, to fight in foreign lands, no dissensions arose either among them or against the prince, whether in his bad or in his good fortune. This arose from nothing else than his inhuman cruelty, which, with his boundless valour, made him revered and terrible in the sight of his soldiers, but without that cruelty, his other virtues were not sufficient to produce this effect. And short-sighted writers admire his deeds from one point of view and from another condemn the principal cause of them. That it is true his other virtues would not have been sufficient for him may be proved by the case of Scipio, that most excellent man, not only of his own times but within the memory of man, against whom, nevertheless, his army rebelled in Spain; this arose from nothing but his too great forbearance, which gave his soldiers more licence than is consistent with military discipline. For this he was upbraided in the Senate by Fabius Maximus, and called the corruptor of the Roman soldiery. The Locrians were laid waste by a legate of Scipio, yet they were not avenged by him, nor was the insolence of the legate punished, owing entirely to his easy nature. Insomuch that some one in the Senate, wishing to excuse him, said there were many men who knew much better how not to err than to correct the errors of others. This disposition, if he had been continued in the command, would have destroyed in time the fame and glory of Scipio; but, he being under the control of the Senate, this injurious characteristic not only concealed itself, but contributed to his glory.

Returning to the question of being feared or loved, I come to the conclusion that, men loving according to their own will and fearing according to that of the prince, a wise prince should establish himself on that which is in his own control and not in that of others; he must endeavour only to avoid hatred, as is noted.

CHAPTER 18

Concerning the way in which princes should keep faith.

Every one admits how praiseworthy it is in a prince to keep faith, and to live with integrity and not with craft. Nevertheless our experience has been that those princes who have done great things have held good faith of little account, and have known how to circumvent the intellect of men by craft, and in the end have overcome those who have relied on their word. You must know there are two ways of contesting, the one by the law, the other by force; the first method is proper to men, the second to beasts; but because the first is frequently not sufficient, it is necessary to have recourse to the second. Therefore it is necessary for a prince to understand how to avail himself of the beast and the man. This has been figuratively taught to princes by ancient writers, who describe how Achilles and many other princes of old were given to the Centaur Chiron to nurse, who brought them up in his discipline; which means solely that, as they had for a teacher one who was half beast and half man, so it is necessary for a prince to know how to make use of both natures, and that one without the other is not durable. A prince, therefore, being compelled knowingly to adopt the beast, ought to choose the fox and the lion; because the lion cannot defend himself against snares and the fox cannot defend himself against wolves. Therefore, it is necessary to be a fox to discover the snares and a lion to terrify the wolves. Those who rely simply on the lion do not understand what they are about. Therefore a wise lord cannot, nor ought he to, keep faith when such observance may be turned against him, and when the reasons that caused him to pledge it exist no longer. If men were entirely good this precept would not hold, but because they are bad, and will not keep faith with you, you too are not bound to observe it with them. Nor will there ever be wanting to a prince legitimate reasons to excuse this non-observance. Of this endless modern examples could be given, showing how many treaties and engagements have been made void and of no effect through the faithlessness of princes; and he who has known best how to employ the fox has succeeded best.

But it is necessary to know well how to disguise this characteristic, and to be a great pretender and dissembler; and men are so simple, and so subject to present necessities, that he who seeks to deceive will always find some one who will allow himself to be deceived. One recent example I cannot pass over in silence. Alexander the Sixth did nothing else but deceive men, nor ever thought of doing otherwise, and he always found victims; for there never was a man who had greater power in asserting, or who with greater oaths would affirm a thing, yet would observe it less; nevertheless his deceits always succeeded according to his wishes, because he well understood this side of mankind.

Therefore it is unnecessary for a prince to have all the good qualities I have enumerated, but it is very necessary to appear to have them. And I shall dare to say this also, that to have them and always to observe them is injurious, and that to appear to have them is useful; to appear merciful, faithful, humane, religious, upright, and to be so, but with a mind so framed that should you require not to be so, you may be able and know how to change to the opposite.

And you have to understand this, that a prince, especially a new one, cannot observe all those things for which men are esteemed, being often forced, in order to maintain the state, to act contrary to fidelity, friendship, humanity, and religion. Therefore it is necessary for him to have a mind ready to turn itself accordingly as the winds and variations of fortune force it, yet, as I have said above, not to diverge from the good if he can avoid doing so, but, if compelled, then to know how to set about it.

For this reason a prince ought to take care that he never lets anything slip from his lips that is not replete with the above-named five qualities, that he may appear to him who sees and hears him altogether merciful, faithful, humane, upright, and religious. There is nothing more necessary to appear to have than this last quality, inasmuch as men judge generally more by the eye than by the hand, because it belongs to everybody to see you, to few to come in touch with you. Every one sees what you appear to be, few really know what you are, and those few dare not oppose themselves to the opinion of the many, who have the majesty of the state to defend them; and in the actions of all men, and especially of princes, which it is not prudent to challenge, one judges by the result.

For that reason, let a prince have the credit of conquering and holding his state, the means will always be considered honest, and he will be praised by everybody; because the vulgar are always taken by what a thing seems to be and by what comes of it; and in the world there are only the vulgar, for the few find a place there only when the many have no ground to rest on.

One prince of the present time, whom it is not well to name, never preaches anything else but peace and good faith, and to both he is most hostile, and either, if he had kept it, would have deprived him of reputation and kingdom many a time.

CHAPTER 19

That one should avoid being despised and hated.

Now, concerning the characteristics of which mention is made above, I have spoken of the more important ones, the others I wish to discuss briefly under this generality, that the prince must consider, as has been in part said before, how to avoid those things which will make him hated or contemptible; and as often as he shall have succeeded he will have fulfilled his part, and he need not fear any danger in other reproaches.

It makes him hated above all things, as I have said, to be rapacious, and to be a violator of the property and women of his subjects, from both of which he must abstain. And when neither their property nor honour is touched, the majority of men live content, and he has only to contend with the ambition of a few, whom he can curb with ease in many ways.

It makes him contemptible to be considered fickle, frivolous, effeminate, mean-spirited, irresolute, from all of which a prince should guard himself as from a rock; and he should endeavour to show in his actions greatness, courage, gravity, and fortitude; and in his private dealings with his subjects let him show that his judgments are irrevocable, and maintain himself in such reputation that no one can hope either to deceive him or to get round him.

That prince is highly esteemed who conveys this impression of himself, and he who is highly esteemed is not easily conspired against; for, provided it is well known that he is an excellent man and revered by his people, he can only be attacked with difficulty. For this reason a prince ought to have two fears, one from within, on account of his subjects, the other from without, on account of external powers. From the latter he is defended by being well armed and having good allies, and if he is well armed he will have good friends, and affairs will always remain quiet within when they are quiet without, unless they should have been already disturbed by conspiracy; and even should affairs outside be disturbed, if he has carried out his preparations and has lived as I have said, as long as he does not despair, he will resist every attack, as I said Nabis the Spartan did.

But concerning his subjects, when affairs outside are disturbed he has only to fear that they will conspire secretly, from which a prince can easily secure himself by avoiding being hated and despised, and by keeping the people satisfied with him, which it is most necessary for him to accomplish, as I said above at length. And one of the most efficacious remedies that a prince can have against conspiracies is not to be hated and despised by the people, for he who conspires against a prince always expects to please them by his removal; but when the conspirator can only look forward to offending them, he will not have the courage to take such a course, for the difficulties that confront a conspirator are infinite. And as experience shows, many have been the conspiracies, but few have been successful; because he who conspires cannot act alone, nor can he take a companion except from those whom he believes to be malcontents, and as soon as you have opened your mind to a malcontent you have given him the material with which to content himself, for by denouncing you he can look for every advantage; so that, seeing the gain from this course to be assured, and seeing the other to be doubtful and full of dangers, he must be a very rare friend, or a thoroughly obstinate enemy of the prince, to keep faith with you.

And, to reduce the matter into a small compass, I say that, on the side of the conspirator, there is nothing but fear, jealousy, prospect of punishment to terrify him; but on the side of the prince there is the majesty of the principality, the laws, the protection of friends and the state to defend him; so that, adding to all these things the popular goodwill, it is impossible that any one should be so rash as to conspire. For whereas in general the conspirator has to fear before the execution of his plot, in this case he has also to fear the sequel to the crime; because on account of it he has the people for an enemy, and thus cannot hope for any escape.

Endless examples could be given on this subject, but I will be content with one, brought to pass within the memory of our fathers. Messer Annibale Bentivogli, who was prince in Bologna (grandfather of the present Annibale), having been murdered by the Canneschi, who had conspired against him, not one of his family survived but Messer Giovanni, who was in childhood: immediately after his assassination the people rose and murdered all the Canneschi. This sprung from the popular goodwill which the house of Bentivogli enjoyed in those days in Bologna; which was so great that, although none remained there after the death of Annibale who were able to rule the state, the Bolognese, having information that there was one of the Bentivogli family in Florence, who up to that time had been considered the son of a blacksmith, sent to Florence for him and gave him the government of their city, and it was ruled by him until Messer Giovanni came in due course to the government.

For this reason I consider that a prince ought to reckon conspiracies of little account when his people hold him in esteem; but when it is hostile to him, and bears hatred towards him, he ought to fear everything and everybody. And well-ordered states and wise princes have taken every care not to drive the nobles to desperation, and to keep the people satisfied and contented, for this is one of the most important objects a prince can have.

Among the best ordered and governed kingdoms of our times is France, and in it are found many good institutions on which depend the liberty and security of the king; of these the first is the parliament and its authority, because he who founded the kingdom, knowing the ambition of the nobility and their boldness, considered that a bit in their mouths would be necessary to hold them in; and, on the other side, knowing the hatred of the people, founded in fear, against the nobles, he wished to protect them, yet he was not anxious for this to be the particular care of the king; therefore, to take away the reproach which he would be liable to from the nobles for favouring the people, and from the people for favouring the nobles, he set up an arbiter, who should be one who could beat down the great and favour the lesser without reproach to the king. Neither could you have a better or a more prudent arrangement, or a greater source of security to the king and kingdom. From this one can draw another important conclusion, that princes ought to leave affairs of reproach to the management of others, and keep those of grace in their own hands. And further, I consider that a prince ought to cherish the nobles, but not so as to make himself hated by the people.

CHAPTER 22

Concerning the secretaries of princes.

The choice of servants is of no little importance to a prince, and they are good or not according to the discrimination of the prince. And the first opinion which one forms of a prince, and of his understanding, is by observing the men he has around him; and when they are capable and faithful he may always be considered wise, because he has known how to recognise the capable and to keep them faithful. But when they are otherwise one cannot form a good opinion of him, for the prime error which he made was in choosing them.

There were none who knew Messer Antonio da Venafro as the servant of Pandolfo Petrucci, Prince of Siena, who would not consider Pandolfo to be a very clever man in having Venafro for his servant. Because there are three classes of intellects: one which comprehends by itself; another which appreciates what others comprehend; and a third which neither comprehends by itself nor by the showing of others; the first is the most excellent, the second is good, the third is useless. Therefore, it follows necessarily that, if Pandolfo was not in the first rank, he was in the second, for whenever one has judgment to know good or bad when it is said and done, although he himself may not have the initiative, yet he can recognise the good and the bad in his servant, and the one he can praise and the other correct; thus the servant cannot hope to deceive him, and is kept honest.

But to enable a prince to form an opinion of his servant there is one test which never fails; when you see the servant thinking more of his own interests than of yours, and seeking inwardly his own profit in everything, such a man will never make a good servant, nor will you ever be able to trust him; because he who has the state of another in his hands ought never to think of himself, but always of his prince, and never pay any attention to matters in which the prince is not concerned.

On the other hand, to keep his servant honest the prince ought to study him, honouring him, enriching him, doing him kindnesses, sharing with him the honours and cares; and at the same time let him see that he cannot stand alone, so that many honours may not make him desire more, many riches make him wish for more, and that many cares may make him dread changes. When, therefore, servants, and princes towards servants, are thus disposed, they can trust each other, but when it is otherwise, the end will always be disastrous for either one or the other.

CHAPTER 23

How flatterers should be avoided.

I do not wish to leave out an important branch of this subject, for it is a danger from which princes are with difficulty preserved, unless they are very careful and discriminating. It is that of flatterers, of whom courts are full, because men are so self-complacent in their own affairs, and in a way so deceived in them, that they are preserved with difficulty from this pest, and if they wish to defend themselves they run the danger of falling into contempt. Because there is no other way of guarding oneself from flatterers except letting men understand that to tell you the truth does not offend you; but when every one may tell you the truth, respect for you abates.

Therefore a wise prince ought to hold a third course by choosing the wise men in his state, and giving to them only the liberty of speaking the truth to him, and then only of those things of which he inquires, and of none others; but he ought to question them upon everything, and listen to their opinions, and afterwards form his own conclusions. With these councillors, separately and collectively, he ought to carry himself in such a way that each of them should know that, the more freely he shall speak, the more he shall be preferred; outside of these, he should listen to no one, pursue the thing resolved on, and be steadfast in his resolutions. He who does otherwise is either overthrown by flatterers, or is so often changed by varying opinions that he falls into contempt.

I wish on this subject to adduce a modern example. Fra Luca, the man of affairs to Maximilian, the present emperor, speaking of his majesty, said: He consulted with no one, yet never got his own way in anything. This arose because of his following a practice the opposite to the above; for the emperor is a secretive man—he does not communicate his designs to any one, nor does he receive opinions on them. But as in carrying them into effect they become revealed and known, they are at once obstructed by those men whom he has around him, and he, being pliant, is diverted from them. Hence it follows that those things he does one day he undoes the next, and no one ever understands what he wishes or intends to do, and no one can rely on his resolutions.

A prince, therefore, ought always to take counsel, but only when he wishes and not when others wish; he ought rather to discourage every one from offering advice unless he asks it; but, however, he ought to be a constant inquirer, and afterwards a patient listener concerning the things of which he inquired; also, on learning that any one, on any consideration, has not told him the truth, he should let his anger be felt.

And if there are some who think that a prince who conveys an impression of his wisdom is not so through his own ability, but through the good advisers that he has around him, beyond doubt they are deceived, because this is an axiom which never fails: that a prince who is not wise himself will never take good advice, unless by chance he has yielded his affairs entirely to one person who happens to be a very prudent man. In this case indeed he may be well governed, but it would not be for long, because such a governor would in a short time take away his state from him.

But if a prince who is not experienced should take counsel from more than one he will never get united counsels, nor will he know how to unite them. Each of the counsellors will think of his own interests, and the prince will not know how to control them or to see through them. And they are not to be found otherwise, because men will always prove untrue to you unless they are kept honest by constraint. Therefore it must be inferred that good counsels, whencesoever they come, are born of the wisdom of the prince, and not the wisdom of the prince from good counsels.

CHAPTER 24

Why the princes of Italy have lost their states.

The previous suggestions, carefully observed, will enable a new prince to appear well established, and render him at once more secure and fixed in the state than if he had been long seated there. For the actions of a new prince are more narrowly observed than those of an hereditary one, and when they are seen to be able they gain more men and bind far tighter than ancient blood; because men are attracted more by the present than by the past, and when they find the present good they enjoy it and seek no further; they will also make the utmost defence for a prince if he fails them not in other things. Thus it will be a double glory to him to have established a new principality, and adorned and strengthened it with good laws, good arms, good allies, and with a good example; so will it be a double disgrace to him who, born a prince, shall lose his state by want of wisdom.

And if those seigniors are considered who have lost their states in Italy in our times, such as the King of Naples, the Duke of Milan, and others, there will be found in them, firstly, one common defect in regard to arms from the causes which have been discussed at length; in the next place, some one of them will be seen, either to have had the people hostile, or if he has had the people friendly, he has not known how to secure the nobles. In the absence of these defects states that have power enough to keep an army in the field cannot be lost.

Philip of Macedon, not the father of Alexander the Great, but he who was conquered by Titus Quintius, had not much territory compared to the greatness of the Romans and of Greece who attacked him, yet being a warlike man who knew how to attract the people and secure the nobles, he sustained the war against his enemies for many years, and if in the end he lost the dominion of some cities, nevertheless he retained the kingdom.

Therefore, do not let our princes accuse fortune for the loss of their principalities after so many years' possession, but rather their own sloth, because in quiet times they never thought there could be a change (it is a common defect in man not to make any provision in the calm against the tempest), and when afterwards the bad times came they thought of flight and not of defending themselves, and they hoped that the people, disgusted with the insolence of the conquerors, would recall them. This course, when others fail, may be good, but it is very bad to have neglected all other expedients for that, since you would never wish to fall because you trusted to be able to find some one later on to restore you. This again either does not happen, or, if it does, it will not be for your security, because that deliverance is of no avail which does not depend upon yourself; those only are reliable, certain, and durable that depend on yourself and your valour.

CHAPTER 25

**What fortune can effect in human affairs, and
how to withstand her.**

It is not unknown to me how many men have had, and still have, the opinion that the affairs of the world are in such wise governed by fortune and by God that men with their wisdom cannot direct them and that no one can even help them; and because of this they would have us believe that it is not necessary to labour much in affairs, but to let chance govern them. This opinion has been more credited in our times because of the great changes in affairs which have been seen, and may still be seen, every day, beyond all human conjecture. Sometimes pondering over this, I am in some degree inclined to their opinion. Nevertheless, not to extinguish our free will, I hold it to be true that fortune is the arbiter of one half of our actions, but that she still leaves us to direct the other half, or perhaps a little less.

I compare her to one of those raging rivers, which when in flood overflows the plains, sweeping away trees and buildings, bearing away the soil from place to place; everything flies before it, all yield to its violence, without being able in any way to withstand it; and yet, though its nature be such, it does not follow therefore that men, when the weather becomes fair, shall not make provision, both with defences and barriers, in such a manner that, rising again, the waters may pass away by canal, and their force be neither so unrestrained nor so dangerous. So it happens with fortune, who shows her power where valour has not prepared to resist her, and thither she turns her forces where she knows that barriers and defences have not been raised to constrain her.

And if you will consider Italy, which is the seat of these changes, and which has given to them their impulse, you will see it to be an open country without barriers and without any defence. For if it had been defended by proper valour, as are Germany, Spain, and France, either this invasion would not have made the great changes it has made or it would not have come at all. And this I consider enough to say concerning resistance to fortune in general.

But confining myself more to the particular, I say that a prince may be seen happy to-day and ruined to-morrow without having shown any change of disposition or character. This, I believe, arises firstly from causes that have already been discussed at length, namely, that the prince who relies entirely upon fortune is lost when it changes. I believe also that he will be successful who directs his actions according to the spirit of the times, and that he whose actions do not accord with the times will not be successful. Because men are seen, in affairs that lead to the end which every man has before him, namely, glory and riches, to get there by various methods; one with caution, another with haste; one by force, another by skill; one by patience, another by its opposite; and each one succeeds in reaching the goal by a different method. One can also see of two cautious men the one attain his end, the other fail; and similarly, two men by different observances are equally successful, the one being cautious, the other impetuous; all this arises from nothing else than whether or not they conform in their methods to the spirit of the times. This follows from what I have said, that two men working differently bring about the same effect, and of two working similarly, one attains his object and the other does not.

Changes in estate also issue from this, for if, to one who governs himself with caution and patience, times and affairs converge in such a way that his administration is successful, his fortune is made; but if times and affairs change, he is ruined if he does not change his course of action. But a man is not often found sufficiently circumspect to know how to accommodate himself to the change, both because he cannot deviate from what nature inclines him to, and also because, having always prospered by acting in one way, he cannot be persuaded that it is well to leave it; and, therefore, the cautious man, when it is time to turn adventurous, does not know how to do it, hence he is ruined; but had he changed his conduct with the times fortune would not have changed.

Pope Julius the Second went to work impetuously in all his affairs, and found the times and circumstances conform so well to that line of action that he always met with success. Consider his first enterprise against Bologna, Messer Giovanni Bentivogli being still alive: The Venetians were not agreeable to it, nor was the King of Spain, and he had the enterprise still under discussion with the King of France: nevertheless he personally entered upon the expedition with his accustomed boldness and energy, a move which made Spain and the Venetians stand irresolute and passive, the latter from fear, the former from desire to recover all the kingdom of Naples; on the other hand, he drew after him the King of France, because that king, having observed the movement, and desiring to make the Pope his friend so as to humble the Venetians, found it impossible to refuse him soldiers without manifestly offending him. Therefore Julius with his impetuous action accomplished what no other pontiff with simple human wisdom could have done; for if he had waited in Rome until he could get away, with his plans arranged and everything fixed, as any other pontiff would have done, he would never have succeeded. Because the King of France would have made a thousand excuses, and the others would have raised a thousand fears.

I will leave his other actions alone, as they were all alike, and they all succeeded, for the shortness of his life did not let him experience the contrary; but if circumstances had arisen which required him to go cautiously, his ruin would have followed, because he would never have deviated from those ways to which nature inclined him.

I conclude therefore that, fortune being changeful and mankind steadfast in their ways, so long as the two are in agreement men are successful, but unsuccessful when they fall out. For my part I consider that it is better to be adventurous than cautious, because fortune is a woman, and if you wish to keep her under it is necessary to beat and ill-use her; and it is seen that she allows herself to be mastered by the adventurous rather than by those who go to work more coldly. She is, therefore, always, woman-like, a lover of young men, because they are less cautious, more violent, and with more audacity command her.

CHAPTER 26
An exhortation to liberate Italy from the barbarians.

Having carefully considered the subject of the above discourses, and wondering within myself whether the present times were propitious to a new prince, and whether there were the elements that would give an opportunity to a wise and virtuous one to introduce a new order of things which would do honour to him and good to the people of this country, it appears to me that so many things concur to favour a new prince that I never knew a time more fit than the present.

And if, as I said, it was necessary that the people of Israel should be captive so as to make manifest the ability of Moses; that the Persians should be oppressed by the Medes so as to discover the greatness of the soul of Cyrus; and that the Athenians should be dispersed to illustrate the capabilities of Theseus: then at the present time, in order to discover the virtue of an Italian spirit, it was necessary that Italy should be reduced to the extremity she is now in, that she should be more enslaved than the Hebrews, more oppressed than the Persians, more scattered than the Athenians; without head, without order, beaten, despoiled, torn, overrun; and to have endured every kind of desolation.

Although lately some spark may have been shown by one, which made us think he was ordained by God for our redemption, nevertheless it was afterwards seen, in the height of his career, that fortune rejected him; so that Italy, left as without life, waits for him who shall yet heal her wounds and put an end to the ravaging and plundering of Lombardy, to the swindling and taxing of the Kingdom and of Tuscany, and cleanse those sores that for long have festered. It is seen how she entreats God to send some one who shall deliver her from these wrongs and barbarous insolencies. It is seen also that she is ready and willing to follow a banner if only some one will raise it.

Nor is there to be seen at present one in whom she can place more hope than in your illustrious house, with its valour and fortune, favoured by God and by the Church of which it is now the chief, and which could be made the head of this redemption. This will not be difficult if you will recall to yourself the actions and lives of the men I have named. And although they were great and wonderful men, yet they were men, and each one of them had no more opportunity than the present offers, for their enterprises were neither more just nor easier than this, nor was God more their friend than He is yours.

With us there is great justice, because that war is just which is necessary, and arms are hallowed when there is no other hope but in them. Here there is the greatest willingness, and where the willingness is great the difficulties cannot be great if you will only follow those men to whom I have directed your attention. Further than this, how extraordinarily the ways of God have been manifested beyond example: the sea is divided, a cloud has led the way, the rock has poured forth water, it has rained manna, everything has contributed to your greatness; you ought to do the rest. God is not willing to do everything, and thus take away our free will and that share of glory which belongs to us.

And it is not to be wondered at if none of the above-named Italians have been able to accomplish all that is expected from your illustrious house; and if in so many revolutions in Italy, and in so many campaigns, it has always appeared as if military virtue were exhausted, this has happened because the old order of things was not good, and none of us have known how to find a new one. And nothing honours a man more than to establish new laws and new ordinances when he himself has newly risen. Such things when they are well founded and dignified will make him revered and admired, and in Italy there are not wanting opportunities to bring such into use in every form.

Here there is great valour in the limbs whilst it fails in the head. Look attentively at the duels and the hand-to-hand combats, how superior the Italians are in strength, dexterity, and subtlety. But when it comes to armies they do not bear comparison, and this springs entirely from the insufficiency of the leaders, since those who are capable are not obedient, and each one seems to himself to know, there having never been any one so distinguished above the rest, either by valour or fortune, that others would yield to him. Hence it is that for so long a time, and during so much fighting in the past twenty years, whenever there has been an army wholly Italian, it has always given a poor account of itself; the first witness to this is Il Taro, afterwards Alexandria, Capua, Genoa, Vaila, Bologna, Mestri.

If, therefore, your illustrious house wishes to follow those remarkable men who have redeemed their country, it is necessary before all things, as a true foundation for every enterprise, to be provided with your own forces, because there can be no more faithful, truer, or better soldiers. And although singly they are good, altogether they will be much better when they find themselves commanded by their prince, honoured by him, and maintained at his expense. Therefore it is necessary to be prepared with such arms, so that you can be defended against foreigners by Italian valour.

And although Swiss and Spanish infantry may be considered very formidable, nevertheless there is a defect in both, by reason of which a third order would not only be able to oppose them, but might be relied upon to overthrow them. For the Spaniards cannot resist cavalry, and the Switzers are afraid of infantry whenever they encounter them in close combat. Owing to this, as has been and may again be seen, the Spaniards are unable to resist French cavalry, and the Switzers are overthrown by Spanish infantry. And although a complete proof of this latter cannot be shown, nevertheless there was some evidence of it at the battle of Ravenna, when the Spanish infantry were confronted by German battalions, who follow the same tactics as the Swiss; when the Spaniards, by agility of body and with the aid of their shields, got in under the pikes of the Germans and stood out of danger, able to attack, while the Germans stood helpless, and, if the cavalry had not dashed up, all would have been over with them. It is possible, therefore, knowing the defects of both these infantries, to invent a new one, which will resist cavalry and not be afraid of infantry; this need not create a new order of arms, but a variation upon the old. And these are the kind of improvements which confer reputation and power upon a new prince.

This opportunity, therefore, ought not to be allowed to pass for letting Italy at last see her liberator appear. Nor can one express the love with which he would be received in all those provinces which have suffered so much from these foreign scourings, with what thirst for revenge, with what stubborn faith, with what devotion, with what tears. What door would be closed to him? Who would refuse obedience to him? What envy would hinder him? What Italian would refuse him homage? To all of us this barbarous dominion stinks. Let, therefore, your illustrious house take up this charge with that courage and hope with which all just enterprises are undertaken, so that under its standard our native country may be ennobled, and under its auspices may be verified that saying of Petrarch:

> Virtù contro al Furore
> Prenderà l'arme, e fia il combatter corto:
>   Che l'antico valore
> Negli italici cuor non è ancor morto.

A STUDY GUIDE TO MACHIAVELLI'S THOUGHT

1. In what sense is Machiavelli an idealist?
2. What is the sentiment expressed in "Tercets on Ambition"?
3. How can Machiavelli's republicanism be reconciled with his *Prince*?

4. What are Machiavelli's principles of historical interpretation?

5. Why should men study history?

6. What effect does fortune have on men?

7. Can men have any effect on fortune?

8. Is a principate always more desirable than a republic?

9. Why is reform necessary?

10. Is the service of a prince always required?

11. Why does Machiavelli disapprove of the mercenary system?

12. Does the last chapter of Machiavelli's *Prince* belong with the rest of the work?

13. Was Machiavelli really a good observer of human nature?

14. Who are some of the historical figures upon whom he bases his model of a prince?

15. What are some of the principles a successful prince must follow?

16. Do you approve of Machiavelli's philosophy?

5

MODERN COMMENTARY ON DANTE

Etienne Gilson

To be sure, the ideological framework of the *Divine Comedy* explains neither its origination nor its beauty, but it is there, and it alone enables us to understand the poem's contents. Virgil holds sway in Limbo over the poets and Aristotle over the philosophers, but Boniface VIII has a place all prepared for him in Hell, while Manfred, who died excommunicate, waits patiently in Purgatory for his daughter's prayers to shorten the years that still stand between him and the sight of God. The fact is, as Villani said, that this Manfred was "an enemy of Holy Church, of clerics and of monks, seizing the churches as his father did before him". His crimes and those of Boniface VIII have no common measure: the one relieved the Church of possessions to which it had no right, and so he could be exonerated; but the other had attempted to violate the majesty of the Empire: hence it was impossible to save him. The same laws of the same Dantesque universe explain Siger's proximity to Thomas Aquinas, or rather they demand it, since Dante's allocation of authority makes it necessary. Everything encourages us to attribute to him the fundamental convictions that we have mentioned, for they are the convictions that animate the whole of his work. The *Convivio* having restored in its entirety the moral authority of the Philosopher over the Emperor, the *Monarchy* having restored in its entirety the political authority of the Emperor over the Popes, the *Divine Comedy* provides a fresh reminder of the rights and duties of all, but here Dante is no longer content, as in his previous works, with founding them in law on the absolute notion of divine justice; by the magic of his art he actually

Source: Etienne Gilson, *Dante and Philosophy*, pp. 278–281. Copyright, 1949, Sheed & Ward, Inc., New York. Reprinted with permission of the author and the publisher.

shows the movements of this Justice—the eternal custodian of the laws of the world, which it preserves in the form in which it created it. For it is certainly this Justice that beatifies the just with its love, as it crushes the unjust beneath its wrath. If it is only too true that in the poem it does not always seem to us equitable in its judgments the reason is that this divine Justice is, after all, merely Dante's conception of justice, but we are concerned rather with understanding the work and its author than with judging them.

If the essence of these conclusions should by right be regarded as true, Dante's general attitude towards philosophy would be less that of a philosopher anxious to cultivate it for its own sake than that of a judge desirous of rendering it its due, so as to obtain from it the contribution which ethics and politics are entitled to expect it to make to the great cause of temporal human happiness. Here, therefore, as in all his speculative work, Dante adopts the attitude of a defender of the public weal. His special function is not to promote philosophy, nor to teach theology, nor to demonstrate the working of the Empire, but to inspire these fundamental authorities once more with the mutual respect which their divine origin exacts from them. Whenever any one of them, out of greed, exceeds the limits imposed by God on its domain, it enters a state of revolt against an authority no less sacred than itself, an authority whose jurisdiction it usurps. This is the commonest and most pernicious crime committed against justice, which is the most human and the best loved of the virtues, even as injustice in all its forms—treason, ingratitude, treachery, theft, fraud and peculation—is the most inhuman and the most hateful.

Understood in this sense, the virtue of Justice signifies in Dante above all fidelity to the great authorities whose divine origin renders them sacred, injustice, on the contrary, consisting in every sort of betrayal of these authorities, which he himself never mentioned save in tones of submission: philosophy and its Philosopher, the Empire and its Emperor, the Church and its Pope. When he attacks—and how harshly he does so!—one of the representatives of these cardinal authorities, his sole object is to shield one of them against what he regards as a transgression on the part of its human representative. The savage freedom of his invective against the leaders springs from his love for the great spiritual realities which he accuses them of undermining through failure to respect their limits, since each of these realities destroys itself by usurping the power of another no less than it destroys that power by usurping it. We may certainly argue about the actual idea that Dante formed of these dominant authorities and of their respective spheres of influence, but once this idea has been accepted we are no longer justified in mistaking the nature of the feeling by which he was actuated. Those who accuse him of pride misinterpret his outbursts of invective, for his violence is indicative of a passionate submission that demands of others a like willingness to submit. His verdict descends on the adversary not from a pinnacle of self-aggrandisement, but from that pinnacle to which he raises his three great ideals. We offend him only if we offend them. The torment of this great spirit was to be ceaselessly in conflict with what he loved most in the world in consequence of his very longing to serve it; his enemies were Popes who betray the Church and Emperors who betray the Empire. It is in response to this stimulus that Dante's invective is unleashed to smite traitors, for in this universe in which the gravest of evils is injustice, the gravest injustice is treachery, and the gravest treachery of all is not betrayal of a benefactor, but betrayal of a leader. Every betrayal of this kind shakes the fabric of the world in that it shakes the authorities on which God Himself wills that it should be founded and which, together with order, ensure its unity and peace. The foulest denizen of the depths of Dante's hell is Lucifer, who has betrayed his Maker, and the three arch-criminals whose eternal chastisement Lucifer ensures are also the arch-traitors: Judas Iscariot, the betrayer of God, and Cassius and Brutus, the betrayers of Caesar. How can we mistake the implications of this terrible symbolism? It is most certainly a greater crime to betray the majesty of God than to betray the majesty of the Emperor, but it is the same class of offence, and in either case it is the crime of crimes: the betrayal of majesty.

In thus making sure what it is that Dante despises more than anything else in the world, we learn what he esteems above all things: loyalty to the powers established by God. This has been too often forgotten by expositors of his works, especially when their philosophical, theological and political content has been involved. It is idle to attempt to identify the single master whose disciple he is supposed to have been. Dante cannot be regarded as having less than three simultaneously. In fact, in a given sphere, he submits always to the supreme authority in that sphere: to Virgil in poetry, to Ptolemy in astronomy, to Aristotle in philosophy, to St. Dominic in speculative theology, to St. Francis in affective theology and to St. Bernard in mystical theology. Many others could be found answering to the description of guides. It matters little to him who the man is, provided that in every case he is sure of following the greatest. Such is the chosen system to which the only truly authentic Dante seems always to have adhered. If, as is asserted, a "unifying vision" of his work exists, it cannot be identified with any philosophy, or with a political cause, or even with a theology. We shall find it rather in his peculiarly personal conception of the virtue of justice and of the allegiances which that virtue exacts. Dante's work does not constitute a system, but is the dialectical and lyrical expression of all his loyalties.

Joseph A. Mazzeo

Thus the hierarchies of being, truth, beauty, perfection, indeed of all value, are reduced to a hierarchy of light ascending to the very Primal Light itself, spiritual, uncreated, divine, the vision of which is the vision of all. The doctrines we have considered are the bare bones of the most important part of Dante's universe. The flesh and substance are the *Paradiso*, to which we now turn.

While the *Inferno* and *Purgatorio*, in their respective ways, are concerned with the correction of moral error, the *Paradiso* as a journey through the intelligible universe celebrates truth and involves the correction of intellectual error. Here Dante rectifies his mistakes of thought and knowledge on such questions as the ordering of the celestial hierarchy, the origin of the spots on the moon, and the language of Adam. The *Paradiso* is thus philosophical poetry, both in the obvious meaning and in the most exact sense of this term. It solves the problem of rendering a systematically ordered world of pure thought in terms of images. To the extent that the *Inferno* and *Purgatorio* deal with virtue, they bear on the ethical realm and are dramatic and psychological. Readers of the *Paradiso* are sometimes disappointed because it lacks those dramatic qualities which dominate the previous *cantiche* and which, we generally assume, are central to literature.

For Dante, however, the ethical realm and the life of conflict and choice prepare the way for a life of ideal emotional and intellectual activities. The ultimate objects of desire are not actions but states of mind and spirit—understanding, love, joy. The *Paradiso*, so to speak, evokes "a life beyond life," pure spontaneity which transcends morality and the ordinary forms of human experience. Hence comes its lyrical and evocative character, the subjective mode in which Dante describes this part of the universe. He is, in a way, the single character here, the only one still capable of surprise. What we feel about his experience at this stage of the journey we feel through the effect his various experiences have on him.

If the problem of the *Paradiso* was the reduction of objects of thought to objects of vision, how was this accomplished? First, the ladder of light constituted an ontological principle which ran through the whole of reality, from the sensible to the intelligible to God. Light metaphysics also unified and made continuous these two orders of reality, by positing light, in its various analogical forms, as the single strand running through the whole universe. To the various forms of light

SOURCE: Joseph A. Mazzeo, *Medieval Cultural Tradition in Dante's "Comedy,"* pp. 103–105, 113–118. Copyright © 1960 by Cornell University. Reprinted by permission of Cornell University Press.

corresponded various forms of apperception, both sense and thought being explained by the union of "inner and outer lights." There was thus no truly sharp cleavage in light metaphysics—at least for the imagination—between the realms of matter and spirit, sense and thought. Thought was not a world of pure colorless concepts, but one of even brighter light than the world of senses. Thus the intelligible world was supersensuous both in a privative and in a positive sense. Clearly, the solution to Dante's problem lay at hand in the concepts and images of the light-metaphysics tradition. He could shape the ladder of light— the ultimate principle of all value in the universe—to render his own universal vision in terms of shapes, grades, and kinds of light.

The second mode of rendering the celestial universe was to make the heavenly host *manifest* itself in space and time during the journey through the spheres. The *Paradiso's* imagery thus functions as symbolism since it refers to a higher reality than language can formulate. Dante's images, however, far from being arbitrary are drawn from the world of knowledge and observation; they mean what they say and simultaneously point to a reality which transcends them. Dante shapes light to build the universe of the *Paradiso*, but this light has the same properties and obeys the same laws as the light of the universe according to the knowledge of his time. His universe is thus simultaneously an imaginative creation and a world about which one might ask the same questions as one asks about the real world.

The eyes whose function it is to be lured by beauty discern it through its garment of light, the latter a reflection or incarnation of the immaterial, uncreated light that is God. Luminosity in matter is simply a defective manifestation of the same power as it exists detached from matter. Thus in canto a ray of immaterial light from the immaterial tenth heaven or Empyrean materializes itself at a point in the concave surface of the ninth sphere "which derives from this ray light and power." At this point time and space begin, as well as causality and natural law, for in the Empyrean "where God rules directly, natural law is of no effect." This light is the "lume" or "splendor of God" . . . . This power communicates existence and activity to the entire universe through the agency of the *primum mobile*, which, spinning within the Empyrean, transmits its *virtù* to all the lower spheres that it encloses and through them to all other beings . . . . Thus the unitary power and efficacy of the heaven of light are diffracted through the stars and planets, constituting a graded ladder of light as causal power. . . .

Clearly, light is here a function and correlate of love and therefore functions as beauty—indeed, it is the principle of beauty itself. The circular operation of the triad light-love-vision, or beauty-love-knowledge, is made clearer by St. Peter Damian. A divine light centers upon him, penetrating the light of which he is made. Its power, joined to his sight, so uplifts him that he is able to see the divine essence from which it comes. This light produces the joy with which he is aflame; the clearness of the flame matches the clarity of his sight . . . . The union of the "inner" lights of the faculties of apprehension with the "outer lights" constituting reality releases joy (*delectatio*), in the tradition of light metaphysics—a special application of the general scholastic principle that joy attends the union of a thing with that which befits it (*coniunctio convenientis cum convenienti*). Thus the wisest of men and the great contemplative expound a complementary doctrine. Increase of vision-knowledge results in an increase of love which in turn demands more and higher light. This circular process is characteristic of the ascent from heaven to heaven and ends only when the infinite eternal Light is reached.

The circularity of vision-love-light is adumbrated early . . . when Dante asks Beatrice whether unfulfilled vows can be compensated for by other means besides fulfillment, such as good works. Before answering, she increases in luminous beauty, a beauty which overpowers him. At the very start of canto 5 she explains her beauty, which blinded him, as a function of love and vision or truth. It is the flame of love, an "exterior light" which derives from the perfect and immediate vision of the Eternal Light, a vision which kindles love or, more precisely, is an amorous vision. Beatrice observes that she can already see in Dante's mind the implied "interior light," a shining of the eternal light of truth.

Dante here explains the activity of the beatified consciousness partly in terms of his own, partly in terms of Beatrice's, but (witness the souls of Solomon and Peter Damian) the process also takes place in each consciousness separately. Beatrice in effect tells us that Dante now shares more fully in the eternal light and is thus prepared for the reception of the truth she is about to divulge. As Nardi demonstrated, Dante's epistemology is Augustinian and posits some form of divine illumination as the actualizing principle in the process of knowledge. Beatrice concludes by explaining that the eternal light of truth is the true object of love and that any other becomes such only because the Eternal Light shines through it in its beauty. . . .

Happiness also manifests itself as light, and the brightness of a soul grows with increase of joy. Beatrice shines with greater splendor when she sees the Eternal Light of truth shining in Dante's mind . . . ; Justinian glows with joy when ready to impart a new truth to Dante . . . . As Beatrice's joy rises while she leads Dante closer and closer to ultimate reality, her beauty and luminosity increase with each ascent. But light here as everywhere in the *Paradiso* is no simple external sign of an inner state but is functional as the principle of truth, beauty, and being.

This circularity is, then, both a convenient metaphor and a structural rhythm permeating the *Paradiso*, at once the pattern of expanding consciousness and of ascent through the intelligible universe. The expanding spiral of growing awareness has a triadic structure, being constituted of moments of increasing light-beauty, followed by growth of love and knowledge and of a fresh desire which demands greater beauty. Each ascent is accompanied by an increase in knowledge and so leads toward God through the intelligible universe. We journey simultaneously through the ladder of love, the scale of being, and the hierarchy of all value rendered as light.

The virtuous triadic circularity of the *Paradiso* describes the way in which consciousness extends its range both *qualitatively* and quantitatively. It describes the progress of consciousness as the development of perception already known and as the successive introduction of new dimensions of insight not derivable from the preceding state. Each moment of Dante's "blindness" as he ascends from sphere to sphere is really the moment of superrational ecstasy which precedes conscious awareness of a new and higher level of reality; this sort of "blindness" comes from an excess of light.

But the *Paradiso* actually has a linear as well as a circular rhythm: these correspond to two simultaneous journeys, one through the sensible, the other through the intelligible, world. As the spirits of the blessed only manifest themselves in the universe of space and time but reside in the Empyrean, so the architecture of the intelligible universe is gradually revealed through its sensible analogue. Finally, with the acquisition of a new sense of vision, once the limits of the universe of space and time have been passed, all reality is simultaneously grasped in one flash. Dante's linear ascent frequently comes to life through the imagery of wings and of the arrow seeking its mark. It is interrupted as Dante, upon entering each sphere, is carried along for a time by its diurnal motion. Circularity—a "motion" proper to spiritual and incorruptible substances—manifests itself in the moment of transition from sphere to sphere primarily in Dante the pilgrim's consciousness and, upon completion of the journey, as the "motion" of his desire and will after they are "revolved by the Love that moves the sun and the other stars". . . .

The state of blessedness, in the very presence of God, is not identical with the activity of consciousness on the road to God. It is rather the activity at the journey's term. This state begins with grace which rectifies and makes good the will. A good will and grace constitute merit which determines the degree of vision or "sight" of God's essence. This sight, in its own right, awakens love. . . . The circularity which Solomon and Peter Damian describe, also ultimately a gift of grace, may be said to have a fourth phase as the presupposition of its triadic movement. However, the state, as distinct from the attainment of blessedness ends with the love which follows vision, for the angels and the blessed are completely filled with beatitude, and their vision is as complete as it can be. In the process of ascent, the emphasis is placed on love's demand for more light as beauty and knowledge, since vision is not yet complete and love must therefore demand and obtain more of the light which is beauty . . . .

This light is a reflection of the infinite, eternal light. It is divine goodness which reveals its beauty through its burning and sparkling . . . and the Primal Light irradiating the angels and eliciting their love . . . . Every lesser good is as a light from its ray, and more than any other it moves the mind to love . . . . It operates through all the lesser lights and beauties of creation, including Beatrice.

Beatrice's blinding supernatural beauty is but the light in which, like Peter Damian and the other saints, she is "embosomed," the light of which she is now made. Now that Beatrice has put off the corruptible body, that inner splendor shines in all its power. The incorruptible body she, along with Solomon and the other saints, will put on after the resurrection will be even more beautiful because it will have still more vision and its inner flame of love will shine yet brighter.

From the two sources of light, material and immaterial, there radiate being, actuality, excellence, blessedness, and the luminosity which is beauty itself. All, *pari passu*, constitute various hierarchical orders and are reducible to properties of the analogical forms of light. The ladders of light, being, love, knowledge, and beauty are all actually fused; this fusion permits Dante to ascend to God as poet, lover, philosopher, and mystic seer all at once. For each step in the ladder includes and transcends the qualities and perfections of the one below it until Perfection and Reality themselves are reached and found to be a "simple light," from whose virtuous radiation the entire universe is ultimately derived. The ladder of light and beauty is thus, in one way, the *scala Dei* par excellence, for if all the distinctions in reality are traceable to light, so Dante's distinctions in forms and modes of apprehension and appetition are reduced to a kind of *sui generis* unitary faculty which transcends and unifies sense and thought, love and knowledge, and is the faculty for perceiving this supersensuous immaterial light. Paradise contains no object of thought which is not at the same time an object of "sense," no object of love which is not fully an object of knowledge. To light, as the principle of All, corresponds this faculty as power of simultaneously grasping all (*totum simul*).

The light that is beauty motivates the ascent to "simple light" by engendering the desire which drives the soul to God. The light is ultimately the radiated light (*lume*) of God, His grace . . . . But light as motive power resides mediately in Beatrice's beautiful eyes which have lifted Dante from planet to planet through the heavens . . . . The beauty of her eyes comes into play especially as the poet mounts from sphere to sphere. The surge from the earthly paradise to the heavens begins when Beatrice fixes her eyes on the heavens and Dante fixes his own upon hers. They had previously both been looking at the sun together, she first and he imitating her.

Dante, in his reconstituted unfallen nature, can bear to contemplate the sun in all its splendor, along with Beatrice. Suddenly the sky is doubly bright, as if two suns were shining in it; Dante then fixes his eyes on Beatrice's; she, in turn, is looking heavenward . . . . Her aspect transforms, divinizes him, an indescribable experience the nature of which he suggests only by analogy with the story of Glaucus and allusion to St. Paul's experience . . . . Only after gazing on her eyes is he transhumanized and he hears the music of the spheres. Simultaneously he sees a further increase in light which arouses his desire to know the cause of his experience . . . .

The pattern here described repeats itself at every stage of the journey through the spheres: Beatrice looks toward a higher reality, Dante gazes into her eyes and, as light increases, reaches another sphere. At first she has to tell him that he is ascending; later, from any increase of light he gathers that he has reached a higher sphere. Such an increase of light is always accompanied by a growing desire or love and by a change in the "spiritual gravity" or natural love of the soul, which, free from sin, shoots off like a bolt of lightning toward its natural place. In the explanation which follows, Beatrice describes the doctrine of the *pondus amoris*, the internal principle of all things, corporeal and intellectual, prompting them to seek their proper place, moving to different ports over the great sea of being, each with a guiding instinct of its own . . . . As Glaucus became a sea-god, Dante, extending the image, intimates that he has become a god in the sea of being. Beatrice concludes by explaining that his natural motion upward is no miracle. It is as natural for him to rise as it is for fire to ascend to its sphere . . . .

The process of ascent is thus a version of the same virtuous circularity of Peter Damian's and Solomon's light-love-vision. Dante "sinks" himself in Beatrice's eyes which themselves are "sunk" in the vision of the Eternal Light. An increase of light is accompanied by an increase of love, which in turn demands more light. To clarify this process, let us examine the various moments of transition from star to star.

In ascending to the moon, Dante simply describes some aspects of the process later stated more emphatically. He fixes his eyes on Beatrice's and in an instant is carried to the lunar sphere by the "inborn and perpetual thirst for the godlike kingdom." He recalls her happiness and beauty and describes his entry into the body of the moon, still uncertain whether *he* is in his body. Weighing the possibility of the miraculous interpenetration of bodies, he likens the physical process of ascent to a ray of light passing through water without breaking it. The light of this sphere calls to mind a pearl and a diamond sparkling in the sun . . . .

George Santayana

Without passing beyond the sphere of learned criticism, I think we may say this: the various interpretations, in this matter, are not mutually exclusive. Symbolism and literalness, in Dante's time, and in his practice, are simultaneous. For instance, in any history of mediaeval philosophy you may read that a great subject of dispute in those days was the question whether universal terms or natures, such as man, or humanity, existed before the particulars, in the particulars, or after the particulars, by abstraction of what was common to them all. Now, this matter was undoubtedly much disputed about; but there is one comprehensive and orthodox solution, which represents the true mind of the age, above the peculiar hobbies or heresies of individuals. This solution is that universal terms or natures exist before the particulars, *and* in the particulars, *and* after the particulars: for God, before he made the world, knew how he intended to make it, and had eternally in his mind the notions of a perfect man, horse, etc., after which the particulars were to be modelled, or to which, in case of accident, they were to be restored, either by the healing and recuperative force of nature, or by the ministrations of grace. But universal terms or natures existed also *in* the particulars, since the particulars illustrated them, shared in them, and were what they were by virtue of that participation. Nevertheless, the universals existed also after the particulars: for the discursive mind of man, surveying the variety of natural things, could not help noticing and abstracting the common types that often recur in them; and this *ex post facto* idea, in the human mind, is a universal term also. To deny any of the three theories, and not to see their consistency, is to miss the mediaeval point of view, which, in every sense of the word, was Catholic.

Just such a solution seems to me natural in the case of Beatrice. We have it on independent documentary evidence that in Dante's time there actually lived in Florence a certain Bice Portinari; and there are many incidents in the *Vita Nuova* and in the *Commedia* which hardly admit of an allegorical interpretation; such as the death of Beatrice, and especially that of her father, on which occasion Dante writes a

SOURCE: George Santayana, *Three Philosophical Poets* (Cambridge, Mass.: Harvard University Press), pp. 93–99. Copyright, 1910, by Harvard University; renewed 1938 by George Santayana. Reprinted by permission of the publishers.

sympathetic poem. I can see no reason why this lady, as easily as any other person, should not have called forth the dreamful passion of our poet. That he had loved some one is certain. Most people have; and why should Dante, in particular, have found the language of love a natural veil for his philosophy, if the passion and the language of love had not been his mother-tongue? The language of love is no doubt usual in the allegories of mystics, and was current in the conventional poetry of Dante's time; but mystics themselves are commonly crossed or potential lovers; and the troubadours harped on the string of love simply because it was the most responsive string in their own natures, and that which could most easily be made to vibrate in their hearers. Dante was not less sensitive than the average man of his generation; and if he followed the fashion of minstrels and mystics, it was because he shared their disposition. The beautiful, the unapproachable, the divine, had passed before him in some visible form; it matters nothing whether this vision came once only, and in the shape of the actual Beatrice, or continuously, and in every shape through which a divine influence may seem to come to a poet. No one would deserve this name of poet—and who deserves it more than Dante?—if real sights and sounds never impressed him; and he would hardly deserve it either, if they impressed him only physically, and for what they are in themselves. His sensibility creates his ideal.

If to deny the existence of an historical Beatrice seems violent and gratuitous, it would be a much worse misunderstanding not to perceive that Beatrice is *also* a symbol. On one occasion, as we read in the *Vita Nuova*, Dante found himself, in a church, in the presence of Beatrice. His eyes were inevitably fixed upon her; but as he wished to conceal his profound passion from the gossiping crowd, he chose another lady, who happened to stand in the direct line of vision between him and Beatrice, and pretended to be gazing at her, in reality looking beyond her to Beatrice. This intervening lady, *la donna gentile*, became the screen to his true love. But his attentions to her were so assiduous that they were misinterpreted. Beatrice herself observed them, and thinking he was going too far and not with an honourable purpose, showed her displeasure by refusing to greet him as he passed. This sounds real and earthly enough: but what is our surprise when we read expressly, in the *Convito*, that the *donna gentile*, the screen to Dante's true love, is philosophy. If the *donna gentile* is philosophy, the *donna gentilissima*, Beatrice, must be something of the same sort, only nobler. She must be theology, and theology Beatrice undoubtedly is. Her very name is played upon, if not selected, to mean that she is what renders blessed, what shows the path of salvation.

Now the scene in the church becomes an allegory throughout. The young Dante, we are given to understand, was at heart a religious and devout soul, looking for the highest wisdom. But intervening between his human reason and revealed truth (which he really was in love with, and wished to win and to understand) he found philosophy or, as we should say, science. To science he gave his preliminary attention; so much so that the mysteries of theology were momentarily obscured in his mind; and his faith, to his great sorrow, refused to salute him as he passed. He had fallen into materialistic errors; he had interpreted the spots on the moon as if they could be due to physical, not to Socratic, causes; and his religious philosophy had lost its warmth, even if his religious faith had not actually been endangered. It is certain, then, that Beatrice, besides being a woman, was also a symbol.

But this is not the end. If Beatrice is a symbol for theology, theology itself is not final. It, too, is an avenue, an interpretation. The eyes of Beatrice reflect a supernal light. It is the ineffable vision of God, the beatific vision, that alone can make us happy and be the reason and the end of our loves and our pilgrimages.

A supreme ideal of peace and perfection which moves the lover, and which moves the sky, is more easily named than understood. In the last canto of the *Paradiso*, where Dante is attempting to describe the beatific vision, he says many times over that our notion of this ideal must be vague and inadequate. The value of the notion to a poet or a philosopher does not lie in what it contains positively, but in the attitude which it causes him to assume towards real experience. Or perhaps it would be better to say that to have an ideal does not mean so much to have any image in the fancy, any Utopia more or less articulate, but rather to take a consistent moral attitude towards all the things of this world, to judge and coordinate our interests, to establish a hierarchy of goods and evils, and to value events and persons, not by a casual personal impression or instinct, but according to their real nature and tendency. So understood, an ultimate ideal is no mere vision of the philosophical dreamer, but a powerful and passionate force in the poet and the orator. It is the voice of his love or hate, of his hope or sorrow, idealizing, challenging, or condemning the world.

It is here that the feverish sensibility of the young Dante stood him in good stead; it gave an unprecedented vigour and clearness to his moral vision; it made him the classic poet of hell and of heaven. At the same time, it helped to make him an upright judge, a terrible accuser, of the earth. Everything and everybody in his day and generation became to him, on account of his intense loyalty to his inward vision, an instance of divine graciousness or of devilish perversity. Doubtless this keenness of soul was not wholly due to the gift of loving, or to the discipline of love; it was due in part also to pride, to resentment, to theoretical prejudices. But figures like that of Francesca di Rimini and Manfred, and the light and rapture vibrating through the whole *Paradiso*, could hardly have been evoked by a merely irritated genius. The background and the starting-point of everything in Dante is the *intelletto d'amore*, the genius of love.

A STUDY GUIDE

1. According to Gilson, what is the significance of justice in the philosophy of Dante?

2. What does Mazzeo mean by "the cult of light" in Dante? How was this related to the idea of hierarchy?

3. What does Mazzeo mean by the circular and linear rhythms of Dante's *Comedy?*

4. According to Santayana, what is the meaning and significance of love in Dante's *Comedy?*

6

MODERN COMMENTARY ON MACHIAVELLI

J. W. Allen

In his preface to the *Discorsi* Machiavelli announced that he had resolved to start upon a road hitherto untravelled by anyone. What was it that he thought of himself as doing for the first time? We hold antiquity, he says, in great reverence; we study the law and the medicine of the ancients and their works of art; and yet no one goes to them for instruction in the arts of government and war. This is not due so much to our wretched education or to our apathy about things political, as to our failure to understand what we read in history and to see its practical value. Not Athens but Rome was, to Machiavelli, the eminently successful State of antiquity. The experience of the Romans could not but be rich in suggestion, alike as to the causes of success and of failure. We must study Roman history and see what profit can be made of it for our own use. So he called his book *Discourses upon Livy*. Actually there is not very much of Livy in it, and it seems clear that it was from Italy and not from Livy or Polybius, Plutarch or Cicero, Aristotle or Xenophon, that Machiavelli derived his main conceptions and conclusions.

But his own explanation of his image was inadequate. The road he was taking was, at least for the world outside Italy, even stranger than he seems to have thought it. He insisted upon the need of studying history because, for him, the experience of himself and of others, past or present, was the only guide. He was proposing to concern himself only with things as they actually are. He was not troubled by any doubts as to what that may mean. Man is the very stuff of politics and man's nature may be judged of by his conduct. In thinking of the State he would think only of actual States, past or present. For a thousand years and more men had been thinking of politics theologically and juristically. Machiavelli will do neither. "He takes the data of his own experience and checks the conclusions which he learns from

SOURCE: J. W. Allen, *History of Political Thought in the Sixteenth Century* (London: Methuen & Company, Ltd., 1960), pp. 451–456. Reprinted with permission of the publishers.

them by reference to certain canons derived from a study of history." That, in fact, is all he does. From knowledge of man as he is and always has been, from knowledge of the constitution of States as they are and have been, of their modes of action and good or evil fortunes, one can draw conclusions, valid and positive, as to the causes of political success and failure, as to the greatness and decline of States, as to the most efficient form of government, as to what makes for stability and what for disorder and ruin. What we need is positive knowledge of these things and this can only be arrived at by looking at things as they are, without fear or preconceptions. This is the only road to whatever we desire to attain. This is the new road of Machiavelli; and certainly it had not been trodden for a long time, except by Italians. In Italy it did not seem strange. Machiavelli's "realistic" mode of thought was only an extreme illustration of a tendency visible in Italian thought since the days of the last Hohenstaufen Emperor.

Machiavelli was not a systematic thinker. He was a man of extremely acute perceptions and capable of subtle and searching analysis of the concrete. Failure to co-ordinate his observations is conspicuous throughout the *Discorsi* and the *Principe* and shows itself in the confusion of their structure. He seems to have paid little or no attention to the implications of what he said. Consequently, in spite of his lucidity of statement, he falls easily into inconsistency. The elusive quality of his writing, which accounts for a good deal of the disagreement about him, arises, I think, from the fact that, in spite of the sharpness of his vision of the actual, his thought was at bottom confused.

Fundamental in his thought would seem to be his notion of the origin and purport of the sense of good and evil in action and his conception of the quality of man's will. The two are intimately connected, in the sense that the latter is unintelligible till the former is understood. At some early stage of human history, he informs us, men, considering that the injuries they saw done to others might be done to themselves, protected themselves by the establishment of laws, with penalties for their infringement, and hence arose the recognition of justice. From this establishment of government and legal justice "was born the knowledge of what things are good and honourable in distinction to those that are evil and shameful." Generalized notions of right and wrong, in fact, developed from the effort to repress forms of activity, recognized as dangerous to himself by every individual. In course of time, it is true, men came to think of certain kinds of action as good or evil absolutely. But this, it is implied, is a delusion, due either to confusion of mind or to religious superstition. There is no absolute good. Goodness is simply that which subserves, on the average or in the long run, the interests of the mass of individuals. The terms good and evil have no transcendental reference; they refer to the community, considered as an association of individuals, and to nothing else. At bottom, ap-

parently, they refer only to the universal desire for security. Such a
view involves, of course, an absolute denial of the validity of the conception of natural law. For Machiavelli there was no *lex aeterna* and
therefore no *lex naturalis*. He never even thought it worth while to refer
to that conception. There was nothing new, it must be remarked, in
his way of putting the matter. It was at least as old as the *Defensor Pacis*.
Yet Machiavelli himself does not seem to have had a clear grasp of the
implications of his own doctrine or even always to remember what he
had said. From this primary assertion of his, his view of morals in
politics can be derived quite simply. But that he himself understood it
so, is by no means clear. As I hope to show, in discussing his political
ethics, his language is not wholly consistent with that interpretation of
his meaning.

If we take Machiavelli to mean that "goodness" in action signifies
simply a tendency to promote the general welfare of the community,
then we can give definite meaning to his oft-repeated assertion that
men are radically bad. It is proved, he says, to demonstration, and all
history confirms it, that in ordering a State, this must always be assumed. Men will always show themselves wicked unless they are compelled to goodness. The ligament of obligation is a thing which, men
being the poor creatures they are, is broken upon every occasion for
their own personal profit. He means, apparently, that every man is
always ready to act in a manner detrimental to the community if he
sees any advantage to himself from doing so. Good is that which, in
my own interest, I wish my neighbour to do; but my neighbour and I,
in our own interest, are always ready to do evil. It would be difficult
to give any other meaning than this to Machiavelli's declaration that
all men are wicked. Man's will must be conceived as at bottom, anti-
social and anarchical: and it is this fact that constitutes the central
problem of politics and the difficulty of actual government.

Yet it cannot be said that Machiavelli held this view without quali-
fications; which, indeed, he himself supplies. Evidently he did not
think that man's will was wholly anarchical. Man, he thought, cares
for nothing but himself; he is a rascally, mean, greedy, sensual creature,
more ready to forgive the murder of his father than the seizure of his
property: gratitude for him is but the hope of benefits to come and what
he calls his love is but love of himself. But the selfish will is a will to
order and security and all men, therefore, may see the general interest
as their own. Man wills government and the State for his own profit
and protection. He is, furthermore, a timid creature and a creature of
habit. He dislikes what he is not used to and seeks the lines of least
resistance. He tends to follow well-beaten tracks. It is a fact of great
importance, practically, that it is generally easier and safer to conform
than to rebel.

Too much stress has sometimes been laid upon Machiavelli's

insistence on the predominance of the purely selfish will in man. He knew, even, that there were men, though certainly few, capable of labouring for the common benefit without regard to their personal interests. He even claimed to be one of them himself. But what is, in this connection, of the greatest importance, is the fact that man's capacity for developing public spirit to a point at which mere personal interests are wholly subordinated, is implied everywhere in the *Discorsi*. It was on just such a development that, in Machiavelli's view, the stability and the strength of the State depended. It is his own fault that he has been misread. So convinced was he that the ferocious egotism and egregious lack of public spirit prevalent in his Italy, was the main general cause of the land's weakness and disorder, that he was led to lay disproportionate stress on the selfishness of man. None the less is it true that he actually measures the strength of a State mainly by the amount of public spirit developed within it. It was, he thought, just such a development that had constituted the strength and ac-counted for the success of the great Roman Republic. There is, as usual in the *Discorsi*, a failure to state the matter fully; but there is, I think, no real inconsistency. Public spirit may be developed in a com-munity and so long as it lasts, and in the measure of it, a State is likely to be strong and flourishing. On the other hand, he insists that it is unlikely to last long. Everything tends to corruption: nothing lasts except the radical selfishness of man.

That was in the beginning and shall be as long as man lasts. It is a supposition of the greatest importance in Machiavelli's thought that the quality of man's will never changes. It remains constant through all time; it is, in fact, unalterable. It is true, Machiavelli admits, that in different parts of the world, the character of men to some extent differs. But he adds that men of the same region retain through all ages almost the same character. It is mainly upon this supposition that he bases his opinion of the practical value of history in teaching by examples. Owing to the constant character of humanity man's history tends constantly to repeat itself, with mere circumstantial differences.

> The judicious are wont to say that he who would foresee what is to happen should look to what has happened: for all that is has its counter-part in time past. This is so because all happenings are brought about by the will of man, whose desires and dispositions remaining in all ages the same, it follows that like results are produced continually.

Not only does human history tend to repeat itself but all States tend to move as it were on a circular track. The suggestion of this cycle would seem to have come from Polybius, but to Machiavelli it appeared that it must actually be a fact. He conceived it as resulting from the unchanging nature of man and from the special quality of his will acting under changing conditions. Action and reaction alternate and out of prosperity comes decay and out of dissolution rebirth. Every human institution, like every individual, has inherent defects which must eventually destroy it. But new growth follows. States normally commence as monarchies; but monarchy becomes tyrannical and is overthrown by a combination of magnates, who form an oligarchy. All goes well so long as the oligarchs are animated by public spirit. But degeneration follows inevitably. The oligarchs in their turn are overthrown and a popular government is established. Then liberty passes into license and so into anarchy; and the result of anarchy is a reversion to monarchy and the dreary round recommences. Machiavelli points out that the cycle is only rarely actually completed. At one of its moments of greatest weakness the State will probably be destroyed or conquered by aliens. Assuming this not to happen, it might hopelessly continue to infinity to turn on its circular course. In any case, men remaining always the same poor creatures, no real progress is possible.

The finally inevitable ruin that awaits all States seems to be conceived by Machiavelli as partly the result of another peculiarity of human nature. The appetite of man is for ever insatiable. By nature he desires all things, but fate allows him little. Man is eternally desirous and eternally unsatisfied, raging at the present, extolling the past, hoping in the future. No human community, no human government, any more than any single human being, is ever content with its position. Hence arises a constant effort after aggrandisement and domination which leads, sooner or later, to ruin. But this ruinous effort is unavoidable. It results partly from man's everlasting discontent and partly from the fact that conflict and war are necessary to the health of the body politic. War and fear are what give the State such vital unity as it has and counteract the anarchic tendency which is rooted in the nature of man's will. Peace is relaxing and disruptive: 'Damn braces, bless relaxes.' Under these circumstances, equilibrium is impossible, all human affairs being in perpetual motion and never remaining for an instant as they were. The movement of the State must needs be upward or downward. Hence, though the better its laws and the more intelligent its ruler, the more stable will be the State, there is yet no possible escape from ultimate ruin.

Herbert Butterfield

The thought of the Renaissance reaches at certain points an extraordinary emancipation from religious authority and medieval prepossessions; but it has curious features which seem to savour now of the

SOURCE: Herbert Butterfield, *The Statecraft of Machiavelli* (New York: The Macmillan Company, 1960), pp. 37–46. Reprinted with permission of the publishers.

occult and now of the archaic, and even when it is irreligious we must not be too ready to call it modern. To free oneself from the tyranny of the past or from the dominion of the written and spoken word is never easy. Even today it requires a great exertion, a genuine effort of will, if not always actual originality of mind. And the men of the Renaissance we must remember, the humanists in particular, did not wish to be so emancipated. To consult the classics on all matters, to imitate the ancient world, was indeed for them the great adventure—the source and secret of that intellectual exhilaration which was the glory of the Italy of this time. The Protestants, who pushed their reverence for the ancient Scriptures to that extreme which came to be described as Bibliolatry; the followers of Aristotle who, for over a century after this, resisted novel theories concerning the physical structure of the universe; the medical students who now despised medieval science and turned the Arabians into a by-word, because they had found a more direct route to ancient Greece; the humanists who so deprecated the use of the vernacular that they checked the brilliant course of Italian literature and made imitative Latin verses the fashion, and who attempted, by copying Cicero, to turn Latin into a dead language—the Latin which for centuries had been rough and alive, a handy means of international communication for scholars—all these are only extreme examples of what was in fact a general adoration of antiquity.

In their devotion to the ancient culture the men of the Renaissance were most like their medieval predecessors. Perhaps it is true to say that their subservience to the classics was even more complete. We must note that the idea of a progressive development taking place in the course of centuries—the world moving forward to an unimagined future, to wider horizons and opening vistas—is a modern one. The idea of history as an ascending process was not part of the equipment of a Renaissance mind. In any case such a view of history could not congenially combine with current assumptions concerning the tendency of all composite bodies to disintegrate. The self-conscious development of the sciences in the seventeenth century; the rising importance of a knowledge that grows by sheer accumulation and deepens as one man takes up the researches of his predecessors; the technical progress that comes to be achieved in finance and industry and organization; the cumulative results of inventions, discoveries, better communications, speedier interchange of thought—these are the factors that have helped men to believe in a future big with the promise of better things. It was not until the seventeenth century that the world finally faced the problem of the Ancients versus the Moderns. And perhaps we owe the currency of the idea of progress chiefly to the grand hopefulness and complacency of the French 'philosophic' movement. We to-day can see the results of a portentous speeding-up of those processes which cause mutation in society. Perhaps life and the world, and the general appearance of the country-side, change more quickly now in one generation than at one time they changed in the course of many centuries. It is more easy now than in the more static world of the sixteenth century to believe that apart from the ups and downs of cities and states, apart from variations in mere clothing and custom, there is process in history, something more than cycle and succession, something more than Rome replacing Greece. Machiavelli, like his contemporaries, naturally assumed that apart from superficial variations of an external character, the world throughout the ages remains substantially the same. In the Preface to Book II of the *Discourses* he writes:

> And when I meditate upon the workings of these matters, I come to the conclusion that the world always remains in very much the same condition. The good and the bad balance one another, but each varies from region to region, as anybody can see who pays attention to the kingdoms of antiquity; for though these might have differed in their customs, the world as a whole continued its course in much the same way. The only difference was that, whereas at one time this virtue was assembled in Assyria, it passed to Media, then to Persia, and then to Italy and Rome. And if since the Roman Empire there has been no enduring empire, and no place in which all the virtue was assembled at one time, that virtue is nevertheless scattered about amongst the many nations [not including the Italy of the Renaissance, we may note] in which life is meritoriously carried on.

Further than this, having no principle of progress, these men possessed and were bound to possess, the converse conception which regards history as normally a process of decline. According to the current belief, it was in the nature of compound bodies to disintegrate; and human societies and institutions were compound bodies in this sense. It is apparent in the work of Machiavelli—in the early part of the *Discourses*, for example—and in the thought of the age, that the ascent of states, the rise to prosperity and virtue, was regarded as something of a miracle, a wonderful over-riding of the normal working of things in nature; on the other hand decline was in the ordinary processes of time, only to be checked by unsleeping vigilance and extraordinary endeavour. A great lawgiver, a mighty act of volition, a stroke of fine fortune, might bring a state to a condition of greatness and power; by a grand intervention—a cataclysmic event—a decadent people might be restored to a condition of soundness and of public morality; but a degenerate people, ordinarily speaking, could not recover themselves again (any more than water could rise above its own level), as Machiavelli pointed out; and, even when greatness had been achieved, it was held that corruption soon set in, by an automatic process, if vigilance was relaxed for a moment and extraordinary energy was not continuously displayed.

So the men of the Renaissance believed in a closed culture, and did not imagine that civilization could be indefinitely expanding—continually producing new things. The boundaries of that culture had been reached in ancient Greece and Rome, and men could only revolve ancient things anew, could only hope to travel over the same ground and win the old truths back again, could only dream of equalling perhaps the achievements and the prowess of the ancient days. More strongly than the generations that preceded them they believed that since classical times the whole world had been wandering in darkness; and though when they said that wisdom lay in "antiquity," it might seem that they had in mind the prudence and the knowledge that come with the multitude of years, it did not occur to them to see that the world of Greece and Rome was on this view younger than theirs— that, as the centuries advance, mankind in fact gets older and wiser. It was a generation after the death of Machiavelli that Giordano Bruno in *La Cena de le Ceneri* thought it worth while to expose the current fallacy in regard to this matter:

> If you properly understood what you were saying you would see that from your principle there follows a conclusion which is exactly the contrary to the one you have in mind: I mean that it is we who are older and who have a greater multitude of years than our predecessors; at any rate as regards certain topics, like the one with which we are dealing at the moment [the Copernican theory]. The judgement of Eudoxus who lived shortly after the rebirth of astronomy (if the renaissance did not actually take place through him) could not be so mature as that of Callippus, who lived thirty years after the death of Alexander the Great; and who, as year succeeded year, could add observation to observation. Hipparchus for the same reason must have known more than Callippus. . . . More has been seen by Copernicus, almost in our day.

It is not too much to say that the thinkers of the Renaissance were undoubtedly right in the main general conclusion that they drew from their theory of history. From their point of view the classical world was the peak of civilization; and devotion to it had not yet become mere bondage for the scientific mind. Also, we may add that in many of their aspects the classics became, and long remained, one of the important constituents of the modern world. In any case English students should glance sympathetically even upon the prejudices of the Renaissance on the subject of the historical process; for these may be said to have become blended with our own fortunes and embedded in our political consciousness. When the Whigs emerged victorious in England towards the close of the seventeenth century, they did not stand out as the apostles of modernity and progress. Renaissance views on the processes of history were part of the make-up of their minds. The theory of decline which we are examining at the moment was part of the structure of their interpretation of history. Always the Golden Age would seem to have been behind them, if even occasionally one could only impute it to a dim and unspecified past. Always it was said that the Glorious Revolution "restored our constitution to its primitive vigour" and recovered the liberty that our ancestors had enjoyed. The Revolution indeed brought our government "back to its first principles" and reasserted the rightness of an ancient law. Furthermore, the Whigs who believed that liberty ever tends to decline unless men are constantly vigilant, that, if liberty is to be preserved in a new age, fresh laws and institutions must be devised to guard it against unforeseen dangers, that no laws can preserve liberty if the people themselves have become corrupted, saw the force of these maxims with special vividness because they were near to a view of history that stressed the tendency to decline. Into English Whiggism, in fact, passed the most benevolent of the maxims of Machiavelli himself; who had discussed the decay of liberty, the policies that would serve to arrest decline, and the whole problem of corruption in the state.

These ideas upon the classical world and the historical process are the background against which we must see the work of Machiavelli; and in the light of them it becomes the more remarkable that this man should have reproached his contemporaries for their indifference to the ancient world. In pursuing the cult of antiquity into the realm of statecraft and urging that imitation should be definite and detailed, he outstripped his generation; here he himself claimed to be unique and his contemporaries seem to have regarded him as such; and this we have seen was the very thing which he specified as the contribution that he had to make. Whereas the philosopher and scientist looked to ancient Greece, he, as a political teacher, put all his faith in republican Rome. The principal exposition of his statecraft is a commentary on Livy. His treatise on the *Art of War* is an essay on the imitation of the Romans. Perhaps the greatest effect of the isolated reading of *The Prince*, and the special notoriety that this book has enjoyed in so many generations, has been an underestimation of the strength of his devotion and the greatness of his debt to antiquity. For in *The Prince* his obligations to classical history and ancient writers are for the most part concealed; and the statecraft—though it is always the same statecraft—has been given a more topical bearing than in the other treatises. A generation ago a German writer, Ellinger, however, traced some of the classical borrowings in *The Prince* and many such borrowings are noted in Burd's edition. It will be seen below that Machiavelli's indebtedness to the Romans is not any less remarkable in this book than in the rest of his political writings.

In general Machiavelli's statements on the imitation of the Romans are remarkably specific, and unmistakable in their insistence:

> From all these considerations the true method appears to be the one which the Romans used, and it is all the more remarkable in that it has never been adopted by any other people before or since. . . . We might add by way of conclusion that many other rules which the Romans observed in conducting their affairs both at home and abroad are not only not imitated in these days but are treated with definite lack of consideration; some of them being looked upon as mere fables, others as impossible and others again as not appropriate or of no utility; and to this ignorant attitude we owe the fact that our country of late has been the prey of every invader who cared to come.
>
> *Disc. II 4.*

In the sixth chapter of the first book of the *Discourses,* he shows that in founding a state it is better to follow the Romans and establish the state for purposes of aggrandizement and not merely for long duration. It had already been suggested in the preceding chapter that "if the state be designed to extend its dominion . . . the conduct of the Romans must be imitated in every particular."

Machiavelli's argument for the adoption of his maxims is the assertion that by following them the Romans achieved their success and renown. The question as to which form of government he preferred is an easy one to answer both from his own statements and by inference from the principles he puts forward. He did not admire ancient Rome because the Romans had a republic; he admired republican government because it was the form under which ancient Rome had achieved unexampled greatness and power. He admired Switzerland, and feared her designs on Italy, and was once reproved for suggesting that she would "do what the ancient Romans had done"; and this was because from ancient Rome he had gained a high opinion of what he called "armed republics" and considered Switzerland to stand in this class. And there is no contradiction when Machiavelli tells us in one place that a mixed form of government—a combination of monarchy, aristocracy, and democracy—is best; for he had learned from ancient writers to consider republican Rome in this very light, stressing the combination of consuls, senate, and plebs. One might have inferred from Machiavelli's beliefs on the subject of history and fortune that if a race like the Romans had existed as an example of happy achievement and public well-being, he would have opposed the view which tended to ascribe this success to good fortune and combinations of circumstances; he would have preferred to attribute it to virtue and good policy which he would enjoin future generations to copy. This is what actually happens in the *Discourses* though Machiavelli has to differ from both Plutarch and Livy on the point.

HERBERT BUTTERFIELD **215**

His imitation of the ancients implied the acceptance of their precepts as well as their practice, and in particular the acceptance of many of the maxims or historical comments of ancient writers. Those who like to think that he merely pretended to possess the authority of ancient examples, which he did not use save as cover for policies of his own, cannot deny that he followed ancient precepts even in numerous cases where he did not pretend to be doing so at all. *The Prince* itself, which has such close relations with Machiavelli's period of active political service, contains a remarkable assortment of quotations, imitations, paraphrases, or variations of the teaching of antiquity. The very idea of the "new prince" as the founder of a new state and a new condition of things is based upon classical writers; and the application of this idea to the special purpose of the amelioration of the condition of Italy has been ascribed to the influence of Xenophon's *Hiero*. This book, which Machiavelli had certainly read, and which he called by the title *De Tyrannide*, dealt with the situation and problems of a new prince who had gained power in a state that had hitherto been free; and it influenced *The Prince* in a number of details if not in the general lines of the theme. The dedication to *The Prince* opens with a passage which we are told is modelled upon Isocrates, and the final chapter exhorting the new prince to deliver Italy from the barbarians has resemblances to Isocrates' exhortation to Philip, though the direct connection has in this later case been disputed. The dictum that the prince must imitate the fox and the lion; the recurring suggestion that conquests can be maintained if only the family of the dispossessed ruler is wiped out; the view that the prince can avoid hatred if he does not usurp the property and the women of his subjects; the claim that a prince should have no other aim or thought or preoccupation but war —all these and many others too numerous to mention have been shown to be close reproductions of the opinions of ancient writers.

Finally the very method by which Machiavelli proposed to discover statecraft from the examples of history, and all the principles upon which his "lessons of history" were based—the doctrine of imitation, the view that human nature is constant, the idea that history runs in cycles and that similar situations and problems recur—all are a heritage from the ancient world, a further proof of his discipleship. And I do not think we realize how often even when Machiavelli seems to be inductive, seems to be describing the contemporary world, he is really only making deductions from classical theses concerning human nature or the historical process . . . . We must not regard his statecraft in the first place as the result of observation of the contemporary world. It is rather Guicciardini who is the modern observer standing already in the clear light of day. Machiavelli is that other kind of person who can be so troublesome to the practising politician—the assured and insistent historian, the dogmatic disciple of the ancient ways. And he created his science of statecraft only because he was less modern than Guicciardini—entering more fully and with an almost medieval rigidity into the Renaissance cult and imitation of ancient Rome.

Federico Chabod

The primordial, ultimate character of this world—devoid of great moral and political motifs, uninfluenced by the masses, having its being solely in the isolated virtue of scattered individuals, who left their own imprint on material that was flabby and incoherent—finds its true expression in *The Prince*. The latter is not exactly a history of the Seigniories and Principates, if by history we mean the detailed examination and the minute and constant assessment of specific events. Rather does it summarize and illustrate the consequences of history, revealing them in broad outline, stripped of all irrelevancy. Naturally, it does not go into details—Machiavelli is not at all concerned now with writing history—and these must be sought elsewhere, just as we have to look elsewhere for a precise, factual account of the course which Italian life pursued in the fourteenth and fifteenth centuries. Here we have merely the fundamental principle which determines and informs the various immediate manifestations of that life—a principle that is at the same time a consequence.

But Machiavelli, with that powerful creative imagination of his, manages to escape from the realm of mere diplomacy, to which Guicciardini, on the other hand, will confine himself exclusively. He sees beyond the Court events of the last fifty years and, by a wonderful intellectual effort which remained incomprehensible to his contemporaries and caused him to be described as "extravagant to a degree in his opinions and a discoverer of new and unusual things," succeeds in re-creating the possibility of a great political struggle.

Just as the expansion of the seigniorial State had not been accompanied by a corresponding increase of political virtue, so he too deals only in superficialities; but at least that is something. The grandiose ideal which the Visconti had sought to realize—the establishment of a unitarian State in the Po valley—recurs in Machiavelli as an intellectual concept. Indeed, its realization becomes a certainty; it is seen as the object of a faith that reveals all the passion in the writer's soul—for his discretion and composure are not always sufficient for him to con-

SOURCE: Federico Chabod, *Machiavelli and the Renaissance* (Cambridge, Mass.: Harvard University Press), pp. 61–70. Copyright, 1958, by Federico Chabod. Reprinted by permission of Harvard University Press and Bowes & Bowes Publishers, Ltd., London.

ceal the true nature of his feelings. Not for him the cut-and-thrust of diplomacy, the ebb and flow of negotiations in which the point of equilibrium is sought through the shrewd assessment of possibilities, but rather the clear, positive affirmation of a system which, while availing itself to the maximum degree of the arts of government, human speculation, and back-room intrigue, aims not at a balance of forces but at its own undisputed supremacy. Such are Machiavelli's guiding principles; and in this way he abandons the limited aims of the Italic confederation and of Lorenzo de' Medici and goes back to Gian Galeazzo Visconti and Ladislao of Naples.

Accordingly, he will reject neutrality as being the most pernicious of doctrines, and will refer to the Italian political equilibrium of former years as a mistake that should be rectified and consigned to oblivion.

Such is the origin of the treatise *De Principatibus*, in which political strife, in its most blatant connotation of a struggle for victory and power, is reduced to a schematic form; but experience brings with it a new vigour, which, accepting the basic principle, seeks to carry it out in the surest way possible, and so exposes the uncertainties and mistakes of the past.

There could be no doubt as to the correct ways of putting the idea into practice. In the complete absence of any collective force by which the new edifice could be supported, and assuming, as Machiavelli did, that the virtue of the Prince was to be the supreme controlling factor of life, it was essential to follow the paths already trodden by man, through whom the revival must be brought about. Hence the minute, cold, incisive analysis, centring round the figure of the presumed ruler; hence, too, the careful examination of the position in which the latter would find himself in relation to his subjects and to foreigners. The details necessarily preserve that personal quality which characterizes the points of departure and arrival.

And just as for two hundred years of her history Italy had been dominated by the figures of the great Seigneurs, who were unsustained by the power of tradition or of any myth, so in the treatise the thing that serves to illuminate the general background of events, even if the latter are not determined solely by an individual, is the character of the Prince, all sinew and thought, cold and impenetrable, like one of those fine suits of armour made of delicately-wrought steel in which warriors used to encase themselves before a battle: the *new* Prince, sustained not by the memory of his ancestors, not by the recollection of long years of suffering shared with his people, but solely by his own wit and strength of will, his warlike prowess and diplomatic wisdom. Men are more "beholden" to virtuous actions than to "ancient blood."

The people, who bring the first book of the *Discorsi* to life and condition its thought, so much so that Machiavelli justly regards the struggle between patricians and plebs as the source of Rome's greatness, are absent from *The Prince*. They do not even appear in the distance as a social and political entity. We have the Prince's subjects, isolated beings, fragments, as it were, of a vast whole which no longer exists, opposed to the sovereign, but as man to man. Hence the necessity for the Prince to humour them, not to dishonour them or violate their property, to keep their friendship. But where is there any reference to the strength that derives from collective action? When the author seems at first sight to be returning to the theme of the organizing capacity of the masses we find ourselves confronted not with the people but with a confused rabble, not with a party, rich in native energy, abounding in enterprises of its own, seeking to fulfil clearly-defined political aspirations and therefore capable of facing the disputes and the free clashes of opinion on which the fortunes of the Republic depend, but with a mob that "does not wish to be oppressed" and judges "a thing by its result." Compare Chapter 9 of *The Prince* with the passage in Chapter 4 of the first book of the *Discorsi* in which Machiavelli speaks of the struggle between patricians and plebs in Rome, or with Chapter 6. These last-named chapters breathe a living force, ever-present and self-conscious, a force that creates its forms of life and overcomes individual passions by welding them into the compact unity of a common passion, a force that can also err "through excessive love" of its liberty— but in a Republic that is not corrupt its very error is a source of great good "and enables it (the Republic) to lead a free life." In Chapter 9 of *The Prince*, on the other hand, we have an amorphous, scattered and truly anonymous mob, in which nothing has any significance except the feelings of individual persons, who are incapable of perceiving the collective mind that transcends their own, or of aspiring to the grandeur of political resolution, even if the latter be expressed in the communal strife of parties. We have once more "a brute beast, which . . . not being accustomed to feeding itself, nor knowing the hiding-places in which it might take refuge, becomes the prey of the first man who tries to recapture it."

Nor is the nobility any less irresolute and aimless. It is reduced, in short, to engaging in a battle of wits with princes and people, to hatching plots designed to further only immediate interests of limited scope, beyond which there is now nothing. These Italian *Grandi* lack even the pride—a pride not devoid of a certain heroic quality—which united the French feudatories against the Monarchy; the latter at any rate had a pride of caste—as Machiavelli noted. Hatreds and passions are aroused by personal, trivial and therefore fleeting dissensions. The *Grandi* cannot mould their desire to dominate the people into a clear line of conduct, and in the end they bow the knee to the Prince, after which fresh disorders quickly supervene.

Finally, the Prince must gain the friendship of the people, so that he may keep them "alive"; but the mob must derive this "life" from a virtue that is outside itself, from a power that stands above it. For what life remains in those "guilds" or "tribes", the ancient and glorious corporations of arts and arms, potent symbol of the creative capacity of the Communal *bourgeoisie?* The Prince must take these people into account, so that he may sometimes talk to them and give examples of humanity and magnificence, as if he were a juggler who has to win the favour of an indifferent public.

The emotional invocation at the end itself brings out, once and for all, this lack of spiritual energy: "Here is great virtue among individual members of the community"; but meanwhile these are not capable of any action unless the genius of a single *condottiere* is forthcoming to arouse them; and they wait "open-mouthed" for the "manna in the desert".

Machiavelli, then, is impelled to keep his eyes fixed on the Man alone; and while he propounds some of the general principles that have occurred to him as a result of his long meditation—above all that of the necessity of a State militia, which he regards as fundamental—he is faced with the task of discovering the specific human laws on which the difficult art of government will henceforth be based. In this way the treatise on Principates takes the form of a relentless analysis, a kaleidoscope of humanity.

Not that we do not discern even in this the continual expression of a creative imagination that is induced to reconstruct analytical detail through its own power of synthesis. Moreover, the inexorable necessity of reducing an impression that is beautifully complete in itself to the form of a rigid principle is clearly revealed. Just as Machiavelli transforms the historical fact into a theoretical precept, so he remoulds the closely-observed detail into the maxim of unvarying significance, with the result that the contrast with the "discretion" of Francesco Guicciardini becomes newly apparent; but in the event the axiom, possessing a clearly-defined factual foundation, has a vitality that often disguises its general character, making it as immediate as a psychological observation.

Thus the argument is coloured by human impressions, rapid, clear and complete. Machiavelli, who has spent many years in the service of the Florentine Republic, has met a great number of men, especially the kind of men who hold the tangled threads of the political skein in their hands. Perhaps he is not by nature very diplomatic, not inured to subtle disputations in which care is always taken to keep the language within the limits of a formality that never yields place to the Horatian *fides perlucidior vitro*. Perhaps he lacks the temper of a merchant, having acquired through long practice the habit of remaining impassive and indifferent, with an indifference that terrifies those who have to face it. Perhaps he does not always succeed in restraining the vehemence of his feelings with that calm, lordly mastery which is characteristic of Guicciardini. Yet the sometimes painful experience of many years has removed his rough edges, made him civilized, enabling him to perform the most difficult manoeuvres with ease and accustoming him to assume that cold inscrutability which is essential to those who wish to gamble at Court with the lives and destinies of nations. Sometimes, it is true, he forgets what he has learned, and has sudden outbursts of enthusiasm and bitterness which a true diplomat would never permit himself; and indeed his natural confidence re-appears in *The Prince* alongside the acquired manner, moulding the calm and severe analysis into periods that are often animated, vivacious and unexpected. But at any rate the prolonged constraint of public life, combined with the natural perspicacity of his judgment, have taught him to measure carefully the acts and words of those who sit in government over cities and to calculate exactly the effect of the subtle interweaving of the sometimes discordant thoughts and feelings from which the event proceeds—though the process is invisible to the mob.

And so, even when the axioms seem general to a degree, we discern the concrete, precise foundation, unwavering in its detail. The very turn of the clear, laconic phrase, whose every accent is endowed with colour and form, reveals the perfection of the psychological inquiry, which permeates the canvas on which the new State is gradually taking shape.

Moreover, Niccolò does not have much trouble in describing the characters and sketching in the lines of the different figures. It is enough for him to fix his gaze on the various Italian princes, on that crowd of men who had in many cases risen from the humblest circumstances to prosperity, as was possible in those days, by rapid jumps—men who had made themselves the wonder of their contemporaries and had appeared before Machiavelli himself in the privacy of a closed room, like Valentino, or in the crowded halls of another Seigneur, like the princes and ambassadors at the Court of Maximilian. Such fragments of human life present themselves almost automatically, ready to be re-assembled into an organic whole, to one who recalls, for example, men like Sigismondo Malatesta or Federigo da Montefeltro, both "fox" and "lion" at once. Failing all else there is the portrait of Piero della Francesca; the living image of the Prince with his broad face, prominent canine jaw, and glassy, impassive stare. As for his mind, Machiavelli can reconstruct it with certainty merely by contemplating the image as it appears roughly outlined against the luminous background.

He finds Valentino truly perfect—partly because in the character of this son of a Pope, "le plus desloyal filz de Prestre qui fut onques",

perfect poise was combined with a prodigious blending of cold calculation and passion, so that he was able to indulge his passion for sensual
pleasures without prejudice to his wise imperialistic plan; but most of all
because Caesar Borgia tried to create a strong unitarian State, pursuing
that goal to which, in the solitude of his villa, the writer's thoughts
were likewise directed. Final ruin can barely dim the brightness of the
vast stage upon which moved the figure of the *condottière sans peur et sans
remords*. Machiavelli explains his ruin as a caprice of fortune—"fortune" being an obscure, indeterminate idea to which he never succeeded in giving clear expression in a bold spiritual affirmation, sometimes regarding it as the force and logic of history, but more often as a
mysterious, transcendent grouping of events, whose incoherence is
unintelligible to the human mind. Fortune has "reproved Valentino";
and the writer is not concerned to examine the fundamental justice
of her condemnation.

Thus the picture remains serenely sculptural. It is dominated from
afar by the mocking figure of the Borgia, inscrutable in his smile as in
his meaning look, with his great black beard that climbs up his pale
cheeks and gives his face a sombre setting, even as his mind is circum-
scribed by his fixed imperial resolve, which is dimly reflected in his
every gesture.

He dominates the picture, yet only from a distance; for *The Prince*
is no more a glorification of Caesar Borgia than of all those other
Seigneurs who come upon the scene—some returning again and again,
so that we glimpse the hard, angular features of Francesco Sforza and
Ferdinand of Aragon. But since the State can only be founded upon a
specific personage—for it has to be conditioned first and foremost by
the virtue of an individual, and the inert material awaits the imprint
of an "excessive" excellence—it is natural that the analysis should
centre round a figure who will confer on the scattered fragments, which
are endowed both with reason and with emotion, a sense of community;
and naturally the dominating figure is the son of Alexander VI, who
has so often been reviled by the Republicans of Florence.

Friedrich Meinecke

This kind of naturalism can easily lead to a harmless and unreflecting
multiplicity in the question of human values. But (in spite of the
offering which he gladly brought to the altar of Venus) Machiavelli
concentrated all his real and supreme values in what he called *virtù*.

SOURCE: Friedrich Meinecke, *Machiavellism*, translated by D. Scott (New Haven,
Conn.: Yale University Press, 1957), pp. 31–37. Reprinted with permission of
Yale University Press and Routledge & Kegan Paul, Ltd., London.

This concept is exceedingly rich in meaning, and although it was taken over from the tradition of antiquity and humanism, it had been felt and elaborated in a quiet individual manner; ethical qualities were certainly embraced in it, but it was fundamentally intended to portray something dynamic, which Nature had implanted in Man—heroism and the strength for great political and warlike achievements, and first and foremost, perhaps, strength for the founding and preservation of flourishing States, particularly republics. For in the republics, of which Rome in its great republican period seemed to him an ideal example, he saw the conditions most favourable for the generation of *virtù*. It therefore embraced the civic virtues and those of the ruling class; it embraced a readiness to devote oneself to the common good, as well as the wisdom, energy and ambition of the great founders and rulers of States. But the *virtù* which the founder and ruler of a State had to possess counted for Machiavelli as *virtù* of a higher order. For in his opinion this kind of *virtù* was able, by means of appropriate 'regulations', to distil out of the thoroughly bad and wretched material of average specimens of humanity the other kind of *virtù* in the sense of civic virtue; to a certain extent the latter was *virtù* of a secondary quality, and could only be durable if it was rooted in a people whose spirit was naturally fresh and unspoilt. This separation of *virtù* into two types, one original and the other derived, is of exceptional significance for a complete understanding of the political aims of Machiavelli. For it shows that he was a long way from believing uncritically in the natural and imperishable virtue of a republican citizen, and that he viewed even the republic more from above, from the standpoint of the rulers, than from underneath, from the standpoint of broad-based democracy. He appreciated the proverb, which was popular in his time, that *in piazza* your opinions were not the same as they were *in palazzo* . . . . His republican ideal therefore contained a strain of monarchism, in so far as he believed that even republics could not come into existence without the help of great individual ruling personalities and organizers. He had learnt from Polybius the theory that the fortunes of every State are repeated in a cycle, and that the golden age of a republic is bound to be followed by its decline and fall. And so he saw that, in order to restore the necessary quantum of *virtù* which a republic had lost by sinking to such a low point, and thus raise up the State once again, there was only one means to be adopted; namely, that the creative *virtù* of one individual, of one *mano regia*, one *podestà quasi regia* . . . , should take the State in hand and revive it. Indeed he went so far as to believe that for republics which were completely corrupt and no longer capable of regeneration, monarchy was the only possible form of government. Thus his concept of *virtù* formed a close link between republican and monarchical tendencies, and, after the collapse of the Florentine Republic, enabled him without inconsistency to set his hopes on the rule of the Medicis, and to write for them the Book of the Prince. In the same way it made it possible for him immediately afterwards to take up again in the *Discorsi* the strain of republicanism, and to weigh republic and monarchy against one another.

Moreover his own special ethic of *virtù*—a product of the joyous worldly spirit of the Renaissance—begins now to throw light on the relation in which he stands to the ordinary Christian, and so-called genuine, morality; this relationship has been the cause of much dispute and a continual subject of reproof to Machiavelli. We have already remarked that he retained the basic Christian views on the difference between good and evil. When he advocated evil actions, he never denied them the epithet evil or attempted any hypocritical concealment. Nor did he dare to embody direct traits of morally wicked behaviour in his ideal of *virtù*. In Chapter 8 of the *Principe*, which deals with Agathocles, he says that to murder one's co-citizens, to betray one's friends, to be lacking in loyalty, piety and religion, cannot deserve the name of *virtù*; these things can achieve mastery, but not glory. And yet in Agathocles, who behaved in this way, he recognized at the same time a real *virtù* and *grandezza dell'animo*, i.e. great virtues of a ruler. The ethical sphere of his *virtù* therefore lay in juxtaposition to the usual moral sphere like a kind of world of its own; but for him it was the higher world, because it was the vital source of the State, of the *vivere politico*, the supreme task of human creativity. And because it was for him the higher world, so it could be permitted to trespass and encroach on the moral world in order to achieve its aims. These encroachments and infringements, these "sins" in the Christian sense, never ceased to be judged by him as immoral, and did not indeed constitute *virtù* itself—but they could in the last resort (as we shall soon see more clearly) arise out of *virtù*.

Let us first look more closely at his theory of *virtù*, and at the striking mixture of pessimism and idealism, of mechanistic and vitalistic elements, which go to compose it. In the *Discorsi* . . . , he says that of their own accord men will never do anything good, unless they are driven to it by some "necessity". Hunger and poverty, he goes on, make men industrious, and laws make them good. The penalties imposed on any infringement of the laws lead on towards a recognition of justice. For him, therefore, moral goodness and justice were produced and could be produced by the constraining power of the State. How high his opinion was of the State, and how little he thought of individual human beings! But this rigid positivist causal nexus was relaxed through the medium of *virtù*, and by a belief in the creative powers of great men, who, through their own *virtù* and the wise regulations which they made, were able to raise up the average level of humanity to a new, secondary form of *virtù*. Then too it was another mechanistic and fatalistic belief of his that, since the world always remained the same and all things were repeated in a cycle, *virtù* did not exist in the world in unlimited supply, but was passed round in the world continually, and now this, now that people was privileged to possess it. This was echoed by Hegel three hundred years later when, in his theory about the 'dominant peoples of world history' (who are entrusted by the World Spirit from time to time with the task of directing its affairs in the world), he made the fatalistic element part of a sublime philosophy of progress and ascent. Machiavelli however contented himself with stating resignedly that only in ancient times did it happen that a single nation was blessed with a preponderance of this *virtù*; in modern times it was divided up amongst a number of nations. This brings out very clearly the similarity and the difference between the centuries. Surrounded by the collapse of the political world in which they lived, both thinkers cast longing eyes on the representatives of strength and efficiency in world history—Hegel with an optimistic belief in progress, the result of the century of the Enlightenment, Machiavelli with the old belief in the everlasting similarity of historical life, a belief which had always been fostered by the Christian disdain for this world and which the vital energy of the Renaissance had not been able to break down. But this vital energy was still strong enough not to lose courage even amid the collapse and in the face of the contempt of humanity, and strong enough to watch out for fresh *virtù*. For the development and creation of *virtù* was for Machiavelli the ideal, and completely self-evident, purpose of the State. To raise his own nation by means of *virtù* from the low point to which it had sunk, and to regenerate the State, if this was still possible (he continually wavered between doubting this and believing it), became his life interest. But this new political idealism was now indeed burdened with the serious problematical element which was inherent in the character of *raison d'état*. This brings us nearer to our real task.

It was certainly impossible, once the moral and religious bond had been severed which held together the mediaeval Christian ideal of life, to set up immediately a new worldly system of ideals which would have the same inner unity and compactness. For, to minds freshly released from the restraints of the Middle Ages, so many provinces of life were now opened up simultaneously that it was not possible at once to find a distinctive point of view, from which the secularized world could be grasped and comprehended once again as a harmonious unity. One made discoveries, first in one place, then in another; one devoted oneself enthusiastically and often quite wholeheartedly to the discovery of the moment and became so completely taken up with it, that one had no opportunity to examine the contradictions and discrepancies between the experiences one had newly acquired and the human values which had held up till now. Machiavelli possessed this one-sided passion for discovery to an extraordinary degree. He threw himself on his particular aim of the moment in such a way that occasionally all he himself had previously thought and said was entirely forgotten. In a quite undaunted, now and then almost fanatical manner, he deduced the most extreme, and sometimes the most terrible consequences from the truths which he had found, without ever testing their reaction on other beliefs he held. In the course of his experimental discoveries he was also fond of changing his standpoint, and identifying himself for the moment with widely different interests in the political struggle, so that for each interested party, whether it be a prince or an enemy of princes, he could devise some powerful remedy, some *medicina forte* (and wherever possible a *regola generale*). His occasional recipes, then, should often be taken as having a certain degree of relativity. And these tendencies of his should be kept firmly in view.

The most serious discrepancy in his system of thought—a discrepancy which he never succeeded in eliminating and which he never even tried to eliminate—lay between the newly discovered ethical sphere of *virtù*, and of the State animated by *virtù*, on the one hand, and the old sphere of religion and morality on the other. This *virtù* of Machiavelli was originally a natural and dynamic idea, which (not altogether unhappily) contained a certain quality of barbarity (*ferocia*); he now considered that it ought not to remain a mere unregulated natural force (which would have been in accordance with the spirit of the Renaissance) but that it ought to be raised into a *virtù ordinata*, into a rationally and purposively directed code of values for rulers and citizens. The *virtù ordinata* naturally set a high value on religion and morality, on account of the influence they exerted towards maintaining the State. In particular, Machiavelli spoke out very forcibly on the subject of the indispensability of religion . . .; at any rate, he was strongly in favour of a religion which would make men courageous and proud. He once named "religion, laws, military affairs" together in one breath, as the three fundamental pillars of the State. But, in the process, religion and morality fell from the status of intrinsic values, and became nothing more than means towards the goal of a State animated by *virtù*. It was this that led him on to make the double-edged recommendation, which resounded so fearsomely down the centuries to come, inciting statesmen to an irreligious and at the same time dishonest scepticism: the advice that even a religion tinged with error and deception ought to be supported and the wiser one was the more one would do it . . . . Whoever thought like this was, from a religious point of view, completely adrift. What final certainty and sure foundation was there left in life, if even an unbelieved and false religion could count as valuable, and when moral goodness was seen as being a product of fear and custom? In this godless world of Nature man was left alone with only himself and the powers Nature had given him, to carry on the fight against all the fateful forces wielded by this same Nature. And this was exactly what Machiavelli conceived his own situation to be.

It is striking and forceful to observe how he strove to rise superior to it. On the one side *fortuna*, on the other *virtù*—this was how he interpreted it. Many people today (he says in Ch. 25 of the *Principe*), in the face of the various blows of Fate and unsuspected revolutions we have experienced, are now of the opinion that all wisdom is entirely unavailing against the action of Fate, and that we must just let it do what it likes with us. He admits that even he himself has occasionally felt like this when in a gloomy mood. But he considered it would be lacking in *virtù* to surrender to the feeling. One must rouse oneself and build canals and dams against the torrent of Fate, and then one will be able to keep it within bounds. Only half our actions are governed by Fortune; the other half, or almost half, is left to us. "Where men have not much *virtù*, then *fortuna* shows its strength clearly enough. And because it is full of change, so there are numerous changes in republics and states. And these will always go on changing, until sooner or later there will come a man who so loves antiquity, that he will regulate *fortuna*; then it will not be able to show every twenty-four hours how much it is capable of accomplishing" . . . . *Fortuna* has got to be beaten and bruised like a woman one wants to possess, and boldness and barbarity will always be more successful there than coldness. But this boldness has got to be united with great cunning and calculation, for each situation of fate demands a method specially suited for dealing with it. He began to meditate very deeply on just this particular problem, for it showed up very clearly both the powers and the limitations of *virtù*, and of humanity altogether. The individual agent cannot escape the nature he is born with. He acts in such and such a way because this nature requires it. Hence it arises that, according to the disposition of Fate, this same method which his character dictates will turn out well one day, and badly the next . . . . An insight of this kind could lead back to fatalism. But the effect on him of all these doubts and impulses was like the bending of a taut-strung bow. He let fly his arrows with all the more force.

Enemies learn to use each other's weapons. *Virtù* has the task of forcing back *fortuna*. *Fortuna* is malicious, so *virtù* must also be malicious, when there is no other way open. This expresses quite plainly the real spiritual origin of Machiavellism: the infamous doctrine that, in national behaviour, even unclean methods are justified, when it is a question of winning or of keeping the power which is necessary for the State. It is the picture of Man, stripped of all transcendent good qualities, left alone on the battlefield to face the daemonic forces of Nature, who now feels himself possessed too of a daemonic natural strength and returns blow for blow. In Machiavelli's opinion, *virtù* had a perfectly genuine right to take up any weapon, for the purpose of mastering Fortune. One can easily see that this doctrine, which appeared so dualistic on the outside, had really sprung from the background of a naïve Monism, which made all the powers of life into forces of Nature. It now became a presupposition for the discovery which Machiavelli had made about the essence of *raison d'état*.

But in order to make this discovery, yet another theory was needed— one which he thought out and applied just as clearly and consistently as he did the theory of the struggle between *virtù* and *fortuna*. This was the theory of *necessità*. *Virtù, fortuna* and *necessità* are three words which keep on sounding again and again throughout his writings with a kind of brazen ring.

A STUDY GUIDE

1. According to Allen, why did Machiavelli believe that his *Discourses* represented a new avenue of thought?

2. What, according to Allen, are the underlying principles of Machiavelli's view of human nature and of history?

3. Can Machiavelli's principles in his *Discourses* be reconciled with his precepts in *The Prince*?

4. According to Chabod, what is the essence of *The Prince*?

5. What is the "Cult of Antiquity" according to Butterfield?

6. How is this "cult" significant in Machiavelli's thought?

7. According to Meinecke, what are the three fundamental principles of Machiavelli's thought?

8. What is Meinecke's interpretation of *"virtù"*?

B C D E F G H I J   5 4 3 2 1 7 0